The
Last Indentured
Servant

ISBN 978-1-7343827-6-1

Author's website: aletheiawrites.bravesites.com

Published by Canyon Rose Press
Benicia, California
email: info@canyonrosepress.com

Book design: Jan Malin

Cover image: Los Angeles, California
Cover Photography: LPETTET

The Last Indentured Servant

Aletheia Morden

Dedication

*To the late Camille and Jerry Fielding
and the Williams Family for their kindness
to this stranger.*

"If you have something to say, wrap it in chocolate."

— *Billy Wilder, Film Director*

Preface

This Memoir is based on letters between my mother and I from 1965 and 1966, as well as my memory of over half a century ago. Also, letters from friends. I incorporate language in common use then with updated terms for today. Thus, "negro" and "colored person" is referenced along with "Black" and "African-American," as well as "Indian" and "Native American."

English and American words are also intermittently mixed in together. They share a common language base, but often have quite different vocabularies and expressions. And I am a product of both.

Aletheia Morden's 1965 English Passport

Her Britannic Majesty's
Principal Secretary of State
for Foreign Affairs
Requests and requires
in the Name of Her Majesty
all those whom it may concern
to allow the bearer to pass freely
without let or hindrance,
and to afford the bearer
such assistance and protection
as may be necessary.

Aletheia's Letter to Employer:

18th May, 1965.

Dear Mrs. Fielding,

I received a letter from the Agency today, stating that they have found me a position with your family. I would be very pleased to accept this offer and thank that I'd better tell you a little about myself ...

The letter from the Agency mentioned something about a car and I must tell you that although I am able to drive, I do not qualify for an International Driving License and therefore will not be able to drive in America without taking your tests. I will also have to have some instruction in your tests. I will also have to have some istruction beforehand as driving in England in on an entirely different scale to that in the States! I hope that it doesn't matter too much from your point of view as I am most willing to learn and I'm sure it wouldn't take me too long.

I don't know if the Agency told you, but I do have a friend who went out to Los Angeles last week and if possible, I'd like to have the same time off as her. She has every Sunday and instead of a half day, her employer gives her every other Saturday off, so that makes it a full weekend one week and just Sunday off the following week. If you have different ideas about this I am sure we can come to an agreement anyway ...

The Agency does not say how soon you wish me to come, but I am ready now and have got everything I need from this side, so whenever you decide is the best time I'm all set to get an interview for my visa etc.

I don't really know what else to say as it is rather difficult to write to someone you don't know, isn't it? However, you can tell me if I have to bring anything special, apart from the usual things or anything I should know before I come, when you write.

Yours sincerely,

Patricia Morden

The Employer's Response:

Dear Miss Morden,

I received your very nice letter and needless to say I was pleased to hear from you, and also to learn that you will soon be entering our employ.

We will go over everything completely when you arrive, but perhaps this information will give you a little hint as to what to expect.

My husband is a musical composer, arranger, and conducter and his schedule is most frantic and quite irregular and demands a lot of our patience and understanding. But I just say, through it all, I think it is a stimulating and fascinating atmosphere to be around and most of all it's rarely dull.

I too was in the theatrical business most of my life. I was a dancer up until Mr. Fielding and myself were married. Now I have my hands full with my new life, my adorable daughter Elizabeth, and my thoughts of the new one who will be here in early October.

I'm sure you will find Elizabeth a lovely and charming child. She may be a little shy with you in the beginning, but I presume that's natural with most children.

I try to run my house fairly normally, but it seems as though, with my husband's business associates coming in and out, personal friends and family, etc., it gets somewhat confusing, plus the fact that sometimes things are planned at the last minute! I will try my best to keep your time off as regular as possible, but I do hope you will be agreeable if it has to fluctuate some. My doctor has given me orders to take my chaotic life a bit more slowly so we will have to work this one out together. I do hope all of this will suit you.

Your duties here will be the same I would suppose as in most homes. I think that you would be able to take over here without too much effort. You and I can work out a daily schedule together so that we will know where we are most of the time. So, that's a brief idea of what it's like on this end...

We are looking forward to your joining us soon. If you can, keep us posted as to when your interview for your visa occurs, and your final plans for leaving England have been decided.

Yours sincerely,

Mrs Camille Fielding

Contents

Cast of Characters

Jerry Fielding, Television and Film Music Composer,
Hogan's Heroes, The Wild Bunch
Camille Fielding, his wife, an ex-dancer
Elizabeth, baby daughter
Claudia, new baby daughter
Essie, the housekeeper
Honey, Camille's glamorous mother
Aunt Pat, her sister and Mrs Reed, Camille's grandmother
Brad, Donna and Dana, Camille's brother, sister-in-law
and niece
Dick Williams, Camille's father, one of the first studio
soundmen in Hollywood films, and his wife, Maggie
Little Doggie, Camille's spoiled poodle
Solomon, the Irish Setter
Joyce, cartoon colorist and Camille's oldest friend from
high school
Leonard, Jerry's business manager
Cynthia, Jerry's bossy nurse cousin
Bette, the realtor
Elsa, the drunken neighbor
Julie (Julia) Dorsey, sometime actress and daughter of
1940s bandleader Jimmy Dorsey

★★★

Aletheia, the British au pair
Betty, her starstruck mother
Avril, Aletheia's friend in England
Karin, German au pair
Rita, another au pair
Myra and Harold, Rita's employers
Sharon, Rita's friend

Appearances By:

Debbie Reynolds, Camille's friend and film star
   Singin' In The Rain
Dan Dailey, Camille's former dancing partner and
   popular actor, especially 1940s/1950s films
Farley Granger, an Alfred Hitchcock favorite actor,
   Strangers on a Train
Richard Dawson, English-American actor *Hogan's
   Heroes* and television's *Family Feud*
Mitzi Gaynor, singer, dancer and actress *South Pacific*
Syd Zelinka, screen and television writer *Sergeant Bilko*
Sam Peckinpah, screenwriter and film director
   The Wild Bunch
Shirley Jones, actress *Oklahoma*

Jose Greco, flamenco dancer

Charlton Heston, actor *Ben-Hur*

Betty Hutton, actress *Annie Get Your Gun*

Agnes Moorehead, actress *Bewitched*

Edward G. Robinson, actor popular during Hollywood's Golden Age *Double Indemnity*, and his grandchildren

Ernest Gold, music composer *Exodus*

Marni Nixon, singer, Ernest's wife and "The Voice of Hollywood"

Fifi D'Orsay, 1920s film actress and poodle lover

The Gangster's Girlfriend, a 1940s singer who shall remain nameless

And Many, Many More

HONORABLE MENTION: Dalton Trumbo, Novelist and Academy Award *winning* screenwriter, *Johnny Got His Gun*

London to L.A.

I arrived in Los Angeles shortly before the Watts riots broke out in 1965.

Los Angeles lay atop a stressed fracture of faults in the earth, building energy, waiting to explode—like the people living on the surface. The fissures and fractures were sleepwalking against each other much like I was, but I wouldn't know that for quite awhile on that hot evening in July when I stepped off the plane at LAX. It had taken three flights and many hours and time zones to get here: London to New York; New York to San Francisco; San Francisco to Los Angeles. A long journey but, like a lot of my friends, I'd wanted to get away from England and have an adventure.

None of my friends had any money for travel and neither did I. Avril, was working as an au pair in Switzerland and had been looking around for a job for me. I had a pen pal in Sweden, who could get me similar work there, but I'd answered an agency ad in a newspaper and ended up with an au pair position in Hollywood, the dream capital of the world. It was the furthest distance from home and the hardest from which to return, I thought blithely. Besides, it sounded more like fun. And, a lot warmer, too; no cold, no snow, no freezing rain.

I'd been working as a secretary for an international building company in London during the day, going out dancing most evenings, staying up all weekend going to clubs and parties. This had gone on for several years, and I needed a change. At nineteen, I was exhausted. Sleep deprivation was catching up with me. One Monday morning my two bosses called me into their office and mentioned that a purchase order had gone out with the wrong box checked. Building materials were usually sent to site, but this particular order had had "send to office" checked.

"Yeah, this great big transport lorry turns up in Knightsbridge on a Saturday morning. Blocked the street." My bosses thought it was hilarious. "It wasn't your fault," they assured me. "Nobody checked it."

I didn't much care if the bourgeois personalities doing their Saturday shopping at Harrod's or the trendy boutiques on Sloane Street had had to pick their way through a traffic jam on the Brompton Road. I was still in recovery from my weekend.

I'd been ill with laryngitis the week before, but the doctor had given me morphine tablets to cope with the pain. They had worked wonderfully well, so well I went to a night club in Soho on Saturday night, at a new place which had recently opened: "Le Discoteque." It was unusual in that you didn't have to be twenty-one to join; anyone over sixteen could go and dance, and membership was free. Soho was dark and dangerous in those days, still full of gangsters, but starting to change with the new generation of Mods and their music, which was popular in England and starting to energize the world. The club was on the second floor of an old building, and had been painted black inside: black walls, black ceiling, and probably a black floor, although that could have been dirt. The lights were very low, the rock and roll music very loud. There were no chairs to sit on, just a few old mattresses against the wall.

I was slow-dancing with a friend at about 3 a.m. We were leaning against each other, propping each other up and shuffling our feet because there wasn't much room to move. Le Discoteque was very crowded with people, most of whom were smoking dope, which was turning the air hazy and acrid-smelling. Suddenly, I felt like I was going to faint. Somehow I made it to the Ladies bathroom painted all over in scarlet: red walls, red ceiling, red floor, red stall doors. With the music loud from outside, it was like a giant heart beating. I leaned against the wall, and slid all the way down. Suddenly, people were screaming in the corridor. The door flung open and two policemen charged in. I heard more pounding feet going up the stairs; it was a raid. Oh, shit! I couldn't move; I felt paralyzed. The bobbies glanced briefly at me, stepped over my legs and started banging on the stall doors, pushing them open. There was nobody inside. Then they rushed out as quickly as they had rushed in without a second glance. They weren't interested in tired-looking teenagers. They were interested in catching prostitutes from the illegal gambling club upstairs.

Avril came into the bathroom. "You've been in here for ages. Get up." She grabbed my arm and dragged me downstairs. Outside, the cool night air was like a kiss on my cheek as we joined our two friends. The street was dark, lit only by a streetlight outside the club, as we started walking to where the boys had parked their Vespa mopeds. A group of people were gathered around something on the curb.

"What's that?" Avril started to walk over in that direction just as someone lifted a dustbin lid off of a slumped-over body. "Oh, my God, he's been stabbed!" she cried, running back towards us.

A siren wailed in the distance. We four looked up and saw the blue flashing light on a police car turning into the far end of the street.

"I'm really stoned," Avril's boyfriend said.

"Me, too," she whispered.

Without a word we all ran across the street, jumped on the boys' Vespas and sped off into the night.

Every city has its own particular smell. Paris sidewalks smell of cigarettes and dog piss in the early morning. London smelled of diesel fumes and sooty grit from the traffic mixed with a damp smell from gently falling rain as we roared through the night toward home.

As I stepped off the plane that summer in 1965, Los Angeles didn't smell of spent jet fuel like it does now; it smelled of night-blooming jasmine and plumeria. Palm trees swayed and rustled under stars shining over the vast Pacific Ocean that rippled like black satin sheets in the hot summer night.

2

The Land of Unabashed Energy

This was my first plane ride ever. Anywhere. I wasn't too sure as to exact procedures, but heck, I'd made it almost seven thousand miles by myself without any alarming incidents. So far, so good. Scared? I'd decided quite some time ago I was a Viking at heart; I didn't allow myself to get scared—even if I was. As I walked slowly through the *Arrivals* section at LAX, a man's arm shot out and shook my hand.

"Hi, I'm Jerry Fielding," he said, recognizing me from a photo I'd sent to the employment agency.

I'd been one of two finalists on his wife's list and Jerry had chosen my application. When I'd filled out the agency's questionnaire, I'd written "sometimes" on the line that asked me if I smoked, and diplomatically written "occasionally" when another question asked me if I drank. I wasn't exactly lying, but I didn't want to end up in an uptight household or one at the opposite end of the spectrum. I wanted to convey that I was a reasonable personality, which I really was. I had no idea what my new employers would look like or what their lifestyle would be like.

A woman's arm reached out around Jerry's. "And, I'm Camille Fielding. Welcome."

She wore a white boucle wool jacket and looked to be about six months pregnant. They both had dark hair, dark brown eyes, and wore black heavy-rimmed glasses. Very American-looking 1960s style. Very cool. Well, this was Hollywood. We shook hands.

"How do you do?" I said politely.

Camille beamed at me. I liked her immediately. Jerry seemed charming and friendly, but was not a man who smiled a lot. Very high-strung. Very creative. A lot on his mind.

We walked towards the baggage section making conversation about my flight as I glanced around. Everything seemed new and very, very bright; overhead lighting blazed down on us as if there was no tomorrow, no shortage of anything. Americans in Europe stood out by a mile. They seemed to move differently, occupied space differently, as if they had a right to be in the world. It had impressed me. I wanted to experience some of that. Now that I was here, it didn't seem as if people strolling by, or just hanging around waiting for others, were taking up more room. Apart from being new and modern and bright, it all looked normal. It all fit. This was the land of unabashed energy. Intriguing. I was an outsider looking in. Up close. Personal. A stranger in a strange land, but I didn't dwell on that too much. It was to be expected. And it wouldn't last long.

"Phew, it's hot in here." Camille started fanning herself. "I'm always hot in my condition, though."

We were walking past a little open-air bar. "It'll take a while for the luggage to come out. I could do with a beer," Jerry suggested.

"Sounds perfect." Camille leaned against the counter.

Jerry signaled the barman and lit a cigarette. "Two beers." He looked at me and I nodded. I was thirsty, too. Besides, I wanted to fit in. I'd heard that American beer was nothing like English beer, more like lager, and I liked lager. It was almost like lemonade.

"Make that three," Jerry added.

Later, Camille would remark that she didn't realize until after the beers arrived that I was under drinking age. "But since you didn't hesitate and didn't look like an L.A. teenager the barman didn't question it."

Standing there in what passed as part of the latest Mod style in London: black patent high heels, a black patent leather handbag on my arm, wearing a beige and white houndstooth check suit over a pink blouse with a loose floppy bow tied at the neck I wasn't aware of exuding a confidence beyond my nineteen years. I was just an English girl stepping out into an adventure, and not that sophisticated or streetwise compared to some of my friends. My long brown hair was tied back with an Italian silk scarf. I wore light makeup, but heavy on the eyeliner and mascara, carefully refreshed before I'd stepped off the plane.

I had been a secretary for two years; now I was an au pair, a mother's helper for the next twelve months. One hundred and fifty dollars a month to start, one hundred and sixty-five after three months if it worked out between the employer and myself, with a hundred-dollar bonus if I stayed the full twelve months. The employer had also advanced the fifty-dollar plane fare deposit, which I had to pay back out of my first month's paycheck. They'd guaranteed the rest, so I owed the Beneficial Finance Company and British Overseas Airways Corporation (B.O.A.C.)

fifty-three dollars a month for the following six months for a total of three hundred and eighteen dollars for the one-way flight and loan fees. It was the 20th-century version of the way some English had been coming to America since the 17th century—working off their passage as an indentured servant—but without the 17th-century involvement of a crime for which they'd been booted out of England in the first place.

Things had changed a lot since then and indentured servitude was about to become moot thanks to Robert Kennedy's recent bill that argued America had plenty of people who could fill jobs like I was about to undertake. I'd just slid in under the gun, so to speak, since the immigration laws were always changing. America even had laws that countermanded those already in place. Who could keep up? A person just needed a bit of luck.

Thus, I arrived in America already in debt. It was the American way. There were no credit cards in those days, unless you were a highly paid business executive with a company-issued Diners Club card. It had not occurred to me to even ask what would happen if I upped and left before my year was up. At the back of my mind I thought I could always go home again. Somehow.

★★★

It had taken over a year of trying to find a way to actually get to America, circumnavigating rules and regulations vis-à-vis the American Embassy in Grosvenor Square. In those days when money was short for most people, young women went abroad—ostensibly to learn about another culture and language—and swopped bed and board, plus a small stipend and a lot of time off, in return for light

housework in a family's home. Since none of us had money
to travel, we got jobs at the places we wanted to visit.

Avril had gone to Switzerland to improve her French.
I'd declined her inquiry about finding me a job there in the
end. I was not in California to learn another language, but
being under the then-legal age of twenty-one I'd had to
have a sponsor, and this was the only position I could get.

My parents had argued about it. "You're going to be a
servant!" My father was horrified.

"But she'll be in Hollywood," my mother said with glit-
tering stars in her eyes.

"I can't go to New York," I explained. "They won't let
me in because they have too many English secretaries
working there. They say they're taking jobs away from
American girls, so I'm banned. It was in the newspaper,"
I added for official weight. I didn't mention that I had no
intention of going to New York anyway, even though I
had an ex-office friend who was working there as a nanny.

California had been my first and last choice. I had
dreamed it as a very young child. When I was four years
old, I'd stand on the beach at Brighton, where we'd lived in
my grandmother's house, and watch the ships sail over the
horizon of the English Channel. I knew there was another
country over there, and many more foreign places, too,
where they spoke different languages and had different
customs. Europe was teeming with displaced foreigners
and refugees for ten years after World War II, and a lot of
them were in England.

During the summer, the onion seller used to come
over from France and pedal around our seaside town
with strings of onions hanging in long strands from the

handlebars. He always knocked on my grandmother's door, and she always bought some onions, usually inviting him in for a cup of tea if he had time. I don't remember if she spoke French, but he spoke some English and they managed to communicate using both languages. Then he would lightly touch his beret with his forefinger, say *au revoir* and disappear over the horizon for a few months. I knew that I would disappear over that horizon, too, one day. When I was grown up.

★★★

"I'm not sure I want you to go." My father sat back in his chair and folded his arms. He liked to be in charge and control what went on in the household. He liked having the last word, too. He'd been sitting at the dining-room table in cotton pajamas when I walked in, his flies open, his penis exposed, but quickly adjusted himself when he heard my mother coming downstairs right behind me.

She recognized the signs of an impending verbal showdown between us. My mother consulted her wrist watch. "Time for me to go to church, otherwise I'll be late." She was in her coat and flowered hat and out the door in ten seconds flat.

I pulled out the immigration form from my pocket and laid it on the dining room table in front of Dad. "Read and sign on the dotted line."

He glanced at the form. "I'm not so sure I will. Says here it needs your father's signature. If I don't sign, you can't go," he said smiling with that touch of malice he had when I wanted something important. When I'd passed the Eleven+ exam that was mandatory for children under twelve in those days and decided whether you went to a school that put you on an academic track, or a school that did not, I was pleased. But my teacher at that time, who definitely favored boys over girls, told me in front of the whole class that I "wasn't as good as I thought I was." I'd felt crushed, and went home and told my parents.

My father had laughed. "I told him to say that at Parents Night," he said. "You're getting too big for your boots."

I was my mother's child; he'd adopted me after they married, but deep down he'd always resented me and any attention my mother gave me. Most teenagers have a secret part of themselves so adults can't trash that part of them they enjoy the most. He'd also denied me the chance of a scholarship to art college when I was fifteen. I would not let this dream be denied.

"If you don't sign the form, I will tell mum about your girlfriends."

He stopped smiling and that cocky, blustering air of his wavered. He worked as a traveling salesman and was often away from home, which was much quieter when he wasn't around. I had found a woman's scarf in his car's glove compartment that was not mine or my mother's and also had figured out that the family of furry mice ornaments on his car dashboard had come from an Austrian girl I had seen him giving a lift to the year before. And I had witnessed endless arguments and denials between him and my mother when his co-worker's wife had phoned my mum and informed her she was getting a divorce from her own husband because of "what the men were getting up to."

This was my D-Day. "I will make your life a living hell," I promised, handing him a pen.

Even when I was seven, I knew where I was headed over that horizon. My aunt had given me a book for Christmas about some children whose father was a professor. He'd accepted a job at a university in Los Angeles for a year, so off they all went singing, *California Here I Come.* I don't remember much of the story about their adventures, which always involved a mystery, but I do remember the description of where they lived: sunny skies and palm trees.

And now, here I was, standing under palm trees. No sun, because it was night time, but I had every confidence that the sun would come up in the morning.

The Fieldings and I walked towards Jerry's 1964 Ford Thunderbird, passing some suntanned teenage boys with longish blonde hair.

Jerry tilted his head towards them. "There's some of your local contemporaries. They look about the same age."

"They look like surfers," Camille said.

I took another look. Their suntans looked really good even in the glare of harsh airport lighting. They wore white t-shirts and had plaid Bermuda shorts on, the kind of shorts I would definitely *not* be wearing in the future. I also had no desire to surf. But I could be the girlfriend of a surfer. Maybe. That would entail a lot of time on the beach. Getting a suntan, socializing. Yeah. I could do that, I thought, remembering a TV show from several years ago with actor Tab Hunter set in Malibu.

We reached the car and Jerry put my suitcases in the trunk as I settled into the back seat.

"I like the Beach Boys music," I said conversationally as he drove toward the 405 freeway.

"Oh, God," Jerry muttered.

"He doesn't write that kind of music. Jerry writes for television shows and film," Camille twisted towards me from the front seat. "It's a different kind of popular music, right Jerry?"

"I'll say." He flicked his cigarette ash out of the window. I got it. Mainstream stuff. It was to be expected. At nineteen, I lived in a rock and roll world. Camille was in her early thirties and Jerry eleven years older. They didn't live in a rock and roll world.

"We'll go over to the studios and watch him record one day," Camille said. "CBS studios are only a few blocks from where we live."

"That would be lovely." I smiled enthusiastically, settling back further in the seat to watch the lights of Los Angeles speed by. It looked totally different from London and would take some adjustment, but that's what I was here for. Something different. I was looking towards the future. It was an adventure.

Jerry asked me what I thought of Los Angeles so far. I glanced up at the skinny palm trees, their fronds waving neon green in the freeway lights and said with satisfaction, "It's just as I imagined."

Job Description Over Beers

*Wh*ite. Everywhere. Everything seemed white and shiny. As we stepped down into the Fieldings' sunken living room I saw white walls. An entire wall of white silk brocade curtains covered the windows from the ceiling to the white wall-to-wall carpeted floor. A crystal chandelier and crystal doorknobs reflected light from the white lampshades. I felt as if I was walking into a cloud. A heavenly cloud. Like a movie set. But comfortable.

A woman with a blue rinse in her gray hair rose up from the long white couch and came towards me.

"This is my mother," Camille said. "Her name's Jeanette, but everyone calls her Honey."

Later, I'd learn that Jerry's last name had been changed from Feldman to Fielding and before that, his grandfather's name had been Lissakoff, which got changed in a single moment as he stood in line for a ticket to America and noticed a Wanted poster for himself on the far wall. He had not turned up at the local induction office for the Russian army some months before. Being Jewish this would have been a fateful conscription since pogroms against Jews were ongoing. The only solution was to escape permanently. Young Mr. Lissakoff had tapped the shoulder of the man standing in front of him and struck up a conversation, asking him his name.

"Feldman," the man had replied.

"That's funny, that's my name, too," he'd said, as they shook hands and the conversation drifted into areas where they might be related.

Well, this *was* America, where people changed their names once or twice, before or after arrival, until they got one that was suitable. America was, after all, a place where people reinvented themselves. I'd been called Lee by friends and family all my life but at that moment in the Fieldings' white living room, I'd change that. I'd use my real name, Aletheia, from now on. I'd become my real self. I'd left the old self behind, or so I thought at the time. I was into a new me, although I was to observe in future years that you could change your name or your country, but you never really left the old you behind. A person just dragged it along with them into the new.

"Hello. Welcome to Los Angeles." Honey extended her arm and we shook hands. She wore a suit and high heels, similar to mine. Ah, sixty and hip. I liked her. She had a vivacious smile like Camille. And, she was *so* slender. Just like the American women I'd seen in the movies.

"I hate to say hello and run, but I have to get up early for work in the morning," Honey apologized.

"Mom babysat for me," Camille explained. "So, how was she?"

"Hardly fussy at all," Honey beamed, gathering up her bag and gloves. "Bye, sweetie." She leaned over and gave Camille a quick kiss on the cheek.

"Nice to meet you," she said over her shoulder to me as the two of them walked towards the front door.

Jerry came in from a back room where he had taken my suitcases. "Hold on, Honey. I'll walk out with you. Got to get back to work," he said looking at his watch. "See y'all later." He gave Camille a quick peck on the cheek and called out "bye" to me. Then he and his mother-in-law were both gone, their footsteps echoing down the path as they walked to the street-level garage below.

"I'm getting another beer from the refrigerator," Camille stated, walking towards what I surmised must be the kitchen. "Do you want one?"

"Yes, please" I replied, wondering if I should walk back there and join her or sit on the couch. I opted for the couch. The house was much larger and grander than my parents' home, but not as large as my Uncle Dennis' house. He lived in half of a manor with spacious grounds that included a small stream flowing into a lake. The other half of the manor had another entrance and another occupant. My mother had always shushed my father's derogatory mutterings of "it's only half a manor," when she boasted about her successful businessman brother.

Camille came back into the living room carrying two Michelobs and sat in a wing chair. "We keep irregular hours around here," she said, handing me one. "Jerry usually comes home about 2:00 a.m. unless he's working all night, and we don't get up until late, 10:00 a.m. at the earliest. I was in the theatrical business myself until I was married, so I'm used to it. I hope it won't be too hard for you to adjust."

I murmured that I was sure it wouldn't as I sipped my beer.

"Jerry might seem a bit preoccupied at times, grumpy even, but that's because he has a lot on his mind. He's writing two shows at once right now and this week he's been pulling a few all-nighters so he's chronically short on sleep."

I nodded sagely. I understood how it was to be short on sleep.

"I try to run my house fairly normally," Camille continued, "but it gets quite chaotic around here with Jerry's business associates running in and out, and our friends and my family dropping by. There's always something unexpected at the last minute. Keeping this in mind, I'll try and give you time off as regularly as possible, but I do hope you'll be agreeable if it has to fluctuate some, especially with the new baby due in about three months. Perhaps at that time we can work something out to where you forego some days off while I'm in the hospital and resting after the birth, and then you can take a week all at once later."

I nodded in agreement. Three months seemed like a long way away at the moment. "How old is your daughter now?"

"Ten months. She may be a little shy with you at first, but I presume that's natural with most children. Elizabeth's very attached to Essie, our housekeeper, who works part-time. You'll meet them both in the morning. Jerry also has two daughters aged nine and twelve from a prior marriage who come over to dinner now and then. Once in a great while they stay over, but it's not often."

I had no idea what the time was but my adrenalin was starting to wane as I finished the beer.

"I expect you're tired from your long journey," Camille said sympathetically. "I've been to Europe several times; it's a long haul. You'll need a few days to recover. By the way, your friend Rita called me this afternoon. The woman she works for has invited you over for the weekend. They have a pool so you can relax. Is Rita an old friend?"

"We worked together in the same office and saw the agency ad in the paper. She arrived a few weeks ago and lives in Mar Vista. Is that far from here?"

"Not too far, about a thirty-minute drive towards the ocean. It's cooler over there. Studio City, where we live, is in the Valley so it's much hotter here." She stood up. "Let me show you to your room. She picked up the empty beer bottles from the coffee table. "I'll take care of these."

I couldn't help myself. "That's the biggest coffee table I've ever seen."

"And the ugliest, I bet," Camille said as we walked across the white carpet towards a hallway on the other side of the room. "Some business friend of Jerry's from Texas sent it as a wedding present. It's supposed to be some kind of rare wood lovingly carved by a designer, but I wouldn't be surprised if it wasn't an old conference table with the legs cut down. It's going out when we move."

I stopped walking. "You're moving?"

"Not yet and probably not far. It'll have to be somewhere nearby. I'm looking for a bigger house, big enough so Jerry can work at home. Unless he takes the job in Denmark," she added after a beat.

"Denmark?" I liked Denmark, but I hadn't just flown over 6,000 miles to turn around and fly back even more.

"It may never happen. But, if it does, I'm not sitting in a hotel for three months while Jerry's working. I intend traveling to Sweden, Finland, Norway and Russia since we'll be so close. You might want to come, too. I'm gonna need help with the babies. The film company's paying all the expenses. "

All expenses paid? Russia? Hmmn. Behind the Iron Curtain. Hmmn. Only for three months. I could pop in and see my family on the way back. My rich cousin was at finishing school in Switzerland, where upper class girls went at that time to have their education "finished" so they could face the world. I'd first asked rich-cousin Jenny's father, manor-house occupant Uncle Dennis, my godfather, if he could lend me the money to come to America, but he'd claimed to have lost too much betting on the horses at Ascot to be of any help. Under legal age but determined to have an adventure, I'd traveled to the western edge of the American continent to have my education finished, although I didn't know it then. I also didn't know what that would entail. I'd never heard of the term "continuing education." It would be a while before I realized that life was a school, a school you attend your whole life long. And how well you learned its lessons was up to you. No one was your teacher, and everyone was your teacher. You were a teacher, too, to everyone you encountered. We all learn from each other in the great cosmic schoolhouse of life.

Camille opened a door at the end of the passage. "My doctor's ordered me to rest since this baby's coming so soon after the last. Not much chance of resting around here, but we try."

I'd stopped in the hallway to look at a black and white photograph on the wall of Camille with Rita Hayworth and Cesar Romero. Next to it was a framed movie poster of *Advise and Consent,* a film by Otto Preminger, "Music by Jerry Fielding." It was a show business photo gallery between my room and the kitchen. I made a mental note to check it out in the morning.

Camille snapped on an overhead light. "This is your room; bathroom's next door with clean towels. I hope you'll be comfortable in here. The TV's new and my father's coming over to hook it up. Don't worry about what time you get up tomorrow." She turned to go. "I left Rita's number by the kitchen phone so you can call her back. Right now I'll say goodnight and hope you manage to sleep well." She walked out of the room, shutting the door behind her.

I stood transfixed for a moment. The room was wallpapered in gold with a dark-red velvet paisley pattern swirling over all four walls. A horrid little glass and gilt chandelier dangled from the ceiling. It looked like a Victorian boudoir. I switched on the bedside lamp and turned off the overhead; it was all too much. What lousy taste the decorator must have had, I concluded, throwing off my clothes and sinking onto the bed. Still, what did it matter? I might not be here too long. Sleep, lovely sleep. It must be lunchtime at the office right about now, I thought as I drifted off. Friday there. Payday. Chinese for lunch. Who knew what Friday would bring here?

4

Home is Like a Film Set. Not.

It was very early morning when I awoke. Daylight stole around the window shades in a thin, white line leaving the room in shadow. It was quiet, the household still asleep. From my bed I made out the outlines of a dressing table, an armchair. The room was small, but adequate. A television stood in front of French windows. I got up, changed into a summer dress and sandals then stood sniffing a strange odor. It was coming from the television. I switched on the light. The brand new orange and white plastic Sears TV clashed with the ghastly wallpaper. I'd never seen anything like it. It was a California thing, I decided. Our television at home had a plain wooden case and so did everybody else's.

I switched off the light, opened the French windows and stepped out onto a small path that wrapped around the side of the house, which stood on a hill with a view of houses tucked in between trees and bushes below. It was like being in the woods, a cross between England and Spain. Behind me, the house was beige stucco and redwood, 'California Spanish' style, Camille had told me. A stone balcony surrounded the second floor, which was slightly recessed.

The sun wasn't up yet, but Los Angeles was coming alive. I could hear a small roar building from traffic in the distance as I wandered around. The back yard was terraced with a stone retaining wall, the lawn gently sloping above it. I discovered the back door—locked—so I continued around the house and re-entered my bedroom by the French doors. Now what? I was tired, but not enough for sleep. I decided to explore a little more.

The hallway outside my bedroom door passed the living room on my left, a full bathroom with gold-colored fixtures and more of the hideous velvety wallpaper on my right, and ended in the kitchen. On the way, I stopped and examined more of the black and white photographs lining the walls. A younger Camille was in many of them, starting when she was about four or five years old standing next to actress Carol Lombard at her dressing room table. A framed foreign newspaper clipping proclaimed "*La Dolce Vita!*" I couldn't read the article since it was in Italian, but could make out something about "American actor and dancer Dan Dailey and his dancing partner." Camille's dress was mid-fifties style and very, very tight as they cha-cha'd down the Via Veneto in series of accompanying pictures. A large framed photo of Jerry taken in a recording studio with Debbie Reynolds was next and then many of him with musicians whose names I was unfamiliar with apart from Ella Fitzgerald.

The kitchen door stood open. More white: white tile, white woodwork and enormous white appliances. I was dazzled by the kitchen gadgets. An electric coffee pot, mixer, toaster for toasting several pieces of toast at once, and an *electric can opener and knife sharpener* stood on the counter. All in white. There was a separate pantry. The baby's high chair (yellow and white) with copious space for toys on three sides of the tray crowded against the wall of a small room situated between the kitchen and a large dining room. Later I would learn it was the breakfast room (*a separate room just for breakfast?*). The sunken dining room, seating at least twelve, led into the entry hall, and the living room was on the other side.

I stepped down onto the white carpet and gently pulled the curtain cord. With an almost imperceptible swish the white silk drapes started to glide back from the windows, then stopped. I pulled the cord again, but they wouldn't budge. I left it. I didn't want to break anything.

The room was still very white in the soft daylight, but as I looked around, I noticed a bookcase lining the wall opposite the windows. It was floor to ceiling black wood. Recessed shelves with books and lots of objects d'art were on the top half, with cupboards below. *How could I have missed that last night?* A glance at the book titles intrigued me: the controversial trilogy by Mikhail Sholokov, *And Quiet Flows The Don,* compared to Tolstoy's *War and Peace* and considered an important work of world literature, sat next to a book published in England about who really killed John F. Kennedy. A little shiver of delight went through me; I was an avid reader. My family didn't spend money on anything so frivolous as books. I'd had my own library card since I was nine-years-old and inadvertently wandered into a library building out of curiosity. My new employment already looked promising.

A silver drinks' tray loaded with crystal decanters of various shapes and sizes sat above the cupboards. Little porcelain tags hung round decanter necks to identify the contents: scotch, bourbon, vodka, gin. The gin decanter had a tall flute, and as I reached for a book, I knocked it over. Quickly, I caught it, but not before a little gin spilled onto the tray. I hot-footed it back to the kitchen, found a dishcloth folded by the side of the sink, quickly wiped up the gin, then ran the cloth over the decanter while I was at it since it seemed a bit dusty. Carefully folding the dishcloth, I placed it back by the sink. My first household duty done, albeit anonymously.

Suddenly, I felt tired. I went and lay down on my bed, and fell asleep as the sun came up. I had wandered into a world I hadn't a clue about, beyond what I knew from movies, television, and my childhood book. But that wasn't to last.

When I awoke, I heard voices coming from the kitchen area. As I walked in, Jerry was in the breakfast alcove on the telephone, an unlit cigarette in his cigarette holder. The baby sat next to him in her high chair, surrounded by small toys and guzzling her bottle. Chewed pieces of toast lay on the floor around her. A small gray poodle had his nose down, hoovering them up as fast as he could.

Camille was in the kitchen talking to a robust-looking black woman in a sleeveless print dress who was making a sandwich. The kitchen clock showed two minutes to noon.

"Ah, you're up. This is Essie, our housekeeper who works part-time. Essie this is Aletheia."

The housekeeper and I exchanged polite hellos. At that moment the baby decided to share more of her breakfast with the dog and dropped her bottle, spilling some milk. Jerry, still on the phone, bent down to retrieve the bottle, throwing his breakfast napkin over the spilt milk. "Someone's gonna slip on this," he called over.

"I've got it, Jerry." Camille picked up the dishcloth, hesitated, frowned then sniffed. "This dishrag smells funny." She looked at Essie, who shrugged. Camille threw it in the sink. "It can go in the laundry."

Jerry slammed the phone down and stood up, patting his shirt pocket. "I gotta go over to Paramount to see that goddamn producer who....do I have my cigarettes?" He picked them up from the table. "See you all later."

Elizabeth made little protest noises and jiggled in her seat. He bent down and kissed her head. "See you later, too, kiddo."

"She thinks he's the nightwatchman," Camille joked, picking up the baby and settling her on her hip after she kissed Jerry goodbye and picked up the napkin. "Elizabeth, this is Aletheia."

The ten month-old looked like a miniature Camille with her dark curly hair, dark eyes and chubby cheeks. She stared at me, clutching onto her mother's blouse.

"Did you feel the earthquake last night?" Camille asked as Elizabeth continued staring.

"What? No! An earthquake?" For some reason, I glanced around to see if everything was in its right place.

"You slept through it, that's good." Camille wiped something from the corner of the baby's mouth with her bib. "They happen all the time. They say the big one's coming in the next thirty years, but they've been saying that for a long time. It's a rocking motion, like you're on a train."

"Oh, okay." I relaxed. Train travel was familiar; I'd traveled on one every day to get to work in London.

Camille put Elizabeth back in her high chair, while I silently digested this bit of information and then put it out of my mind. I had no experience of earthquakes, and what you didn't know you couldn't be afraid of, I reasoned. Besides, nobody else was acting like it was a big deal.

"Listen," Camille turned back to me. "I'm going out to lunch with a friend, but I'll only be gone a couple of hours. Help yourself to what you want to eat." She walked over to the refrigerator and opened it. I followed. "I'm sure you'll find something. The whole household's on a diet "

I glanced over at the sandwich Essie was fixing for herself. Not the whole household.

The front doorbell rang. Camille looked at her watch and went to answer it. I reached for a can of diet black cherry soda and perused the contents of the refrigerator. Lots of salad. A workman followed Camille back into the kitchen. He had a large metal cannister on his back with a rubber hose attached and "Bug Man" written across his shirt pocket. "It's the exterminator," she announced to Essie, then explained to me. "He comes every month, and if he didn't, we'd have creepy-crawlies everywhere."

"This won't take long," the exterminator said to no one in particular and started to spray every drawer and cupboard in sight as he walked quickly around the house.

Essie sat down in the breakfast nook to eat her sandwich. Camille went upstairs. I turned back to the refrigerator. Essie's sandwich looked good to me. Forget breakfast, I was going straight to lunch. Maybe a sandwich and a small salad. I took a few moments examining potential salad fixings. The doorbell rang again.

Someone get that," Camille shouted from upstairs."

I put the soda back and shut the refrigerator door. Lunch would have to wait. I walked past Essie and Elizabeth, who was alternately crooning to some toys on her high chair table and baby-talking to Essie, and went to open the front door. Debbie Reynolds stood on the doorstep holding a brown paper shopping bag in her arms with something wrapped in a towel inside.

Debbie Reynolds
And The Black Madonna

"Hello," Debbie said warmly to me, walking into the house as Camille came back downstairs with her pocketbook on her arm and motioned Debbie inside.

"Oh good, you brought it with you," Camille said eyeing the shopping bag as they greeted each other. After briefly introducing me, she led Debbie into the living room. "I know just where it'll go."

I followed them. I wanted to see what "it" was. Besides, I wanted a closer look at Debbie. My mother would demand particulars when I wrote home. Debbie wore an emerald green silk blouse and beige capris with sandals and carried her handbag, or pocket book as Camille referred to it, over one arm. She'd pushed her large, dark glasses up to rest on her very blonde hair.

Debbie put the shopping bag, along with her pocketbook and sunglasses, down on the coffee table, saying: "This doesn't belong in here, Camille. It's too modern and doesn't go with your Spanish theme."

So that's what they called that style of furniture, I thought, glancing over at the black wooden bookcase.

Spanish. Debbie unwrapped what looked to me like an old block of wood and placed it in Camille's hands.

"Isn't she beautiful?" Camille breathed.

It was a carved wooden statue of a woman with a crown on her head, once painted in brilliant colors of blue, green and red now faded, although the outlines of her face were still visible, the eyes etched in black. What was it, or rather, who was it?

"A black Madonna, from Spain," Camille explained to me.

"She's hundreds of years old," Debbie added.

I hadn't been exposed to antiques. My mother had grown up in an Edwardian row house with old furniture to match. Consequently, she'd furnished our house in Danish modern and very bright colors. This Spanish relic looked like it had a bit of woodworm in its feet to me, but it was certainly lovely, and since they were making such a fuss, possibly quite valuable, even rare.

"D'you think she was looted during the Spanish Civil War?" Camille started breathing more mythology into what she held in her hands.

More likely some locals from the village saw a foreigner coming and seized a chance for some private commerce, I thought, but kept a respectful look on my face. Later I would learn that the African army crossed the Straits of Gibraltar and invaded the Iberian Peninsula in 710 A.D., staying in Europe until 1492 when both Muslims and Jews were forced out of Spain, although some Muslims remained in Europe until the early 17th century. Black Madonnas were no doubt incorporated into Catholic

Spain to help with assimilation (and lots of fighting) that took place over several hundred years.

Debbie shrugged. "We got her from a reputable dealer. She's got a tag on her."

I'd noticed an 8"x10" black-and-white photo of Debbie and Camille in the hallway gallery outside my room earlier. Camille was wearing a Spanish Cordova hat knotted under her chin. So, as well as doing lunch these two went shopping together, I realized. Artifact shopping.

"Where are you going to put her?" Debbie started looking around the room.

Camille indicated a space on the wall between the fireplace and the bookshelf. "I'll need a bracket."

Like a little miracle, Debbie fished down into the shopping bag and brought one out shaped like a small shelf. Then she dug down again and brought out some huge nails. "Now all we need is a hammer."

"Coming right up." Camille put the statue carefully back down on the coffee table, then headed for the kitchen area, calling behind her, "we'll have to move that chest over."

Debbie looked at the carved chest, another dark wood piece, Spanish style, which currently stood between the fireplace and the windows. Then she looked at me. "Come on." In a flash she had her hands on one end of the chest. "We're about the same size. You get on the other end."

God, the chest was heavy. How could she lift it so easily like that?

"Wait a minute." Debbie kicked off her sandals. "Let's go this way."

We moved the chest from one side of the fireplace to the other. A button popped off the back of my dress as I bent to put the chest down.

Camille came back in with a hammer, the little gray poodle trailing behind her. "Oh, you did it already. That was quick. It's pretty heavy."

No kidding, I thought to myself.

"It is, and you couldn't do it in your condition, Camille. She popped a button," Debbie nodded towards me, "but we managed." She picked up the bracket and nails, took the hammer from Camille and hopped up onto the chest. "Now, where do you want this? About here?"

"No, higher. Over to the left a bit." Camille and I stood next to each other as she directed Debbie, who hammered the nails in and made sure the bracket was secure. The dog sat down beside us and watched, too.

"Hand her up to me."

Camille handed over the Madonna. "She is rather heavy."

Carefully, Debbie placed her on the bracket shelf, and gave it a little shake. It didn't move. "You might want to put some museum putty underneath to keep her steady in an earthquake," she advised.

Camille nodded agreement, as Debbie jumped down and came to stand the on other side of her. The three of us, plus dog, contemplated the statue, which I estimated to be about two to three feet high.

"Now you need to rearrange your chairs," Debbie said, looking around the room, then looking pointedly at me. All I could think of was how her energy put mine to shame. Together we moved the wing chairs until she and Camille agreed on the best position for them. I could hardly believe I was moving furniture with "Tammy" on my first day in California. I was already way off the agency's job description: 'some childcare and light housework.'

"Done." Debbie reached for her sandals.

While she was putting them on, I asked Camille what the poodle's name was.

"Little Doggie," she replied.

Doggie?

"Actually, it's Perrito. Little Doggie in Spanish."

Of course it was. It matched the furniture.

Debbie retrieved her pocketbook. "I'm ready for lunch, now."

Me, too, I thought, heading back to the kitchen as the pair of them, both prior *Miss Burbank* in their youth although in different years (plus Debbie had also been *Miss Firecracker* for a July 4th parade), donned their sunglasses and left.

I retrieved a diet soda from the refrigerator, made a sandwich, decided against a small salad, and went to start making friends with Elizabeth. She now sat in a little soft bucket chair on wheels, careening from one side of the kitchen to the other with her bare feet.

"Is that your chariot?" I said, not really expecting an answer. She threw a toy she'd been chewing across the room.

Somewhere in the house a washing machine and dryer were going at full tilt. I recalled Camille telling me Friday was laundry day and Essie was in charge of it. She ironed Jerry's shirts just the way he liked them.

I was telling ten-month-old Elizabeth I had a present for her, but she'd have to wait for it until I unpacked, when Essie came back into the kitchen.

"It's time for her nap. Mrs. Fielding wants me to put her down until she gets used to you."

Fine with me, I nodded, and went to sit back down in the living room and contemplate the Madonna as I drank the soda and ate my sandwich. I felt tired, but not tired enough to lay down on my bed and take a nap. Maybe I'd watch some TV, try it out, see what American television was like since it broadcast twenty-four hours, which was a novelty to me. British television did not start until late afternoon in those days, then stopped until it was time for the evening news, and went off by midnight after a rendition of "God Save the Queen." The phone rang somewhere in the back of the house. I looked over at a French ceramic phone with a dangling cord on the side table by the sofa, plugged it into a nearby wall socket, then picked up the receiver.

"Fielding residence," I said, after swallowing a bite of sandwich.

"My God, you sound as if you're in the office," the voice on the other end of the line had a familiar London accent.

"Hello, Rita, how are you?"

"I'm calling on my Princess phone. It's pink. I'm in my bedroom, for some privacy." She was almost whispering. "Do you have your own phone?"

"No, but there's several of them sprinkled around here, so it doesn't really matter." (Later, I would discover at least six.)

"Where's Camille?" Rita asked.

"Gone to lunch with a friend," I responded, taking a tiny bite of Hebrew-brand salami on corn rye bread, two things I'd never eaten before; three if you counted the Hollywood safflower mayonnaise I'd slathered the bread with.

"Camille and I had a chat on the phone yesterday. She sounds very nice. What does she look like?" Rita sounded curious.

"Tall with dark curly hair. She used to be a dancer," I responded, chewing.

"What's he like?"

"He has dark hair, too. And glasses." I swallowed the bite of sandwich. "Sometimes he smokes cigarettes in a cigarette holder."

"Speaking of cigarettes, hold on a minute, I'm going to light up." At the other end of the phone, I heard a cigarette lighter flip on and an intake of breath, which was then blown out again. "Does he write his music at home?"

"No, Camille told me he has an office over on Chandler Boulevard in North Hollywood, wherever that is, right by the train tracks." I took a sip of my diet black cherry soda, another new taste experience.

"That must be noisy." Rita exhaled.

"Maybe it helps keep him awake. He works late into the night."

"Did Camille leave you with the baby already?"

"No. Elizabeth's with the housekeeper until she gets used to me."

I heard a touch of envy in her voice. "They have a housekeeper?"

"Just three days a week."

"Is it a big house?" Rita took a long inhale of her cigarette.

"It's a mini castle with a lot of antique furniture. And the living room's practically all white." I finished off my can of soda.

"White? Do you have to clean it?"

That hadn't occurred to me. I thought about it for a moment. "Dunno."

"Is she letting you rest or have you had to do anything yet?"

"Just move some living room furniture around with Debbie Reynolds."

There was a moment's silence on the other end of the phone. "Is that the friend Camille's gone to lunch with?"

"It is." I put my bare feet up on the outsized coffee table.

Rita quickly changed the subject. "How was your flight?"

I told her about the new Super VC-10 I'd flown on from Heathrow to New York. I also told her about the woman sitting next to me who was *en route* back to the West Indies, where she managed a private estate. "She wore a lovely turquoise suit that showed off her suntan."

"And that's what we have to work on this weekend, our suntans," Rita interrupted. "Since I've already been here a few weeks and we have a pool and you don't, even though this house is obviously much smaller than the one you're living in, I've already got a good start. In fact, I'm peeling now." There was a scratching sound coming from the other end of the phone as her nails worked a bit of skin loose. "Camille already said you could come over for the weekend, Myra, that's the name of the woman I work for, and I will come and pick you up tomorrow. What would be a good time?"

"Noon?"

"See you then."

We hung up and I lay my head back against the sofa. I'd been in Los Angeles less than twenty-four hours. I hadn't unpacked my suitcase yet, but I'd chatted to a friend and moved furniture with a film star. So far, so good.

I've Just Arrived, But Get The Weekend Off

Rita's employer Myra was a petite twenty-nine-year-old blonde—"not thirty yet,"—who worked in an office Monday to Friday, and suntanned in the backyard on the weekends. She wore a white bikini and was on a permanent diet. Unlike the Fieldings, who were also on permanent diets, but did eat regularly, I never saw Myra with a piece of food in her mouth the whole time Rita worked for her. She smoked Kools, a new type of menthol cigarette, instead.

"What kind of name is Fielding?" Myra asked me as we lay in beach recliners while her three young children splashed in the pool.

I looked at her quizzically.

"What nationality?" she said.

"English, I think," I responded, recalling actor Albert Finney in the *Tom Jones* film from the novel by Henry Fielding.

"Our last name is German, not Jewish," Myra said.

Behind our dark glasses, Rita and I raised our eyebrows at each other. We didn't know the word "anti-Semitism," but recognized the word "prejudice." The world was full of

41

it. Rita and I were born after World War II, but it was still fresh in the world around us. Every family had a war story. I'd grown up seeing men with a suit sleeve cuff pinned to the shoulder where an arm used to be, or a trouser leg folded in half and pinned at the hip where a leg once was. One of our neighbors had a patched-back-together face from burning plane fuel when his plane crash- landed. I'd had a school book with pictures of bodies piled up outside concentration camp crematoriums. Children played on bomb sites where houses had burned down. And food rationing went on until 1953. The day sugar came off the ration books sweet shops sold out of candy in hours.

We knew the U.S.A. was a melting pot, but we'd seen newspaper pictures of policemen beating up black men and women and setting attack dogs on them when they were trying to vote. We knew America was a land of contradictions; we just hadn't expected it to hit us in the face quite so soon.

"What nationality's Camille? She's got dark eyes and dark hair, but her skin's very pale," Myra continued.

"Well, she doesn't sunbathe, Myra," I said.

She gave me a sharp look. Rita had warned me Myra didn't have a sense of humor. That, and the fact she'd spent some time in the state mental hospital in Camarillo, after her third child was born.

"She's on pills prescribed by her doctor," Rita had told me confidentially as we'd changed into our bathing suits in her bedroom. "More than one judging by the number of bottles in her medicine cabinet. She also has a twin sister who looks just like her, one she never mentions," Rita added meaningfully.

"How do you know?"

"Harold told me."

Personally, I thought that this was rather indiscreet of Myra's husband, who'd gone on to say they'd been high school sweethearts at Venice High. Apparently, Harold told Rita a lot of things as they did the weekly shopping or drank a beer together in the kitchen before Myra got home from work. I'd also noted that Harold was a handsome man.

"Camille's whole family originally came from England in the seventeenth century, except for a more recent Indian grandmother on her father's side," I told Myra.

"That would account for the black hair and eyes, then." Myra was satisfied with this explanation. Being part Native American was currently not as shameful as it had once been; in fact, it was now downright celebratory to admit it. At least in some parts of the U.S.A.

Harold barbecued hamburgers at the side of the pool. Rita made a salad. Myra didn't move from her sun lounge, except to rub Coppertone suntan oil on herself from time to time and check her tan line where her bikini met the top of her thighs.

"We're going out tonight," Rita informed me as we ate. "I hope you've brought money."

"Where're we going?" I chewed my hamburger, another new taste experience.

"Movies. Westwood." Rita's mouth was full of hamburger, too.

"Where's that?"

"Over by the university. It's Saturday night and everyone goes out. Lots of people our age."

"Lots of boys, you mean." This evening plan sounded promising to me.

"Exactly. Brainy ones. Ones whose families can afford to send them to college."

"Sounds good."

Rita had made friends with an American girl our own age who lived across the street from her. She could drive and, not only that, had her own car. However, that night her sister was using the Chevy, so Sharon had borrowed their mother's 1965 white Lincoln Continental. It was huge.

"Almost as big as a London bus," Rita commented.

"But a lot more comfortable," I replied, impressed, as we sank into the plush upholstery, also white. I'd only been here two days, but Los Angeles seemed to have a white shimmer about it. Maybe it was something to do with the sun. Or the smog.

Sharon was pretty, a little plump, but she wore what I considered decent clothes: a tight navy skirt and stylish blouse. Her two friends stunned me with their outfits. Deanna wore baby blue chiffon; Shelley lemon yellow. And, wait a minute, were those *white gloves?* I hadn't seen anyone wearing a chiffon dress since the bridesmaids at my cousin's wedding several years before; and wasn't it old ladies who wore white gloves? These girls were just out of high school, I reminded myself. Maybe they didn't have money yet for more up-to-date-fashions. Or a clue, another part of me added cynically. I knew I shouldn't be judgmental, but I couldn't help it. They had sweet smiles, lovely white teeth and perfect ladylike manners like some of those girls in American movies.

★★★

I thought I'd die of saccharin poisoning," I told Camille on the car ride home Sunday afternoon, then wondered if I should have said that. She might not appreciate that kind of cheeky comment. But, I was wrong; Camille loved gossip.

I'd been in the pool when she'd arrived, and was sopping wet. Camille was in a hurry, said not to bother changing, I could dry off on the way back. Her 1958 Ford Fairlane had a Naugahyde front seat. I wrapped myself in a beach towel and regaled her with tales of the weekend as she drove along the recently-opened Santa Monica freeway, through the crazy eight pattern of the Downtown interchange and onto the Hollywood freeway north towards the Valley and Studio City.

"Myra lives in a bikini unless the temperature drops," I rattled on. "Then she puts on shorts. Her husband, Harold, lives in his pool shorts, too, unless he has to go out on-call. Then he throws on a t-shirt and tennis shoes. He's a plumber. He had to go over to Beverly Hills today to deal with Dean Martin's pool problem. Myra almost went with him, but changed her mind when she found out Dean Martin was in Vegas."

Camille chuckled. She especially liked this kind of gossip. "What else?"

"We went to the late show last night and saw *What's New, Pussycat*. Rita and I thought it was very funny. We laughed our heads off at some of the jokes. The American girls didn't laugh as much. I think they thought it was a bit risqué."

I mentioned differences between going to the movies in England versus America. In England you were escorted to your seat by an usher. There were different prices for different parts of the cinema. In America, I'd just learned it was a free for all; everyone paid the same price for a seat (barring children and seniors) and sat where they wanted to.

"The highlight of the evening as far as Rita was concerned was bumping into the actor, James Mason, as she came out of the Ladies Room. She was thrilled."

Camille laughed. "What else. Did you meet any interesting guys?"

"No. They were everywhere on the street, but we didn't actually meet any to say more than two words to. We hadn't been able to get into the eight o'clock show, so we went to a coffee shop for an hour and had peanut milkshakes."

The coffee shop had seemed to be full of kids on dates. I wasn't that keen on peanuts, I told Camille, but everyone else had ordered one, except Sharon. She opted for a glass of water, so she'd be able to keep wiggling into her tight skirt. I'd been astounded to see a long-handled spoon sticking straight up from a mountain of whipped cream on top of the frosted glass when the drinks arrived. In England, a milkshake was exactly that: a glass of flavored milk shaken vigorously. Some of the fashions might be a bit behind what I was used to, but the food was superior, I thought, if not a bit over the top. And there was so much of it. If Rita and I wanted to keep fitting into our bikinis, we'd soon be on diets, too.

★★★

Camille had come back from lunch with Debbie that prior Friday when we'd rearranged the living-room furniture before they went out to eat. After taking Essie to the bus stop (it took her three buses to get home to Watts, only two if Camille drove her into Hollywood), she had declared that she was starving as she came through the front door. "I only had a salad for lunch. Without dressing, just lemon juice," Camille added.

It didn't sound so bad to me, but I was yet to sample the bottles of salad dressing in the refrigerator door and discover the delight of Bernstein's Green Goddess on a wedge of iceberg lettuce.

The phone started ringing in the kitchen, so Camille went to answer it and get a diet soda.

"I'm cooking steaks," she announced putting the receiver down. "Jerry's taking his daughters from his first marriage out to dinner. There's some sort of problem with the twelve-year-old." She consulted her watch. "We can eat on TV trays while we watch the six o'clock news."

"Can I do anything?"

"You can make the salad or feed Elizabeth, your choice."

"I'll feed her," I said, thinking the sooner the baby got used to me in her normal routine, the better.

Camille put Elizabeth in her highchair and tied a bib around her neck. "I keep them in the second drawer down from the cutlery," she explained, then handed me some jars of Gerber baby food. Elizabeth had a heated baby dish, divided into three compartments. "Just plug it in and put the food in each compartment: meat, vegetables, desert. Tonight, we have lamb, green beans and peaches. Yum,

yum," she said to Elizabeth, who kept a close eye on her dinner preparation.

When Rita and I had applied for our jobs we were told they might entail caring for young children or babies. We had both thought the same thing: How difficult could a baby be? They had a limited repertoire and couldn't answer back. As I spooned out the revolting-looking food according to instructions, Elizabeth watched me closely and smacked her little lips. I thought: so far, so good.

"How do you like your steak?" Camille turned from the stove.

I'd never been consulted how I wanted my food cooked at home, so I was at a loss to answer. We rarely ate steak. It was too expensive. My mother cooked a joint of lamb, pork or beef on Sunday only. Well-cooked. Overdone.

"Medium rare?" Camille queried. I had no idea what that meant.

"Just so long as it isn't squeaking," I nodded, joking.

"How is it?" Camille asked as we sat in the living room a short while later with our TV trays loaded with steak, baked potato and salad listening to Walter Cronkite report on the state of the world. What I had thought would be a piece of steak for two turned out to be a steak for one. My plate was loaded with a piece of meat that would have fed our whole family of four at home and was bloody in the middle. Camille had her own enormous T-bone.

I took a sip of the red wine that she always served with dinner, another new experience for me that I had no trouble getting used to. "Fantastic."

Elizabeth was back on the living room floor in the middle of her toys. I always marveled at the way the white carpet stayed white with so many people and so much activity in the household. I never saw anyone actually clean the carpet, although Essie, Camille and I took turns vacuuming , and it was a shag carpet after all.

Meanwhile, Walter was reporting on the Vietnam War. "Oh, this is crazy! Johnson's out of his mind." Camille watched the television, outraged.

I sat and chewed my steak, looking at the lush Vietnamese countryside as American boys my own age were being shot at and dragged into helicopters by friends, their faces and hands streaked with blood and dirt. She was right. It was crazy. We didn't have this where I came from; we didn't watch our relatives getting blown to bits as we ate dinner. We waited until we went to the cinema and watched actors portray historical heroes or fictional characters getting killed and wounded in a film several years after the fact.

"We have no business being over there," Camille continued. "Johnson should get us out before it's too late."

I didn't know much about American politics, only what I read in the newspaper. Politics in my family only ran to the General Election, when both my parents voted for the Conservative party, no matter who the personality standing for it was. There was no political discussion. I'd never paid much attention, since I wasn't old enough to vote.

"I remember that shocking photo of a Buddhist monk setting himself on fire in the streets of Saigon," I said. "It was made into a postcard in Europe. And then President Kennedy was assassinated a few months later," I added.

"Yeah, but that didn't happen because of Vietnam," Camille commented. "There's a book in our bookshelves" she nodded towards it, "that was published in England. It wasn't allowed to be published here. It says it was the Texas oilmen who killed Kennedy."

I looked over at the massive bookshelf. My family had a small one, but it contained holiday souvenirs and the fruit bowl. My family weren't interested in books or reading. But I was.

"We've got John Kennedy's book he wrote, too. You might enjoy reading *Profiles in Courage*," Camille suggested.

I was now remembering another famous newspaper photo, the one of President Johnson taking the oath of office on Air Force One while Jackie Kennedy stood looking on in her bloodied pink suit. It seemed the whole world had mourned alongside the Americans. Then, last year, there had been a picture of Johnson on the front page of the newspaper picking up a Beagle by its ears. It had outraged the English public and ignited debates on television whether it really did not hurt a dog to pick him up by his ears as Johnson had claimed. The general consensus was not on his side. The incident had caused more negative comments than those about the Vietnam War.

★★★

As Camille drove us back to Studio City on that Sunday afternoon, my first weekend in America when I'd stayed with Rita, I had a moment of déjà vu. As we ascended the steps to the house, I mentioned it to Camille.

"I had a dream about two weeks ago where you and I were walking up these steps. Everything looked like it really does except we had bags of groceries in our arms, and your hair was long, not short."

Camille stopped and stared at me. "I had my hair cut two weeks ago. It was long like yours, but curlier, not straight. Perhaps that's why Elizabeth's taking to you so quickly; it's your hair."

Could be, I thought to myself. Could also be the Kewpie doll I'd given her as we watched TV that prior Friday night. "You can chew on it," I remarked as I handed over the rubber baby, "or you can throw it across the room and it won't break." Elizabeth had looked at the doll, looked back at me, then back at the doll as she stuck it in her mouth and bit its leg.

7

Bette the Realtor Drops In For Sunday Cocktails

*M*y friend Joyce is watching Elizabeth, that's why I was in such a hurry when I picked you up from Rita's," Camille explained as we finished climbing the stone steps and she opened the front door. "Joyce and I went to high school together. She works at Hanna Barbera Studios. They make those Saturday morning cartoons you were watching before Rita and Myra came to pick you up yesterday."

"Elizabeth likes those cartoons."

"Joyce will be pleased to know that."

We stepped down into the living room. A woman in what I considered a very hip t-shirt dress of wide purple and green stripes stood by the drinks tray, an empty glass filled with ice cubes in one hand; her other hand paused over the gin decanter. "Oh, good, you're back, Camille. Little Princess here was starting to get anxious."

Indeed, ten-month-old Elizabeth was scooting across the floor towards her mother as fast as she could as Camille introduced me to Joyce.

I'd stuck my head out of the open car window and blow-dried my hair on the drive back from West Los

Angeles. Full of volume, it now floated like a halo around my head. Joyce took in my bikini, also now dry, as well as the hair, which she commented on as "very rock and roll-y." "Did Camille drag you out of a swimming pool?" she asked.

"Almost," I smiled.

"Don't mind me. I always say what's on my mind," Joyce added. "Camille, I'm fixing myself another drink; do you want one?"

"Just my usual scotch," Camille requested, bending down from the waist and keeping her legs straight as she picked Elizabeth up from the floor. It was the dancer in her, I realized, marveling how she could stretch and be that flexible in spite of being over sixth months pregnant. I couldn't have done it.

"Aletheia, would you like something?" Camille straightened up as Elizabeth's chubby little arms tightened around her mother's neck.

"I'm drinking gin and tonic," Joyce told me over her shoulder.

"Sounds good," I replied crossing the room towards the hallway and my room. "I think I better change."

As I shut my bedroom door, I heard Joyce say: "Oh, Camille, she looks so young; but I have a feeling she's going to fit right into this household."

When I walked back into the living room a short while later, Joyce patted the couch beside her. "Come and sit next to me, Aletheia. Your drink's over here. I put ice in it, I hope that's alright. Someone told me the English don't put ice in their drinks."

"That's fine," I said picking up my drink from the coffee table before sinking into the long white couch beside her. "I'm not in England, now. Cheers."

The front door suddenly opened and a woman in a tight dress, heels and a flowered hat, rather like my mother would have worn to church, which covered her hair in colored petals, sailed into the entryway.

"Camille? Yoo-hoo!"

"In here, Bette," Camille called back. "You're just in time for cocktail hour."

"Oh, goody." Bette didn't stop talking as she stepped down into the living room. "Camille, I've found your next house. I'm so excited! You're gonna love it. I just have to persuade the owners to sell it first."

"Aletheia, this is Bette, my realtor. Her sister went to high school with Joyce and I." Camille introduced us. "Bette sold me this house."

"And now I'm going to sell you another house, a bigger house; one that overlooks Hollywood and practically the whole of Los Angeles. Hi, Joyce" Bette eyeballed our beverages. "What're you all drinking?"

"Mine's a scotch, J&B, and they have gin and tonics," Camille replied.

"How very British!" Bette sat down in one of the wing chairs. "I'll have a gin and tonic, too." She smiled brightly at me and I was reminded of bubbly female characters I'd seen in Doris Day movies as a child.

"Don't get up, Camille," Joyce commanded, rising up from the sofa, "I'll get it. I have a feeling I need to top mine up to listen to this." Joyce looked at my drink and raised her eyebrows: *Top yours up too?* I shook my head, *no*.

"Where is it?" Camille looked tired, sitting in the armchair, Elizabeth on her knee, but she perked up as Bette rattled on.

"Outpost Estates, off Franklin between Highland and La Brea, high up in the hills. You can see the Magic Castle down below."

I perked up, too. Castle?

"It's a professional magician's place. They put on shows," Joyce explained from beside the drinks tray.

Bette was full of enthusiasm. "The house is at the end of a cul-de-sac with a ten-foot high wall around it and solid wooden gates that are just as high. You can't see the place from the street when they're closed. I've been up there before and they were open today, so I walked into this charming garden and rang the front doorbell. And, guess what? The lady of the house was home. Oh, it's so darling, Camille! The front looks like a two-story vintage California Spanish with masses of bougainvillea shading the second-story balcony. There's even a patio on one side of the front yard, with a little merry-go-round for the kids,"

"Oh, boy," Joyce muttered handing Bette her drink before sitting down again. She lit a cigarette and leaned her head back against the sofa, blowing out smoke rings.

"There's stairs at the side of the patio, with a little iron gate at the top so the kiddies don't fall down the stone steps leading to a third floor down below that'll be purr-fect for Jerry's office studio. He'll have his own entrance for business associates." She took a quick sip of her cocktail. "I think he'll be able to get his piano down there. You can also access this floor from inside the house, of course. It was built in 1928 for Max Reinhardt, one of those German directors that came over in the 1920's. Darn it, I left my purse in the car. Joyce, can I have a cigarette?"

Joyce handed her the pack and a lighter.

"Menthols. Oh, good." Bette took a moment to light up.

"How many bedrooms?" Camille had a dreamy look in her eyes.

Bette started counting on her fingers, waving the cigarette around dangerously.

"Let's see, one in front with a balcony, one with a little room off of it that must have been a porch at one time before it was enclosed, and those rooms share a bathroom. Then there's a master bedroom suite on the other side that has two bathrooms along with walk-in closets, although the bidet's not working in what would be your bathroom, Camille, but you could fix that."

Bette took a puff of her cigarette as Camille, Joyce and I exchanged looks with arched eyebrows. *A bidet! Wow! Fancy!*

"There's also a fireplace in the master bedroom, and another room adjacent you could use for a private sitting room, or your sewing room, Camille," Betty suggested. "Oh, and the master bedroom suite has a little outdoor porch so you can watch the sunset over the ocean in the distance. Or sunbathe in the nude," she added as an afterthought.

"Jesus!" Joyce exclaimed. "How far up in the hills is this place?"

"Almost to Mulholland," Bette replied, mentioning the road that ran along the top of the Hollywood Hills across to Bel Air.

"This house has four bedrooms, five if you count Aletheia's room, which was the study," Camille pointed out.

"That third floor down below the house I'm talking about also has an additional suite of three rooms and a full bathroom, next to what would be Jerry's office and bathroom, plus a laundry room." Bette continued ticking off more rooms on her fingers. "Then there's a huge sunken living room, twice the size of this one," she estimated, looking around. "Plus, a much bigger dining room than you have now with two sets of French windows, each with its own balcony. Although Mesa, the current owner, says they're not safe to step onto, and I have to agree with her, they're flimsy-looking and rusty. There's a breakfast room off of the dining room and a butler's pantry leading to the kitchen, which has its own porch plus an enclosed pantry...."

"How many bathrooms altogether?" Camille interrupted, the dreamy look getting practical.

Bette counted on her fingers again. "Six, with a facility down by the pool, although that's not currently working and probably hasn't been for a long time."

"A pool?" Camille sat up a little straighter.

I did, too, picturing me working on my California tan while the babies napped.

Bette wasn't finished counting rooms. "It has a library, too, with its own bathroom, and a walk-in cocktail alcove that has a darling hand-painted wall mural, all gold and happy-looking with exotic flowers and palm leaves. Perfect for all your entertaining, Camille. This would be a very comfortable house for you and Jerry."

"Sounds like the Garden of Eden," Joyce snorted as she lit another cigarette, offering me the pack.

I shook my head. "No, thanks. I don't smoke."

Bette wrapped up her description. "Jerry would have a lovely view of the terraced garden from his office, with Los Angeles spread out down below."

I finished my drink and sank deeper into the white sofa. As exciting as all this sounded, the past few days were catching up with me. What did I know about buying houses? I was nineteen and suffering from jet lag.

"How big's the house?" Camille sipped her scotch and looked intently at her realtor.

"About seventy-five hundred square feet."

"For Crissakes, Bette, it's a mansion!" Joyce was certainly not a woman to mince words.

Bette stubbed her cigarette out in the crystal ashtray. "I think you can get it pretty cheap, Camille."

"Why, what's wrong with it?"

Bette pondered the comfy little mansion in her mind. "It needs a bit of fixing up."

"Here we go." Joyce leaned back on the sofa next to me.

"What kind of fixing up are we talking about?" Camille asked, slowly.

"Every room needs a coat of paint. Mesa's two little boys like drawing on their bedroom walls. Women with thirty bosoms on their chest, that kind of thing. The kitchen is original down to the gas oven, circa 1928. Remodeling that could wait for a while, although I'd replace the gas stove as it's very temperamental. When I turned one of the knobs on a flame shot up a foot in the air."

"I could replace it with the one I have now." Camille shifted Elizabeth on her knee. "Why else would the owners sell it cheap?"

"Mesa and husband are building a boat to sail round the world so the children can get a real education. The boat's almost finished, but I got the impression they're running out of money for this trip." Bette finished her drink. "Listen, Camille, I think you ought to move fast on this. It isn't on the market, yet, and I get the feeling they'd rather not bother. You should make them an offer. I've looked up comparable prices in the area and I think you can get the house for a third of what it's worth."

"So they can go sailing." Camille finished her scotch.

"It's in need of paint," Joyce reminded her. "About seventy-five hundred square feet of it."

"What about the outside?" Camille put Elizabeth down on the floor and handed her a toy.

Bette considered. "That painting can wait a few years."

"When can I see it?" Camille's dreamy look sharpened into resolve.

"Mesa said she'll be at home on Tuesday afternoon."

"Perfect."

Camille Buys a Mansion

*A*nd, apparently, it was. Camille fell in love with the house and less than two weeks later she bought it. She also bought new handbags for Essie and myself to celebrate. Since I was used to presents only at birthdays and Christmas, I was surprised by Camille's generosity. I gave her an impromptu thank-you kiss on the cheek which she accepted with an embarrassed giggle.

Jerry was delighted with the prospect of the new house on the hill. He could look down on Hollywood and all the studio businessmen and producers who told him how to write music.

His business office manager was not thrilled. He said: "No, you can't afford it."

Camille pointed out that having Jerry's office at home would be a big tax advantage.

The business office pointed out that Jerry was supporting a wife, three and soon-to-be four children, an ex-wife and her household, a housekeeper and now me; not to mention an aged mother in Pittsburgh.

My grandmother used to say, *where there's a will there's a way.* Camille was determined to find a way. She dug her

heels in and negotiations with the business office began.
So did the economizing.

Camille started by doing her weekly shopping at the
supermarket instead of having everything delivered. I was
awed the first time we stepped into *The Market Basket*.
Apart from the multi-colored flags and streamers hanging
from the walls and ceiling with colorful advertisements
dangling over strategic areas, everything gleamed: the
shiny off-white floor, the shiny off-white walls, the mountain of vegetables and perfect-looking shiny fruit.

"They wax them," Camille told me, weighing out shiny
red apples of identical size.

I ran my finger over a nearby russet potato: no dirt. No
bugs when I picked up a lettuce and inspected it, either.
There was always one small slug hidden in the leaves when
I'd wash lettuce for my mother at home. Camille asked
me what I liked to eat. I pushed the shopping cart down
the aisles as she plucked a giant-sized container of Yuban
coffee off of one shelf, a jar of Hollywood safflower mayonnaise off of another and chose cans of frozen *Minute
Maid* orange juice from the freezer chest.

I shrugged and said, "everything."

"Anything you dislike?" she wanted to know.

I shook my head: "No."

In the first few years after World War II when I was a
small child food had still been rationed, so "dislike" had
never been in my vocabulary. I'd learned to eat what was
put before me, because there wasn't anything else. A sign
announced "nine pounds of oranges for 99 cents." Camille
stood and contemplated this for a moment as we tried to

think what we could do with them. In the end she said, "We'll wait. They'll get cheaper and better soon."

Since Camille's bank was next to the supermarket I opened a checking account at Bank of America, too, with my traveler's checks. The *Continental Domestics* agency, which had furnished me with my job, was just around the corner on Ventura Place.

We walked over, stopping at the post office so I could buy some 11-cent airmail letters to send home to friends and family. Camille had a portable typewriter I could "feel free to use any time it wasn't in the repair shop," which turned out to be often. When I wasn't using it to correspond with all my friends, family, and everyone I'd worked with, Camille was answering some of Debbie's fan mail for her.

"I was just about to phone you," Jackie the receptionist said after Camille had introduced us. Jackie and her mother, Coraline, owned the business and were from London originally. "You need to fill in this form for your health insurance." Jackie waved a piece of paper at me after extracting it from a stack on her desk. "Ask your mum to get a note from your doctor as soon as possible stating you're in good health. You don't want to get caught without insurance in this country, does she Camille?"

"Absolutely not," Camille agreed, watching Coraline plug in the electric kettle and reach for the box of Lipton teabags. "Listen, Aletheia, stay and take care of things. I'm just popping into the antiques shop next door."

She was gone for forty-five minutes while I had two cups of tea as Jackie explained to me that the mandatory doctor's examination and chest x-ray I'd had to pay for at the American Embassy in London for my visa didn't count with Blue Cross. "That was for getting into the country," she said. "Now you have to start paying every month for coverage in case of illness or accident. No National Health here," she added, referring to the British health insurance system that covered everyone and everything, costing just a few shillings a week out of a person's paycheck. Or nothing if you didn't get one. I'd had to also pay for my visa and other Embassy fees, as well as job placement fees with the English employment agency who'd put me in touch with Jackie and her mother, which had cost me another fee. In fact, I'd been shelling money out left, right and center to get to America, and now I understood it was going to continue. It was the American way.

It was also part of being grownup and on your own out in the big, wide world, even if you were relying on the kindness of strangers. Adventures always demanded some kind of token.

Jackie asked how I was getting on at the Fieldings. She and her mother thought I was lucky to have Camille as an employer; she seemed so nice. I agreed. Camille was nothing but kind to me while I worked for her. And so was Jerry.

Coraline asked if I'd paid the Fieldings back yet for the airfare deposit they'd advanced me. Since Camille preferred to pay me every two weeks instead of once a month, I assured both Coraline and Jackie it had come out of my first paycheck. I'd also received the coupon booklet to make monthly payments for the rest of the fare advanced by a finance company which the agency had arranged. They were happy to hear this, and pleased that I was settling in so well. Jackie said to keep in touch and drop in any time.

Camille came to collect me with a broad smile on her face. As we walked back to the car, she steered me towards an antiques shop window.

"What d'you think?" She pointed at some colored cut-crystal wineglasses.

"Very pretty," I replied.

"I put them on layaway," she admitted as the shop owner started removing the wineglasses from the window and wrapping them in tissue paper. "If I don't get them now, someone else may snap them up by next week. They're such a good price. I plan on doing a lot more entertaining after we move."

"You'll need them, then." Her idea of economizing and mine were poles apart, but hers seemed logical to me in a Hollywood kind of way.

"Exactly." Camille was pleased I agreed with her. "I think I can squeeze it out of the housekeeping."

And for the next few weeks, she did. Camille had grown up during 1930's when the Depression was in full swing in America and she knew how to stretch a penny but still keep life looking glamorous. She had worked hard since she was a child. Her father, Dick Williams, had been one of the first soundmen in Hollywood. The studios had taken men from the telephone company where he worked when talkies began.

Sometimes, Camille's father would take his young daughter with him to Warner Brothers where he worked. The doctor had recommended dancing lessons to strengthen her little legs after an illness. It set the four-year-old Camille on a trajectory for life. Pretty soon she appeared in one of the "Our Gang" comedies, and then developed a dancing career. Since she'd now embarked on a new career as wife and mother, she relied on her savings and investments to help out when needed. Jerry's business manager didn't stand a chance. With her dream house in sight, albeit a little shabby, but that could be fixed; nothing was going to stand in Camille's way. I understood that. I was living one of my dreams, admittedly on a much lower level, but where we intersected it was working out for both of us.

We were both wrangling with our budgets. Camille with her household expenses and selling off a few personal stocks and shares, and me making airline and health insurance payments out of my $150.00 a month, while buying dozens of stamps and airmail letters to write to family and friends. Airmails cost 11 cents to send to Europe, and postcard stamps cost eight cents.

I'd been used to wearing the latest London fashions in England. Now I had to restrict my clothing budget, in spite of all the cute clothes I hankered after at the Sherman Oaks Mall where Camille sometimes shopped. It tortured me when Joyce came over in her latest new outfit. Camille took pity on me. She thought the summer dresses I'd brought from home were too good for everyday wear around the house so she suggested two new ones from Macy's. She'd pay for one: a loose black and white checked cotton embroidered with orange and yellow daisies on the pockets. I'd pay for the other: a sleeveless shift in turquoise with large lime-colored polka dots and striped ruffles around the bottom. We cut one ruffle off since hemlines were starting to go up.

"There," she said standing up after pinning the hem, so I could sew it, "that's your uniform."

Essie took one look at me and admitted she loved the colors but stated she was sticking to the standard white nurse's type uniform for her household duties.

9

Scheming How to Pay For It

There was no comparison between living the life I'd left behind in England and my new life in Los Angeles, everything was different, but overall I felt I was navigating the culture shock very well. The Fieldings went out to dinner two or three times a week. They also entertained at home at least twice a week. Camille did the cooking. When she found out I liked to cook she let me fix a meal when there was just the three of us. Lamb cutlets in wine, a recipe out of the *Los Angeles Times* food section, went down very well the first time I made dinner. Shepherd's pie did not. Camille would have a meal the night before her weekly grocery shop that used up all leftovers. Sometimes there was enough chicken to heat up; sometimes different meats went into a casserole. On the night I made shepherd's pie several different meats and vegetables had been camouflaged with a crispy mashed potato crust.

"What's this?" Jerry held up his fork. "Liver?"

Camille had cooked calves liver for us one night when Jerry was out with his two eldest daughters.

"It's leftover night," Camille explained.

"It's shepherd's pie," I added.

"It's shepherd's pants," he decided, good-naturedly, carefully picking through the rest of the food. "Never do that again; I hate liver."

Camille usually kept it simple for dessert: ice-cream. Suddenly I was sampling the delights of Black Cherry Marshmallow, Fresh Peach, Chocolate Chip, Pistachio Nut, and my personal favorite, Rocky Road with chocolate ice cream, nuts and marshmallows. So much for diets, although we did keep the portions small.

When the house went into escrow, apart from scheming and negotiating how to pay for it, Camille started planning and coordinating the rehabilitation and move. Her father agreed to paint the new house just as he'd done with the current one since he was on hiatus from the movie studio. He and Camille estimated it would take three months. All the walls were to be white, except for Elizabeth's room which would be pink. Since the new baby was due in early October, the move was planned for early November.

Essie liked the idea of the new house. "I'll only have to take two buses from Watts to get to work," she commented. "Right now I have to take three."

"I'll be able to just drive down the hill and pick you up on Hollywood Boulevard," Camille realized and they agreed it would be easier on both of them.

Essie had her own routine on the days she came in: mainly vacuuming if it was needed (I hoovered sometimes and so did Camille), mopping the kitchen floor once a week and taking care of Jerry and Camille's laundry and other miscellaneous duties, like cleaning the refrigerator which neither Camille or I ever seemed to get round to doing. I took care of Elizabeth's and my laundry, which was negligible since neither of us wore very much. The temperature kept going up so I often wore my bikini under one of my new housedresses. I'd discovered I could fit into Elizabeth's boat-shaped paddling pool; she was delighted when I climbed in beside her to play on those hot afternoons. It made Camille laugh, too. Elizabeth was fussy with friends and strangers alike so it was a relief to everyone that she took to me so easily.

Camille had been gifted with a diaper service for a year at Elizabeth's baby shower. The *Tidee Didee's* driver picked up the pail full of used diapers put out on the front doorstep every Friday, replacing it with a clean and fresh folded pile ready to go for another week.

We both knew that things would be different when the new baby arrived; I would be busier. And so would Camille, dealing with the new house and planning the move. On the days Essie worked, before escrow for the new house closed, Camille used to take me shopping with her to help me acclimatize to Southern California ways.

Save-on drugstore occupied the same block as the bank and grocery store on Ventura Boulevard. Camille bought most non-food items such as cotton swabs at *Saveon* because they were less expensive than at *Market Basket*. One day as we pushed the shopping cart to the drugstore checkout, Camille stopped mid-aisle by the jewelry counter.

"Look at those beautiful necklaces!"

I stared at ropes of gaudy glass beads as she started picking them up, rhapsodizing over the vibrant colors. Was she losing her mind? I wondered. Did this have something to do with her pregnancy, or the heat? She had diamonds at home; why did she need cheap-looking jewelry?

"I take them apart and make Christmas decorations with the beads," she explained.

"It's still July," I reminded her.

"I know, but I go all out with the festivities so I have to start early. We do a lot of entertaining, so I start planning menus and doing some of the cooking in October and freeze it. Last year I cooked a thirty-five pound turkey for Christmas Day. We're going to be very busy for the rest of the year so we should start preparing now. Christmas will be here before you know it. And look," she held up more strands of ugly baubles, "they're all on sale. Half-price!"

Camille dropped them into the shopping cart. "Single beads at the Arts and Crafts store will cost you a helluva lot more. And Christmas decorations at *Robinsons* in Beverly Hills are expensive."

I saw her logic. Camille was teaching me a lot about a bigger picture as well as planning and preparing for it. Christmas in July? Why not? I started helping her load the shopping cart with glittery colors that I was assured would look wonderful when repurposed as table decorations. We mentally calendared our arts and craft projects to start those last few weeks before the new baby arrived, afterwards during Camille's recovery, and before the house move. At the time, neither of us could guess how even the best laid plans could be abruptly turned upside down and become a serious challenge.

Meanwhile, I talked to Rita almost every day on the phone. Camille encouraged me to visit her as often as I could before the new baby arrived as we'd have our hands full with two children, not to mention everything else. Rita only lived two miles from the beach, but refused to sunbathe there.

"Don't feel thin enough," she admitted.

I mentioned if she stopped running out to the Helms Bakery Van when it came by and buying bread and breakfast pastries that might solve her problem.

"Can't do that." Rita had a stubborn streak.

The siren song of the Helms van's musical horn as it parked in the middle of the street invited all housewives on the block to come running, purchasing their cinnamon rolls, gooey Bear Claws and cheese Danish as they gossiped with each other and made friends. That's how Rita was getting to know people. At eighteen years old she was left alone all day to run the small house and supervise three children under nine after school while Myra and Harold were working. It was a life very different from mine.

★★★

I had my first dip in the Pacific Ocean three weeks after I arrived when Jerry took a Saturday afternoon off from composing to visit a writer friend in Malibu. Camille, Elizabeth and I went with him and sat on the beach while Jerry and his friend discussed business; they were working on a television show and shared commiserations about some of the personalities involved. Like the producer and the director. And the star. Jerry always felt actors were paid more than they were worth. The writer friend felt he wasn't being paid enough.

"But at least you get to work out here," Jerry said, nodding towards the ocean as we got ready to leave.

"Yeah, and it's costing me $400.00 a week to rent this place," the writer replied. "Can you believe they get *Four Hundred Dollars* a week for this shack?"

I thought it was a cozy little seaside bungalow, but then my standards were obviously much lower than the writer's.

Jerry just shook his head and said he had to get back to work, not mentioning that he and Camille had just signed on the dotted line for a new mortgage. Nothing was a done deal until the money was fully secured and escrow closed. Besides, he was working on several projects at once. An afternoon off, even though it was to discuss business as well as pleasure, was a precious commodity. Any time away from his work was a precious commodity, even though it was a necessity. The household revolved around Jerry's work. Camille arranged it that way, and tried to keep everything running as smoothly as possible. Tried. One unexpected surprise a day was a quiet day, a dull day. I didn't know what would happen next, and neither did anyone else.

Jerry was always working on more than one project at a time. He hardly ever turned a job down. There had been too many hard years during the Hollywood Blacklist when most of his friends had been shunned by the studios. Some, like Dalton Trumbo, had worked under other names. Jerry, who had refused to name names or turn anyone in, pleaded the Fifth Amendment to the House Un-American Activities Committee (HUAC) and found himself out of work.

"He mainly survived by taking a band on the road and working in Las Vegas," Camille told me. "Then Debbie asked him to arrange music for her new album and Betty Hutton hired him for her show."

Years later, Groucho Marx apologized in his biography to Jerry for mentioning his name to HUAC. Groucho had given the young Jerry a career break hiring him as musical director for his radio, then later his television, shows. This led to mandatory membership in the Radio Union, necessary for all nationally broadcast radio performers, the crime which eventually brought Jerry before HUAC. That, and hiring black as well as white musicians for the shows, integration being offensive to J. Edgar Hoover and some HUAC members.

"If everyone else in the industry would have got together they could have stopped it," Camille maintained. "It wasn't about patriotism; it was about money. After Trumbo got out of jail and that period of his life was over, he started buying the houses to the left and right of his when they went up for sale until he pretty much owned the whole block. That way he could choose who lived in close proximity to him."

So not only was it all about money in America, it was also about politics.

As July slid into August the constellation of Casa de Fielding swirled at a fast rate. Camille and I established a daily routine based on pure chaos anchored by cocktail hour at four o'clock. Cocktail hour was supposed to be a rest hour where we sat down, whether there were people coming in and out of the house or not. And there were always people coming and going, including a lot of musicians who picked up extra money from copying music for

Jerry since everything was done by hand in those days. Jerry was writing the theme music for a new television show *Hogan's Heroes* as well as a television special starring Gene Kelly and the British pop singer Tommy Steele, for which he'd shortly have to travel to New York. Camille was hoping to go with him for a long weekend at least, but her obstetrician was slow to greenlight that idea.

One Saturday afternoon I returned from shopping in Santa Monica with Rita and opened the front door to absolute chaos. Jerry and his manager were in the dining room with papers all over the table. Some musicians were in the living room with papers all over the floor. A young German Shepherd was corralled in Elizabeth's playpen chewing on a toy. Nobody paid any attention to me. Camille was in the backyard with her friends, smoking a cigarette while her little gray poodle took his bathroom break. Little Doggie started wandering up the hill, sniffing at some gopher holes.

"Get away from there!" Camille admonished. The gardener had put poison down the holes, which was having little effect; every day there were fresh holes in the grass. Little Doggie took no notice of course; he never did. I secretly wondered about inbreeding in his lineage. I didn't care for poodles and this one seemed very spoiled. Little Doggie didn't do stairs of any kind so Camille carried him around a lot. She always carried him up the steps to the lawn when he needed to go outside.

"Can't you just let him out by himself?" I'd commented soon after I arrived to live with the Fieldings.

"He won't go up the steps by himself," Camille explained. "He has a phobia about the retaining wall." She maintained it wasn't Little Doggie's fault. Jerry had gifted her with the little ball of gray fluff when she was pregnant with Elizabeth. "He was *so* cute," she added, "but the first time I took him out he fell off the wall. I feel guilty. I think he suffered a brain injury."

A demented dog. That figured in this household. I felt sorry for Little Doggie and a little bit guilty myself that I didn't pay him more loving attention, but Camille seemed to have that territory well covered. She fed him. He was her dog, and for his part, he didn't care much about anyone else except her, so it was easy for me not to feel too guilty.

A wail came from an open upstairs window.

"Elizabeth's up." Camille said, looking hot and tired as she went to rescue Perrito before he poisoned himself with gopher pellets. "She took a very long nap today."

As I went to retrieve the baby I wasn't surprised. I thought Elizabeth slept a lot for a ten-month-old, but then what did I know? The quieter she was the better. I had come to realize Elizabeth had so much stimulation when she was awake that the crib was her refuge. Babies get worn out, too, and need their dreamtime I reasoned.

As each day passed the temperature climbed. Somehow, the heat didn't affect me as badly as everyone else. I just sweated and climbed into Elizabeth's paddling pool to play with her. She continued to think this was hilarious; I was the only adult who managed to fit into it. During the day, Camille and I closed the curtains and windows opening them during the evening to let in cooler night air.

It got hotter and hotter. Then on the evening of August 11th, the night exploded when a white California Highway

Patrol officer stopped a young black man driving his mother's Buick. The vehicle's passenger, driver Marquette Frye's younger brother, ran to get their mother from their nearby house. The situation quickly escalated: another officer pulled out a shotgun; backup officers arrived. Rumors spread through the neighborhood police were roughing up a pregnant woman as well as Frye. Angry neighbors gathered. A fight between police and local citizens broke out. The Watts riots had begun.

10

Summer in the City: the Watts Riots

*I*t spread like wildfire. Street blockades were quickly established with hand-printed signs on them: "Turn Left Or Get Shot."

"It's like a war zone down here," people told reporters.

Civil rights leaders called for California National Guard and Marshall law for the County of Los Angeles that night. But they were ignored.

"Leadership is virtually absent," ABC News reported as Camille and I sat watching the television, stunned. Mayor Sam Yorty was in San Francisco to address a convention; three city council members were nowhere to be seen.

Jerry came home just as Police Chief Tom Parker compared his "thin blue line" trying to maintain law and order to "fighting the Vietcong."

"He's been drafting southern cops into the LAPD for that area the past year," Jerry commented tersely, reaching for the phone and dialing. "Essie what's going on in your neighborhood? We're watching the late night news."

So was Essie in her little white frame house in Watts. She was angry and frightened, but wasn't about to go outside, even though her particular street was relatively quiet. Her twenty-three-year-old son, Roy Lee, had been roughed up by police the week before when he'd gone out to buy food.

"He's been beaten up before," she'd told Camille and me the next morning, "for doing nothing." I'd listened disbelieving yet comprehending at the same time, recalling horrific photos in the English newspapers reporting on the American civil rights movement. But that was in the south. This was California. Wasn't a colored person supposedly treated better here?

"Don't be fooled by the view of Watts from the 110 freeway of a nice suburban neighborhood with small homes and palm trees," Camille told me later. "Los Angeles has racial covenants which were outlawed by the courts in 1945 but local realtors ignore that." Blacks and Mexicans couldn't rent or buy in certain areas of the city. "Living conditions in Watts are inferior compared to other areas because of over-crowding, plus the schools are inadequate and people can't get jobs. The unemployment rate's forty per-cent."

I didn't know what to say. I knew America was a crazy place, but everything was so much larger than my nineteen years of life and experience. I felt very bad for Essie. She came to work three days a week, got on with her job, then took three buses home to the family she was supporting on forty dollars a week, plus bus fare.

Essie managed to get to work the first morning after the riots began, but the buses stopped running later in the day. She couldn't get home. Governor Pat Brown finally sent in 4,000 California Army National Guard troops later that afternoon and imposed a curfew for all Black neighborhoods. The national news was scathing in its reporting of "the leisurely way" the state authorities had arrived in Los Angeles to see what was going on first-hand. "I'll drive you home before the curfew," Jerry told Essie. Camille grew nervous waiting for his return. Cocktail hour lasted longer that day and we started drinking the wine for dinner as we prepared chicken wings and Spanish rice, listening to updated news on the kitchen radio. Businesses, mainly owned by whites, were being set on fire. So were cars. "I didn't see any cops anywhere," Jerry said when he finally got back close to 9:00 p.m. "Parker's pulled them out." He and Essie had made a plan so she could continue getting to work. "This is gonna last awhile," Jerry told us over dinner. They had arranged a meeting place; Essie would somehow get out of her immediate neighborhood —I never learned how—and Jerry would drive down to the pre-arranged place, pick her up for work and drive her home before curfew.

He went back to composing music at his studio in North Hollywood after dinner while I kept Camille company watching the news on television. It showed streets littered with debris and flames shooting into the sky from burning buildings.

"I feel like I'm watching a Humphrey Bogart movie or a film about 1930's Chicago gangsters," I wrote to my mother on Camille's portable typewriter propped up before me on the coffee table. "It looks like London during the bombing of World War II."

I assured her I was miles away from the area concerned, but watching the chaos unfolding on TV I wrote that it was hard to imagine the lawlessness of it all. On both sides.

Everyone had taken the law into their own hands. People were looting stores before they burned down, "charging about with refrigerators and televisions," I typed, while news helicopters filmed crowds in the streets from above as snipers on both sides let loose. An interviewed official stated no machine guns or anything like that were being used. Fifteen minutes later we watched a television report showing the National Guard in the streets with machine guns.

Essie was glad the National Guard were patrolling she told us the next day. They didn't have as much "inborn hatred" as the cops did. She'd spoken to one and "he was very nice" to her. In Essie's opinion they were much better than the police even if they did go around in groups with their bayonets at the ready.

The situation worsened. The fire department had to withdraw as the LAPD announced it could not protect them. Governor Brown declared law enforcement was confronting "guerillas fighting gangsters."

"Burn, baby, burn" became a rallying chant after a radio disc jockey coined the term. Police Chief Parker, from the back seat of an LAPD cruiser, added fuel to the flames saying the "rioters were acting like monkeys in a zoo."

Camille was able to phone Essie at times on the days she did not come to work, but Essie could not call out. It would later come to light that all calls going in and out of the area were tapped for a week without anyone knowing it. Wiretapping was illegal, but the authorities maintained they needed to detect what was going on. This caused Camille to comment that if she'd realized she was being tapped, she would have said a whole lot more about politics and the situation.

It didn't take long for the electricity to be cut off. Without electricity, Essie's refrigerator would not work and she was soon out of food. Camille and I went to the market and bought provisions for Essie to take home to her relatives. They couldn't get food for themselves. All the neighborhood mom and pop stores were either closed or burnt down. There were no supermarkets in Watts.

Louis Lomax, a black celebrity, made a public appeal on local television for food: the children were starving. When Jerry came home from work at 2:00 a.m. he and Camille went to an all-night market to buy supplies, including baby food and baby formula, then drove down to the drop-off point. I sat up anxiously waiting for them to return.

On August 17th, Governor Brown declared the riot over. Thirty-four people were dead, over a thousand injured, and almost four thousand arrested. The authorities blamed criminals for the riot, but the reality was that most of those four thousand had no prior criminal record. People had just had enough.

Property damage was estimated at $40,000,000, about $300,000,000 in today's money. No homes had been burned unless they'd caught fire from adjacent businesses. The McCone Commission investigating the reason for the riot would later single out the area as one of deprivation and neglect, citing high unemployment, lack of adequate housing and poor schools amongst other things. Their long list of recommendations included emergency literary and pre-school programs, increased low-income housing, more job training, upgraded healthcare services, more efficient transportation and improved police/community relations. Most of the recommendations were never implemented, and those that were took a long time.

I was left with a deep sense of anger at the injustice that could have been prevented. I wrote to my mother that if I was a Negro in America I'd probably have been in the streets, too.

From watching the news reports I was getting the impression that all African-Americans were poor and lived in ghettos. Yet my eyes told me that wasn't so. There were Black entertainers and musicians, and Camille told me a lot of African-American women went into the nursing profession; plus, on my American Airlines flight from New York to San Francisco one of the three elegant stewardesses had been Black. Television was a powerful teaching tool, but what was it teaching?

11

Answering Debbie's Fan Mail

The week after the riots, Jerry left for New York to meet with producers of the Gene Kelly show. Camille's doctor said she couldn't go; she had to rest. We ate dinner on TV trays in in the living room and watched our favorite programs. I liked *Hullabaloo*, a rock and roll show. Camille enjoyed it too, because she liked watching the dancers. We were both interested in the latest fashions. George Hamilton hosted one evening.

"He's very handsome," I said as we ate our half-chicken pieces and broiled tomatoes sprinkled with parmesan cheese and dried parsley topping.

"He's a very sweet boy," Camille commented.

"You've met him?" I squeaked excitedly.

She nodded and said he was as handsome in person as he looked to be on television.

"I like his sweater," I remarked, thinking, *I want one like that*. It was round-necked and long-sleeved, perfect for chilly days when winter came and the temperature dropped but the sun still shone, apart from a couple of weeks in November when it rained, I'd been told.

"It's a velour sweat shirt," Camille said. "They're so popular with the boys they've brought out a line for girls now. You can get them in tons of yummy colors."

"They look soft and velvety," I observed, finishing up my chicken without taking my eyes off of the screen.

"They are, but you can wash them in the washing machine," she told me. "I'm getting one as soon as I get rid of my load. I'm fed up with being pregnant, it's been two years in a row. I'm not going for a third child, no matter what sex this one turns out to be. Two girls would be fine." She smiled down at Elizabeth who was sitting on the floor with some toys, humming away to the music baby-style, then looked at me. "I see you got a letter from your mother today. What did she say?"

"She's getting tickets for Albert Finney in something at the Chichester Festival. She thinks he's a dish," I told her.

"Oh, I've met him. He is. Tell your mother that when you write back."

"She'll love it," I said. "You'll have to tell me some tidbits about some other people you've met. That'll entertain her."

"It's a lot of people, Aletheia. I've been in the business since I was four years old! We could keep your mother entertained for hours."

That would be a good thing, I thought to myself. My mother had also written that she was going to come and visit me before I left California. But I wasn't going to mention that just yet. I pushed it to the very back of my mind. "She really likes Frank Sinatra. Have you met him?"

"Oh yes, several times. He's always been charming to me, but I've seen him be downright rotten to some other girls. You can easily be taken in by his lovely blue eyes and boyish grin. He got a cocktail waitress fired in a Las Vegas nightclub because she put his drink down in front of the friend sitting next to him. It was her first day on the job and she was nervous because he was her first customer. She apologized and switched them but it was no good. I never liked him after that."

I couldn't wait to mention this tidbit to my mother. She'd be furious to learn that her idol had feet of clay.

Hullabaloo had ended. I stood up to take our empty dinner plates to the kitchen, but by bending over and brushing my hair out of my eyes with one hand and reaching for my plate with the other, I dislodged one of my contact lenses, which fell onto the white shag carpet.

"Oh, darn it!" I got down on all fours and started groping around.

Camille was bemused. "What *are* you doing?"

"Looking for my contact lens."

Elizabeth immediately started crawling over to me. Little Doggie trailed behind her.

"You're not helping," I told them as they closed in. Mercifully I found the contact lens before either one of them did.

I went to my bathroom mirror to put it back in, then put the dishes in the sink to soak. Meanwhile, Camille had retrieved her portable typewriter from the bookcase cupboard, plus the stack of letters she'd been diligently working on the past few evenings. It was a little job she did for Debbie.

Elizabeth started fretting, pulling herself up on her mother's armchair. Camille stopped typing. "I don't feel like doing this tonight, but I'm behind on getting these done. Can you type a few of them while I put Elizabeth to bed?"

Answer Debbie Reynolds fan mail? "Me?"

"You were a secretary. It's just copy typing. Most of the letters require the same response but they have to be typed separately." Camille handed me a sample reply and selected a few sheets out of the stack. "When you've addressed the envelopes, there's a rubber stamp advertising her latest film, *The Unsinkable Molly Brown,* so leave room for that at the top. I'll sign the letters. Debbie and I have similar handwriting."

"Okay." My household duties were expanding. Washing the dinner dishes could wait.

I helped Camille type fan letter replies in the few weeks that Jerry was going back and forth to New York for the Gene Kelly show, and before the baby was born and we moved. The studio dealt with the majority of Debbie's correspondence. These letters were only a tiny fraction of Debbie's fan mail and they all begged for money.

In those days, only well-employed businessmen had credit cards, and most of those were given to them and paid for by their companies. Everyone else had to manage as best they could or go without if they couldn't afford to pay cash all at once or put something away on layaway until they'd paid the item off. Small, independent, grocery stores would often extend credit to some of their customers until payday. The fan mail contained a lot of hopelessness and people down on their luck in difficult situations. It was foreign to me that people would actually write to a film star and beg for money to help them out.

I couldn't imagine doing it. I felt embarrassed for them. Growing up in Europe after World War II I was familiar with making do and going without. There was no shame to it; most Europeans were in the same boat. But here in America, the land of extremes, it was different. I'd begun to realize from the Watts riots there was a lot of desperation of all kinds. Being young, employed and out in the world on an adventure, I had no experience of such destitution. My grandmother had always said life wasn't fair, and reading the letters that I typed replies to, I got a glimmer of what she meant.

The portable typewriter got a good work-out. When Camille wasn't using it, and I wasn't helping her with Debbie's fan mail, I was writing airmail letters to friends and family several days a week. My correspondence load was almost equal to hers. When the typewriter broke down, which was often, I sent postcards. Since it was summer in Europe everyone I knew went on vacation and sent postcards back to me. I taped them up around my dressing table mirror and looked at them whenever I suffered a bout of homesickness, which was usually when I got one of those postcards or a letter from home several times a week.

My parents were vacationing on the Italian Riviera and Avril was swanning around on the Cote d'Azur on her way to Spain. I wished I was there. So did Joyce and Camille who enjoyed looking at the postcards, too. Joyce reminisced about the time she spent in Italy and they both drooled over a postcard I received from Monte Carlo. When my mother sent holiday snaps Essie, as well as Camille, was interested in looking at them. I'd only been gone a few weeks, yet I felt as if I'd been in Los Angeles forever, I wrote my mother.

Sometimes I'd suffer little pangs of boredom and loneliness being in the house alone with Elizabeth on the days Essie didn't work and Camille was out lunching with friends or running errands for the new house.

Camille had said she and Jerry would pay for a few driving lessons after my social security card arrived, but that hadn't happened yet. I'd taken driving lessons in England, but had failed the test the first time I'd taken it. Camille told me it was very different here. You got a learner's permit and studied the California Highway Code booklet they handed out. When a person felt confident enough, they went down to the local Department of Motor Vehicles taking the little booklet with them so they could consult it (i.e. look up the answers) as they took the written test. I was appalled at the idea of cheating at first, but Camille said everyone does it and nobody takes any notice. She added that anyone who was honest "must be nuts."

"The actual driving test takes 10-15 minutes. You're allowed three mistakes in your driving. If you don't pass you can go back the next day and take it again," she explained.

I thought that sounded easy enough and couldn't wait to start. If I could drive, it would make all our lives easier.

In the meantime, when it wasn't too hot, I'd put Elizabeth in her stroller and go for a little walk. There weren't any sidewalks until I reached Laurel Canyon and Ventura Boulevard, three or four blocks away. In 1965 a lot of Los Angeles had huge swathes of undeveloped land. It was a wasteland of a different sort compared to the dense concrete wasteland some consider it to be nowadays. The old factory and warehouse buildings downtown spread east across the train tracks and the Los Angeles River, tamed and entombed in a concrete channel in the 1930s, flowed through Studio City and North Hollywood. This seemed strange to me. With all the weed-strewn "lots," compared to London, Los Angeles seemed quite rural in some places.

I asked Rita if she liked being in California more than England. She said she didn't know. It was vacation time for the family he worked for and Rita went with them to the mountains and down to San Diego where they crossed into Tijuana for shopping and a bullfight one weekend. We talked every day on the phone when she wasn't away. I considered visiting her in Mar Vista and swimming in the pool my vacation. My suntan was coming along nicely.

Jerry came home from New York for a long weekend and announced he would not be able to come back again during the show's month-long shooting schedule. Camille didn't like it but there was nothing she could do. Dr. Fox her obstetrician, had outlawed her going to New York, while at the same time assuring them that the baby was nowhere near being due. He had, however, moved the birth date closer to the end of September, instead of in October, which shocked Camille. He told her to rest. She swung into high gear. The new house had just come out of its short escrow.

On Saturday morning, Camille stood in the front hallway handing out cleaning paraphernalia to her sister-in-law, Donna, and best-friend Joyce, who'd both been marshaled into helping clean when they'd expressed an eagerness to see the new place. I stood there, too, with my swimming togs tucked under my arm waiting for Jerry to get off the phone. He was going to drive me to Rita's for the weekend. I'd offered to forego time off while Jerry was gone so I could keep Camille company. I don't think she would have asked me outright, but she and Jerry had both been so nice to me since I arrived, I felt it was only reasonable on my part. They had a lot on at the moment. She had the new house to clean and paint before we moved in; he was now working on three projects that all had looming deadlines, including the new television show that was about to air. Jerry worried about Camille, and Camille worried about Jerry.

Camille thought I should take time off while I could. As it turned out, this would be a wise decision. She had recruited her mother, Honey, to babysit Elizabeth for the day.

Jerry walked into the hallway popping Miltowns for his stomach just in time to see Camille handing out toothbrushes to Joyce and Donna.

"They're for the floors," she explained as Joyce and Donna exchanged glances.

"Camille, you're my oldest and dearest friend, but if you think I'm crawling around cleaning 7,500 square feet of floor with a toothbrush you're out of your cotton-picking mind," Joyce said.

"Yeah, I thought that's what the mops and brushes were for," Donna added in her Mid-Western accent. She was from Illinois, a very nice woman, just a few years older than me.

"Those are for the hardwood floors," Camille told her. "The toothbrushes are for cleaning the filthy Spanish tile floor, which I've discovered has an indent in the middle of each one with a tiny blue and yellow glass flower that you can't see with the naked eye because of the dirt. And it's just the floors in the entryway, the dining room and the butler's pantry. Maybe the library, too," she added. "And the breakfast room."

"In other words, the whole first floor except for the kitchen and living room," Joyce commented cynically.

Jerry stared expressionless at Camille, swallowed his Miltowns then looked at me. "Let's go," he said, walking out the front door fast.

I was also dying to see the new house, but upon reflection, with massive clean-up, it could wait I decided, following him down the steps to the garage.

Jerry had to first swing by his studio to pick up some work he then dropped off at the music copier's house out in the Valley before driving me to Rita's. We took the 101 freeway north before turning onto Malibu Canyon and heading west. The fields and hills had turned yellow from the lack of rain, but as we snaked through the canyon, trees provided a shelter from the scorching sun. I felt like I was in a scene from *The Big Country*.

Every day, every minute, living with the Fieldings had brought something new. Apart from the time in New York, Jerry would go back to his studio and work all day and into the night. Camille was sprucing up her dream mansion in the Hollywood Hills, while I'd spend the weekend sunning and swimming in Rita's employers' pool. The Fieldings were Hollywood people, but I was the one who felt like I was living in a movie. Driving through the canyon, we'd seen no houses for miles and I could imagine the Los Angeles area as it had once been. Raw. Untamed by concrete. Uncluttered with people. It was wild and undeveloped and I could imagine traveling through there in a stagecoach.

"I wonder if Indians used to live in these hills," I mused. "I can imagine them riding through here."

Jerry laughed out loud. "There haven't been Indians around here for well over a hundred years." He was amused by the idea and I suddenly felt foolish.

"A hundred years is not very long where I come from," I pointed out. "My grandmother's house, where my father grew up, was originally a two-room cottage built in the 1700's with a well in the kitchen floor. The rest of the house was added about a hundred years ago."

Jerry lit a cigarette from the dashboard lighter and thought for a while. "You know that Camille's father is half Native-American," he finally said.

"Yes, she told me," I responded.

Camille had talked about her father, Dick Williams, one of the first soundmen in Hollywood, while we'd been watching the Watts riots unfold on television and discussing race in America. When I first met Dick I'd thought him very chic in his Italian leather loafers and Sy Devore cardigan sweater—standard Hollywood industry wear unless you were one of the suits in the offices. He sported a gold watch and drove a late model Cadillac convertible, which he'd been driving when he went to see his relatives in Texas a couple of years before, Camille had told me. He stopped to get something on his car checked in Arizona and stepped into the bar next door to the garage for a cold beer while he waited.

"What color are you, mister?" the barman had asked, requesting to see Dick's driver's license.

"What do you mean, what color am I?" Dick responded, wondering why he needed to show his California driver's license, but producing it nonetheless.

The barman looked from Dick to the license, then back again, then finally asked: "Are you a redskin?"

"Yes," Dick replied, picking up his license from the bar top.

"Get out."

I wasn't surprised at this story, just dismayed. Along with pictures of the civil rights struggles in the south I'd seen in British newspapers over the past few years, I'd grown up with snippets of information about how badly Native Americans had been treated. I'd just had no real context within which to put this. But I was learning.

Camille went onto explain that the reservations and land the Native Americans were given by the government were the poorest, most miserable scratches of acreage they could find. Only in a couple of places they made a mistake: Palm Springs, California and Oklahoma. When oil was discovered in Oklahoma the government offered to buy the land back and also give them alternative land. The tribes said, no deal.

"The Palm Springs land is so valuable now the Indians rent it out," she concluded.

Good for them, I thought.

"There's a huge pow-pow held every July 4th in Arizona," Camille continued. "Lots of tribes in the southwest gather;

it's really impressive. You should try to go while you're here, it's a big attraction. Recently, the Indians wanted to right a few other wrongs, too. The tribes threatened to give up the public event unless the government gave in on a few other deals. Not only would the government look bad, but the locals didn't want to miss out on the money they make from tourists."

I nodded approvingly; I was all for bargaining for justice. After all, it was how I'd managed to get my father to sign the papers so I could come to America.

Camille studied me for a moment. "When I sunbathe, I go the same color you are now."

"Do you think I'd be mistaken for an Indian?" I perused my arms and legs.

She chuckled. "Not with that accent."

12

Home Improvements

$\mathcal{T}$ he house on Reklaw Drive had been put up for sale and Bette brought prospective buyers by regularly. Camille would try to be there if she wasn't running to the hardware store, buying paint or scraping dirt from the hardwood and Spanish tile floors of the new house. Dick had taken one look at the painting job before him the first time he'd seen the house and declared he needed help. Roy Lee, Essie's son, had been hired. Camille also roped in as many friends and relatives as she could to help out, too. She had a self-imposed three-month deadline. My job was to take care of Elizabeth and hold down the fort at the old house.

Bette the realtor added "Open House" on weekends when anyone could walk in and take a look around with a view to purchase. Camille usually stayed to show people around before dashing off to the new place, leaving Bette and myself alone for a few hours.

One Sunday morning, Bette phoned to say she was running late.

"Camille just left," I told her.

"I'll be there in half-an-hour," Bette replied.

"Don't worry about it. Nobody's here," I assured her, putting aside the Sunday edition of the *Los Angeles Times*, and reaching for the latest airmail letter from my mother. I'd already finished reading the latest issue of the showbiz industry paper, *Variety*, something I tried to do every day as a new form of schoolwork or homework to clue myself in a little more to my Hollywood environment. I was sitting on the living-room couch; the radio was on, Little Doggie was snoozing at my feet since we'd now decided to be friends, and Elizabeth was crawling around, playing with some toys on the floor.

"Just having a cup of tea in the garden," my mother wrote. "The sun is out now and quite nice. Just read your letter for the third time!! Will have to start a file for them, then you can read them all when you come home (to remind you what you did)."

She went on to say that she'd taken my younger brother to see the Beatles film, *Help!*, had thought of me when she went to Holy Communion, and that one of her friends had lent her a copy of *Life* magazine which had an article about life in Beverly Hills. It showed "coloured pictures of Tony Curtis outside his home with three Rolls Royces," she wrote. "Carol Baker sunbathing by her swimming pool, Kirk Douglas' home, and George Hamilton sitting in his lounge. It looked something like how you described your house so we got an idea of what it's like." The article "showed a cocktail party on a rooftop building on Sunset Boulevard and it showed the trees; it looked very nice. It said the average salary was £7,000 a year and Butlers earned around £50 a week."

Not quite my lifestyle.

It was amazing how much information could be imparted on those thin, blue airmails, and how much could happen in one week. My mother went on to say that she'd been showing my letters to her friends, and also to my friends, calling on them in the evenings. She'd also lost her job, but not to worry, she'd obtained a shorthand typist position at the firm I'd worked for before I left for America. She mentioned often being waylaid in the corridor or the Ladies restroom by people who'd known me and who loved my letters telling them what my life in California was like.

Instead of writing so many letters to everyone, she suggested "why don't you write one letter to me and I will share it with everyone. It would save postage." I frowned at this thinking, *True, but not bloody likely.* Since she had been the youngest child and the only girl in her family, my mother had always had the habit of demanding all the attention from those around her continuing into adulthood, but inserting herself into my current life and trying to control it from thousands of miles away was going a bit too far.

The radio was tuned to a local rock and roll station. When Jerry was home, I had to keep the volume down as he hated rock and roll. Since he wasn't around on this particular Sunday, I had the volume turned up. Elizabeth loved it. She had pulled herself up and was rocking and humming, moving around the living room holding onto the furniture for support since she wasn't quite walking yet. I put my mother's letter aside and stood up intending to turn the radio volume up higher for the *Top Ten Countdown* currently playing *Hang on Sloopy, Sloopy Hang on!*

The front doorbell rang. I turned the radio volume down, scooped up Elizabeth and went to answer the door. Three realtors stood on the doorstep smiling hellos and offering their business cards. I looked past them down the steps. Where was Bette? Surely it had been over half-an-hour. I stood aside and let the realtors in.

"What a lovely daughter you have," one of them said, cooing at Elizabeth.

"She's not mine, and the lady of the house isn't here. But I can show you around," I hastened to add, since one of them was already walking upstairs, eyeing the entry hall chandelier and inquiring about how many bedrooms and bathrooms as he went. Fortunately, I had read the description sheet Bette had made up and had listened to her and Camille discussing features that needed to be mentioned. One of the realtors was Irish and two of them were English. They were delighted to learn I was English, too.

"How long have been here?" one of the English realtors asked.

"Six weeks," I replied.

I did my best to give them a professional tour of the house while all three regaled me with their life histories and how long they'd been in America (years before I was born, it seemed). We discussed the land across the water and I told them how much things had changed as I pointed out all the crystal chandeliers, the wall-to wall carpeting upstairs, the hardwood floors downstairs, the pantry and the window treatments, including the white silk curtains in the living-room. I added that the Fieldings owned the lot next door, too, and had planned to build a swimming pool before finally deciding to move to another residence altogether.

I must have done a good job because all of them turned up again with clients. Unfortunately, none of them bought the house. Bette, observing me chatting away to a realtor and his client on one occasion while she was showing someone else around, told me I should consider a future career in real estate. I never did, although it was a good idea.

Joyce turned up later that Sunday right after Bette went home. I was in the kitchen helping Elizabeth feed herself.

"Where's Camille?" I asked, wiping Gerber's green vegetable goo from Elizabeth's face.

"Oh, honey, Donna had to take her to the hospital. She was having labor pains," Joyce replied, plonking a bag of hamburgers, fries and salad with ranch dressing from Bob's Big Boy down on the kitchen counter.

I looked up, alarmed. "But the baby's not due until next month!"

"We're gonna need a Plan B," Joyce informed me, opening the refrigerator. "I'm having a beer with my burger. Want one?"

"Definitely," I replied, lifting Elizabeth out of her high chair and placing her in her little chariot so she could practice walking and careen around the kitchen at the same time. Little Doggie removed himself to a safe place near the open door.

While Joyce set out the food and beers in the breakfast nook, the phone rang. It was Jerry calling from New York.

Not knowing what to say, I signaled Joyce to take over the call. Just then, Camille came in with her mother, Honey.

"False alarm," Honey said breezily.

"Here, she comes, Jerry," Joyce waved the phone at Camille.

"I'll take it upstairs," Camille replied from the kitchen doorway turning to go up to her bedroom, Little Doggie's nails tap-tapping on the wooden floor as he followed her.

Honey bent down to pick up Elizabeth from her chariot. "How's my little papagallo?" she chirped as Elizabeth regaled her in babytalk with tales of her day while trying to stick her fingers in her grandmother's mouth.

"Would you like a hamburger, Honey? I got extra," Joyce asked.

"Oh, Lord, no," replied Honey, tickling Elizabeth and smothering her in kisses as the child giggled. "We don't eat things like that, do we?"

Indeed, Camille's vivacious mother didn't. In the next few months, whenever Honey would stay overnight she'd even bring her own breakfast with her. Jerry referred to it as birdseed, which would make Honey smile and tease him about the importance of good health as she topped off her bowl of cereal with fresh seasonal fruit, grapes in winter, peaches from her backyard tree drizzled with honey in summer, and a healthy dollop of plain yoghurt. At age sixty, she still had her girlish figure and a thirty-nine-year-old boyfriend she went dancing with.

"Donna had to go home to get ready for work tomorrow, along with Jerry's cousin, Cynthia, who turned up to help." Honey informed us. "I'm leaving as soon as Camille gets off the phone. I have to be at work bright and early myself, but we've formulated a plan in case the baby comes while Jerry's gone."

"It's obvious to everyone it's not gonna wait until October," Joyce took a bite of her hamburger. "Everyone except Jerry, that is."

"Even her doctor," Honey agreed, "although he won't commit to that opinion."

I nodded silently as I ate. Even Essie, usually not a person to volunteer an opinion, had grunted a skeptical "uh-huh," when Camille stuck to her October due date after her last doctor's visit.

"So the plan is," Honey continued, "Since Jerry's cousin Cynthia is a nurse, she will come and live here while Jerry's gone. She can drive Camille to the hospital if she goes into labor.

"Good idea, since she can't call a taxi," Joyce agreed. She turned to me. "Taxi drivers won't take a pregnant woman to the hospital here."

I was astounded. Where I came from you called an ambulance to come and collect you, unless you were having a home birth. Then, you called the midwife.

"While Cynthia's driving Camille to the hospital," Honey continued, looking at me, "you'll hold down the fort here and telephone everyone starting with Jerry, then Essie, who will bring her overnight bag so you won't be on your own. And Dick and Roy Lee will carry on painting the house and doing what's needed to be done there," she finished up.

Camille was ordered to bed rest by her doctor, which became living-room sofa rest with the telephone right next to her. She and Jerry talked every day when he was in New York. When she wasn't updating him she was dealing with things that had to do with the new house and the move. In between phone calls we both flipped through her stacks of magazines, ordering free stuff, cutting out coupons, and planning future food menus with new recipes. We also started packing for the move. Camille directed and I packed. She didn't feel at all well. Her pelvic bones were moving apart.

"With Elizabeth they didn't move until just before she was born," Camille told me one night as we were watching television while sewing one of our craft projects. "Because I was a dancer my muscles were so strong they didn't move as easily as a normal person. This time I can sit and listen to my bones crunching around inside already, and when I walk around they bang together," she said morosely. She started to call herself Camel instead of Camille. Friends tried to cheer her up, but when she was having dinner at Mitzi Gaynor's one evening and someone asked her when the baby was due. Camille replied "any minute," which sent the dinner guests into a panic.

The mailman brought me letters from family, friends and ex co-workers every day now.

"What's your family up to this week?" Camille asked one evening as she sat pasting sheets of green stamps into a booklet that came free with each gasoline purchase from the 76 station. She counted her booklets. "Another half book and I can get a kitchen step stool for the new place," she muttered.

I was reading a letter from my mother. While she was busy sharing my letters over on her side of the pond, I was equally busy sharing hers on the west coast.

"My parents went on a Ye Olde London Pub crawl with friends last Friday night," I told Camille. "They started off at *The Cheshire Cheese*, a pub rebuilt after the Great Fire of 1666, but there was 'a party going on in the cellars,' so they had to go upstairs and have a have a 'few brandies' before dinner: game pie with a 'superb bottle of wine' that went straight to my mother's head. She writes that she 'never felt so happy.'"

Camille started chuckling. So did I. My mother always claimed she didn't drink. But I have childhood memories of her cooking the Sunday lunch. When she thought no one was looking she'd open the door of the larder where she kept a bottle of brandy "for medicinal purposes." With her back to us, her head would tilt back sharply as she chugged a couple of shots down before dishing up the vegetables.

"What else?" Camille demanded.

"Then they stopped by the *Prospect of Whitby,* a riverside pub where they used to hang pirates in the 17th century, and had after-dinner drinks. Last stop was the *Gilbert and Sullivan*," a pub with walls plastered with operetta memorabilia from the 19th century." I looked up from reading. "Mum's sending pub booklets with pictures for our enjoyment."

"Oh, goody," Camille said. "Anything else?"

"She's been delivering her missionary leaflets and is sending me one showing 25,000 people having Holy Communion on the race course in Barbados."

Camille burst out laughing. Really, I thought, the life I'd left behind was starting to sound more surreal than the life I was living with the Fieldings.

"What are your friends up to?"

I turned to the next airmail letter. "Avril hitchhiked to Spain, where she lost sight of our friend Tosia, but she made new friends and took the ferry to Tangiers for a couple of days. She got arrested trying to steal a bracelet in the souk and almost got her hand cut off. But the shopkeeper had a change of heart and begged the police to release her as he wanted to make her his fourth wife. Whereupon she and her lover, who the shopkeeper didn't know about, beat a fast retreat and hitchhiked to Paris. By that time they were totally broke and she started begging on the Champs Elysees for food money before landing a job at Galeries Lafayette, where she recently served Princess Alexandra."

Camille was shaking her head. "Aren't you glad you're sitting here nice and safe with me in Hollywood?"

Actually, I was. Life with Avril had always been fraught with some kind of danger.

"Who's that other letter from?" Camille nodded at my third blue airmail.

"A friend from my old office," I said, thinking Sandra had probably typed it at work. "There's been a murder."

Camille's head whiplashed up from the green stamps book.

"On a train," I flipped the letter over. "Everyone's now terrified traveling home from work."

13

More Home Improvements

My mother later reported, "We've had Scotland Yard here at work. They say he's a maniac. The girl's handbag was found on Hazelwick Avenue, and some things in the men's toilet at Three Bridges station."

My mother had a flair for the dramatic, perhaps because her father had been an actor as well as a photographer. Still, murder was serious and a sexual predator was later caught and convicted of manslaughter, my mother never mentioning the s-e-x part. She was determined to keep me up regarding home front news, but, really, sometimes it was just too much. Camille loved it, though.

One morning when I'd finished getting dressed and re-reading my mother's letter—she'd also mailed a parcel with some of the clothes in it that I'd had to remove at London airport as my luggage was over the required weight—a furious banging started upstairs at the Fieldings' house.

"My father's repairing a panel on my bedroom door," Camille explained as I walked into the kitchen, where she was conferring with Essie about the weekly grocery list. "Here, Elizabeth, chew on this." She handed her daughter half a toasted bagel, which Elizabeth started drooling on.

She was cutting a new tooth. Little Doggie, who currently had infected ears, had made himself scarce.

"We have to go grocery shopping a day early because it's Elizabeth's first birthday party and Jerry's coming home," Camille told me. "And we have to get going soon, so make it a quick breakfast. What do you need that I should add to my list," Camille continued, picking up her notepad and pencil.

"Apples," I replied, opening the refrigerator door. "The red ones."

I chose a can of strawberry Sego from the refrigerator, a diet drink that tasted like a milkshake. I'd recently weighed myself on the scale in Camille's bathroom and discovered I'd gained weight since I arrived. Camille thought it was the spices and MSG she used in cooking that was the culprit, not that I might be eating differently than I had done back home. Or more.

Camille's father, Dick walked into the kitchen in his painting clothes.

"Okay, that's done. Now I'm off to the paint store."

Camille reached for her purse, pulled out her wallet and handed him some money. "How's the living room at the new place coming along?"

"Another couple of gallons should do it. It's a challenge with that cathedral ceiling in the living room, and the entrance hall is two stories high. Then Roy Lee and I will start on the entrance and upstairs hallway. The dining-room and breakfast room are done. It's a lot of work. I'm sure glad your son's helping me," he said to Essie, who beamed as she silently poured a cup of black coffee for him.

"Thanks, Essie. You look like you've settled in well," he said to me, eyeing the can of Sego, which I was chugging down as fast as I could.

"She has," Camille picked up her purse and threw her notepad inside, as I nodded, 'yes.' She and her father discussed a few more details about the new house, then Camille said, "We gotta get going, Daddy."

"Me, too." He hastily downed the rest of the coffee, then kissed Elizabeth's head. "She looks just you did at that age, Camille. See y'all. 'Bye, Essie."

"'Bye," she replied as we all left. Dick used the front door; Camille and I detoured out the back so she could turn the sprinklers off.

Camille watered every day during the summer. It was the law since the Bel Air fire four years previously. She had explained the fire danger to me the day after I arrived, but said I wasn't to panic "because they give you at least four hours warning to get out; and anyway, this house is built of stone and redwood and won't burn." Besides, there was a fire station two blocks away.

I threw the empty Sego can into the trash before getting into Camille's 1958 Ford Fairlane.

It was never one errand she had to run; it was always several. After we'd ordered Elizabeth's birthday cake from the bakery, picked up the groceries and party supplies, been to the bank and post office, purchasing more blue airmails for me, Camille drove into Hollywood.

"*Pickwick Books* is having a sale," she said, pulling into the parking lot near Musso & Frank's restaurant on Hollywood Boulevard. "I can do a bit of Christmas shopping."

Since Camille had so many friends, family and Jerry's business associates to buy for she had to start early to get everything done. I nodded silently, remembering the jewelry sale at *Save-On Drugstore* a few short weeks ago in July when she'd loaded up on ropes of garish glass beads to pull apart and repurpose for Christmas decorations. Those beads had been catalogued into little boxes, slated for Christmas tree and table decorations, to be crafted after the baby was born while she was recuperating in bed.

There were never any idle moments in the Fielding household. I liked to keep busy, loved arts and crafts, was a creative cook as my grandmother had been (my mother hated cooking, or anything domestic, and was known to routinely declare she should never have had children, usually in her children's' presence). Also, I was being treated as an adult and not ordered around or shouted down as I was at my parents' home. My father's mantra: If you're in my home, you do as I say. And he took part of my secretarial wages every week as his due. But I had nowhere else to go. Until now. The Fieldings never complained about me being a teenager, at least not to my face. Even though I worked in their home, I felt liberated.

I craned my neck at the stars embedded in the sidewalk on the short walk to the bookstore. Camille asked me what I thought of the famous Hollywood Boulevard. I hesitated to say what I really thought: it didn't look very clean to me.

"It's tacky," Camille agreed, as we entered *Pickwick's*, which was the biggest bookstore I'd ever seen, about the size of our local supermarket in England. Camille bought something Jerry had requested, four art books for herself, and a few items for Christmas gifts. I bought a *Kitchen*

Klips: A Personal Recipe Book so I had somewhere I could organize all those cut-out recipes from women's magazines and the *Los Angeles Times'* weekly food page,

"Look up there," Camille said pointing north toward the Hollywood Hills as we came out of the bookstore. "You can see the new house from here. It's at the top. See that white stucco building with the red tile roof and two arched windows peeping through the trees? That's the living-room."

"Oh, yes," I replied after a moment, shielding my eyes as I gazed upwards. Although I wore sunglasses, the sun was fierce and it was almost a hundred degrees where we stood on the sidewalk.

"Come on, we'll drive back along Mulholland and make a short stop there on the way. I can check on how the painting's going," she added.

Ten minutes later, as Camille scrutinized the progress her father and Roy Lee had made, I stood in one of those arched living-room windows and looked out. Bette, the realtor, had been right. The house had a tremendous view from city hall downtown in the east all the way to the ocean in the west; and right below me, past other houses nestled in the trees and the Magic Castle, was Hollywood Boulevard where we had stood just minutes before. As Camille gave me a quick tour of the rest of the house, I realized Joyce had been right, too. Camille had bought herself a mansion, even if the kitchen stove shot flames a foot high in the air, the bidet in her bathroom didn't work, and a lot of paint was needed to cover up all the rude pictures of naked women that the prior occupants' little boys had drawn all over their closet and bedroom, now slated to be my bedroom.

"We're gonna be having a lot of parties," Camille said, her eyes gleaming as we got back in the car. "Christmas will be wonderful, you'll love it!

I smiled broadly. I could hardly wait. Let the entertaining begin!

14

Meet the Relatives
Plus Boring College Boys

Summer was almost over, although it was scarcely noticeable in Los Angeles. Elizabeth turned one year old. At her birthday party, I took a few photographs and chatted to Camille's family as I waited for Rita and our American friend, Sharon, to pick me up for a sleepover. Sharon's family had invited me to a barbecue to christen the new swimming pool they'd just had put in.

Dick's second wife, Maggie, was at the party keeping pace with Joyce on the gin and tonics, a break from her current diet where she only drank orange juice and ate a sliver of cheese for lunch. Maggie usually wore mu-mu's, long and loose Hawaiian dresses she accessorized with outsized costume jewelry, patent leather flip-flops and a flower-decoupaged straw purse from which she drew an endless supply of Lucky Strikes cigarettes; but, today she wore a pair of raw silk slacks and matching blouse to show off her weight loss. Maggie was from the south and had a deep Alabama drawl. She was always nice to me, but I was a little wary of her cupcakes and razorblades manner, and her critical remarks.

"She can't help it," Joyce told me confidentially as we stood at the drinks tray fixing more G&T's. "She's jealous of Camille's mother."

I looked over at Honey, briefly chatting to her ex-husband about how the painting was going at their daughter's new place, then at Maggie taking extra-long draws on her cigarette holder and blowing out smoke rings as she narrowed her eyes at Dick, and thought this was probably true.

"Here, Maggie," I said, walking over and handing her a refreshed gin and tonic.

"Thank you, darlin'." She patted the sofa beside her. "Come and fill me in about what's been happening around here. How are you getting on with Camille? Does she have you painting, too? I hardly ever see Dick any more. All Camille has to do is crook her little finger and he goes running to her."

Ah, the power of guilt—Camille's parents' divorce had been acrimonious when she was a young teenager. And, the power of darling daughters, I thought as I watched Jerry interact with Elizabeth. I wished I'd had it growing up, but my family weren't demonstrative in that way.

Fortunately, providence intervened at that moment and any acrimonious gossip was avoided. "Oh, excuse me," I told Maggie. "My friends are here."

There were so many people dropping by to converse with Jerry, see how Camille was doing, and/or to wish Elizabeth a Happy Birthday that we had left the front door open. Rita and Sharon stood in the entrance hall trying not to look like deer in headlights as they surveyed the noisy living room scene.

"Is Debbie here?" Rita asked.

"No."

"Any other stars here?" Sharon scanned the room hopefully.

"No, just family and industry business people," I replied, retrieving my overnight bag from where I'd stashed it in the hall closet, ready to go.

At that moment Camille came into the hallway carrying the birthday cake. "Hi, girls," she said. "Gonna stay for some cake?"

"Is it chocolate?" Rita asked.

"For a one-year-old? No way," Camille responded, stopping so Joyce could light the candles before they both stepped down into the living-room and started singing "Happy Birthday."

"It's white cake," I told my friends. "So the crumbs match the carpet and the sofa."

"Then, let's just go," Sharon said. "I don't like white cake and my mom needs the car as soon as we get back."

Sharon had arranged for us to meet "some college boys" after we spent the next day shopping in Santa Monica. I was looking forward to spending time with the opposite sex of my own age. Alas, they were deathly dull. I should have realized it when Sharon said they were from her accounting class at Santa Monica College. Their idea of something interesting to do on a Saturday night was going to see the new Mormon Temple in West Los Angeles, but how could I have predicted that? Like many other things, I'd barely heard of the word "Mormon." A suggested night-time stroll on the Santa Monica Pier or along the cliff-top was either too creative or too threatening in some way to these guys. Dancing was out of the question, as was anything to do that might cost money. The money bit I could understand. My conversation about the *Malcolm X* biography I'd read on the way over on the plane fell on deaf ears. The only books they read were accounting manuals. I realized I was stuck in a no-man's land: Too many American kids my own age were too young and inexperienced for me, and Jerry and Camille's friends were too old. But much more interesting. And not so serious. I couldn't understand why young Americans didn't have more of a sense of humor, either.

I don't think I was the only one who was bored. We were back at Sharon's house by 10 p.m. for another round of hamburgers and swimming, sans the guys. The warm Southern California night seemed endless as we swam, played records on Sharon's portable record player, and lay around the pool on lounge chairs talking until we fell asleep in our bathing costumes.

Sharon's mom, Jean, shaking my shoulder, woke me up. "You've had a phone call from someone called Joyce. They need you back at the house as soon as you can get there."

I went to the wall phone in the kitchen and tried calling Joyce back at "the castle," a name Sharon and Rita had dubbed the house in Studio City, but no-one picked up.

Sharon and Rita were now awake. "We could drive you back right now," Sharon suggested. Rita nodded in agreement, so we all got dressed and I gathered my things.

It was still dark when they dropped me off. The outside lights were on, but I opened the front door on Reklaw Drive to quietness and darkness. It was a little spooky. I flipped on all the downstairs lights, then saw Honey standing at the top of the stairs in one of Camille's nightdresses.

"I thought you were Jerry," she said.

"What's happened?" I asked. "Is everything okay?"

"Camille's had the baby," Honey told me, coming down the stairs so she could talk quietly and not disturb Elizabeth. "A little girl. Seven pounds."

"The day after Elizabeth's birthday!"

Honey nodded. "I'll be fetching Camille and the new baby home tomorrow. Meanwhile, I have to take Jerry to the airport first thing this morning."

"Is Essie here?"

"Joyce is picking her up as soon as it gets light. The buses don't run in Watts on a Sunday."

"What about Cynthia?"

Apparently, Jerry's bossy-boots nurse cousin was doing overtime at her hospital this weekend and hadn't been able to get away. So much for all the well-laid plans. Little new-born Claudia Camille had fooled everyone.

The front door opened and Jerry came in with his briefcase and a bundle of handwritten sheet music he needed to take to New York. Upstairs Elizabeth woke up and started singing in her crib.

"God, that kid's got a pair of lungs," he said, checking his wristwatch. He dumped his briefcase and work down on the hall table. "And thank God that's over. I'm glad I was here. I'm not so sure those producers would have let me leave otherwise. Camille and the new baby are both well," he told me. "Thanks for coming back right away.

"I'll go see to Elizabeth, settle her down and say goodbye; then I have to pack," he told Honey.

To me he looked as if he hadn't slept all night, and precious little the night before.

"I better go and get dressed," Honey said to me. "Can you put the kettle on for some tea?

"It'll be interesting to see how Elizabeth reacts to the new baby," I said as Honey and I watched Jerry go upstairs. "She's used to getting all the attention."

"And so much of it," Honey added, turning to follow her son-in-law.

The New Baby

On Monday afternoon, I was sitting in the living room embroidering a woolen sunflower on one of the tapestry cushions Camille and I had mail-ordered as part of our crafts projects, when the Lady of the House herself came through the front door. Her arms were empty. Her mother, solemn-faced, followed.

"Where's the baby," I said, getting up from the armchair, my welcome smile fading. Camille looked distraught. Honey put Camille's overnight bag down by the stairs.

"They wouldn't let me bring her home. She threw up as I was feeding her this morning. We don't know what's wrong."

"Oh, no!" I didn't know what else to say.

Camille looked as if she'd been crying. "I need to lie down."

Honey helped her up to her bedroom. Little Doggie followed. He slept on her bed when Jerry wasn't around.

It was two weeks before little Claudia came home. The baby was having seizures and the hospital wouldn't release her until she'd gone a full week without one. In the interim, Camille spent a lot of time on the phone, and a lot of time crying.

"It was some kind of bacteria in her blood," she told Jerry in New York. The producers of the show he was working on weren't letting him interrupt scoring the show by coming back to California again even though he'd told them he had a sick newborn. Essie was unusually subdued on the days she came to work, and was very attentive to Camille's needs, bringing her anything she needed while she rested in bed, the telephone in active use beside her. Later, I would find out that Essie had once had a baby who died shortly after birth. I tried to be as quiet and helpful as I could, not playing my rock n' roll music loud, staying off the phone, and entertaining Elizabeth, as I reflected on the sadness people carried in their lives that never showed.

★★★

I'd just put Elizabeth down for her afternoon nap when Camille came back from the hospital carrying her new daughter wrapped in a white lacey shawl. Honey had driven them home on her lunch break from work.

"I'll call you later," she told Camille. "Right now I have to make a quick stop and check in on Mom on my way back to the office."

Camille's grandmother, Mrs. Reed, was in her late eighties and now lived with Honey and her sister, Aunt Pat, who worked for the telephone company. Mrs. Reed had come to California via the Oregon Trail in a covered wagon when she was a little girl, Camille had told me. Everyone loved Camille's grandmother, especially Jerry who thought she was the sweetest old lady he'd ever met;

they always engaged in long conversations, heads together on the couch, when she visited.

"The pediatrician's coming by any minute to talk to us." Camille looked upset as we walked into the living-room. She seemed exhausted, and said she badly need to sit down. I held out my arms for the baby. "Can I hold her?"

I was going to place Claudia in the carry-cot since she was sleeping, but couldn't resist taking a good look at her first. She was very pretty with a lot of dark brown hair, but as I pulled back the blanket I could see most of it had been shaved off. There were needle marks on her scalp and bruises with specks of dried blood. I uncurled her tiny fingers; her little palms were one big massive bruise with multiple needle marks. The backs of Claudia's hands were bruised from the intravenous needles, too. I pulled up her nightgown. The little feet were a mass of bruises top and bottom, with more holes where fluids had been drawn. I was horrified.

"She looks as if she's been crucified," I said in a small voice as the doorbell rang.

Camille let the doctor in.

"There's nothing wrong with her." The pediatrician, Dr. Zukow, sat next to Camille on the living-room couch while I sat in a wing-chair holding the still-sleeping Claudia.

"The baby's been seen by the best doctors, had all the tests, and received the best care possible," the doctor continued. "There's nothing to worry about."

"I keep thinking there *is* something wrong with her," Camille said.

"No, she's all right," he assured her. "These things happen sometimes and they grow out of it." He went on to talk about a few more hospitalization details.

While Camille asked more questions, I looked down at the baby. She was starting to twitch and going stiff, trying to sit bolt upright, it seemed.

"Dr. Zukow, I think she's having a seizure," I said, watching her pale face turn pink, then red.

He looked over. "No, she's just having a BM."

I didn't know what a BM was, and I'd never seen someone have a seizure, but I felt alarmed. Something wasn't right. "I think she's having a seizure," I said again. Claudia's little face was starting to turn purple.

Dr. Zukow looked over at her again. "It's a BM, a bowel movement."

I started to doubt myself, after all, he was the doctor. No, he was wrong. I got up from the chair and started walking towards him. The baby was turning from purple to blue.

"I think she's having a seizure," I repeated. I didn't know what to do.

He looked at the baby and checked himself from saying, "Oh, My God," out loud as I handed her to him. But his eyes said it. Camille didn't move. She was literally frozen in place on the settee, staring horrified as Dr. Zukow slapped the baby on her back.

"This is what you have to do if she has a seizure," he told us both. Claudia was still blue.

"And if she hasn't taken a breath yet, tap the bottom of her feet." Claudia was turning a darker blue. "And if she still isn't breathing, do this." He supported her head with one hand and flung his arm down fast and then brought her up quickly.

Claudia's little arms were outstretched and she shuddered, but started turning from blue back to pink as the doctor held her in an upright position against his chest. "You have to shock her neurological system into breathing again," he told us. "You can fling her down again if she still doesn't take a breath, as many times as you need to." He looked at the baby's face. It was pale again. "She's all right now; she's over it. She's asleep."

Passed out seems more like it, I thought, as he handed her back to me. Camille couldn't move. She was still frozen in place and looked like she was having a hard time breathing herself. I didn't know enough to be really frightened, but I was very concerned albeit slightly scared. This was all new to me, and I hadn't a clue about American medical procedures.

"I wish Jerry was here." Camille was trying not to cry.

Dr. Zukow said she wasn't to worry; Claudia would be all right. Neither of us believed him.

Before he left, Dr. Zukow gave us the phone number for the rescue squad. I memorized it. Camille shut the front door behind him, and burst into tears. I was holding Claudia. I looked down at her. She looked peaceful, just like a little sleeping baby should.

"I can't deal with it," Camille sobbed. She was trembling.

Just a few short weeks before, I remembered Camille telling me she'd been distressed to find herself pregnant again so soon after Elizabeth was born. We were sitting in the living room. The temperature was climbing to 100 degrees outside; Camille was in pain and didn't feel well.

She had a fit of pique and grumpily referred to her current pregnancy as "this silly baby." Camille had grown up in a family of Christian Scientists. Her mother, grandmother and Aunt Pat were still practicing. Camille wasn't.

"Call your mother," I said.

16

Trouble Never Sneaks Up By Itself. It Always Brings Friends

The baby had another mild seizure that day, but none the next day. Then six seizures on Monday. Every time Claudia had a seizure, Camille started crying. She couldn't help it.

Honey, on hastily-arranged vacation time from work, and I were taking care of the baby, with me deferring to Honey. Not only was she older and wiser, but she had two grown-up children, and three grandchildren. I'd never been married and definitely did not have any children, but I'd had a baby brother and therefore had a rudimentary knowledge of childcare. They taught things like that in school in those days, along with how to wash clothes properly, clean a house the right way and cooking from scratch, no short cuts with cans or packaged ingredients. I'd learned to knit at age six, embroider with wool at age eight, and made my mother a tea tray cloth with silk thread by the age of ten. Most of us schoolgirls had hands-on experience with helping out at home. But in America things were done a little differently. In those days, babies slept on their fronts, not their backs, for instance, I learned.

Jerry flew in from New York Saturday night and announced that he didn't have to go back for a few days. Since Claudia seemed better, and since Jerry's eldest daughters aged nine and twelve hadn't met their newest sister yet, he invited them over for dinner Monday night. Jerry worked writing music for *Hogan's Heroes* all day. The show had turned out to be a hit but I never watched it since the first episode as I thought it was silly, although I never said so. Hollywood was already an unpredictable paradise in my eyes and I wasn't qualified to judge it or Jerry's work, even if he did ask my opinion regarding popular music from time to time.

Jerry picked up his eldest girls in the late afternoon. Claudia had been having seizures that day, but, following Dr, Zukow's protocol, she came out of them without too much trouble and, like the doctor said, seemed to be all right.

Jerry's oldest children always had colds, although they appeared to be all right at the moment, so Camille didn't object to the visit. It was just a couple of hours for dinner, Jerry told her. He hadn't seen his eldest daughters for several weeks.

We put the baby in my bedroom since it was downstairs and closest to the dining-room. About ten minutes into dinner, I said I was going to check on Claudia. When I opened the door she was laying in the carry cot trembling; she was having a seizure in her sleep.

After taking his girls home, Jerry and Honey took her back to the hospital that night. Camille couldn't stop crying. Her mother, Joyce and Essie spent hours sitting with her.

Jerry was an intellectual, a man of deep thinking and few words, a man whose mind usually ran in musical notes. When he went to the heart of a matter he spoke in volumes. He'd been in show business since he was a teenager and had wised up early in his youth when he'd been blacklisted in Hollywood after refusing to name names to the House Un-American Activities Committee (HUAC). He knew a lot about chicanery and boundaries. He smelled a rat somewhere.

While Claudia was in the hospital, Jerry had lengthy conversations with Camille's ob/gyn, Dr. Fox, who was fast becoming a reliable family friend. Camille, who had briefly reverted to her Christian Science roots after being comforted and counseled by her mother and was now anti-hospital, wanted a change of pediatricians. Jerry concurred. Dr. Fox recommended a Hungarian-born woman pediatrician for Claudia. Both Jerry and Camille liked her. I forget her name now, but when I met her, I liked her, too. She dug into the hospital medical records and obtained copies of Claudia and Camille's records. She told the Fieldings that Claudia wasn't the only sick baby. Three others had fallen ill. One baby had died. It was due to a staph infection, which the doctor explained could only be contracted in a hospital.

Camille understood you couldn't sterilize hospital walls, but was angry at not being told the truth. Dr. Zukow was dismissed. Camille's "baby blues," the common name they gave to post-partum depression in those days, morphed into fury when she and Jerry were handed a $1200 bill for Claudia's first hospital stint. Her current stay would be extra. A lawsuit was filed.

But trouble never sneaks up by itself; it always brings friends.

Jerry's ex-wife filed a lawsuit against him for more alimony and child support. "You have an English nanny," she contested. True, I was English, but I wasn't a nanny. That didn't move her lawyers or the judge.

"She hates me," Camille relayed to me. "She told her kids I was a prostitute because I wore red tennis shoes."

"What!" I laughed. This sounded absurd to my young ears.

When Camille was upset, she didn't hold back. "She told Jerry it was his fault they couldn't have kids. I thought to myself, well we'll just see about that. Then I had Elizabeth thirteen months after we were married."

I was puzzled. "What about his oldest girls?"

"They're adopted."

That explained everything. "And then you went and had another baby."

"Yeah." It was cocktail hour. Camille took a big sip of scotch and soda. "I hope Claudia's gonna be all right," she said worriedly. "I hope these seizures aren't going to leave her mentally retarded or something."

"I think she'll be okay," I ventured optimistically. "In spite of everything, she appears to be a very strong baby to me."

I knew I was talking off the top of my head, but I wanted to keep things positive for Camille. She'd been so kind since I'd arrived and we'd developed what I considered a reasonable and friendly employer/employee relationship before Claudia was born. Camille nodded slightly.

She wanted to believe what I'd said was true. She wanted
to believe that her baby was strong and ultimately healthy.

Claudia spent four additional days in the hospital
and had all the tests re-done. The new pediatrician put
the baby on anti-seizure medications: Phenobarbital and
Dilantin. "They'll help manage the seizures," the doctor assured
Camille. "They're quite safe and have been used for decades
with success."

Camille was skeptical. "Does she have to stay on this
stuff the rest of her life?"

"No. She'll outgrow it, and she'll outgrow the seizures."
The doctor was very reassuring and we all calmed down.

Everyone was instructed on how many times a day
to administer the medicine and how many cc's Claudia
should have. I felt a momentary panic; the measurements
weren't marked on the dropper; it was blank. I didn't want
to give the baby an overdose, so I made sure Honey administered the medicine while I watched the first few times. It
looked to be roughly half a dropper to me, so I eyeballed
it when it came to my turn.

"Am I doing it right?" I held the dropper up for
inspection.

Honey assured me I was doing a great job with the
baby. This was just as well because she had run out of
vacation days and had to return to her job and her own
home. It had been suggested that Jerry and Camille hire
a proper nurse for Claudia, but they couldn't afford it.
The old house hadn't sold and they were now paying two
mortgages while fixing up the new house so we could

move in. Private school fees were due immediately for the oldest girls, plus the extra maintenance and alimony that had been awarded which amounted to thirty percent of Jerry's gross income before he paid for music copying costs, musicians and recording costs. Jerry's aged mother in Pittsburgh had also been making noises regarding her need for increased annual maintenance. Camille, Essie and myself would have to handle things.

Then Essie's mother died.

"Jerry gave her the money for the train fare back to Texas and the funeral," Camille told me. "What else could he do? Essie's had a hard life. She's always worked, but she doesn't have enough money to bury her mother."

"Essie had a baby girl once," Camille continued. "But she died because Essie couldn't keep her warm enough. The family lived in an old wooden shack, like one of those pictures you've seen of the South. As Essie lay in bed recovering from the birth and trying to keep her newborn warm, she listened to six-year-old Roy Lee outside in the bitter winter frost trying to chop wood for the fire, and prayed that the axe wouldn't slip."

How awful! No wonder Essie often got tears in her eyes over Claudia, although she tried not to let Camille see that.

"Essie and Jerry have known each other a long time," Camille explained. "She once worked for him and his ex-wife. After we moved into this house and Elizabeth was born, Jerry found out she needed a job. That's why she came to work for us part-time."

I nodded. Overall, I felt powerless in this brave new world of grownups, but here was another of life's lessons in "do the right thing."

While Claudia was in the hospital, and before Essie
returned from Texas, Joyce invited me over for lunch one
Saturday so I could have a break from the house. I hadn't
been out in several weeks. A friend of hers, Julie Dorsey,
was also there. She worked as an extra in the movies and
was the daughter of Jimmy Dorsey, the 1940's bandleader.

"My mother used to dance to your father's music,"
I told her, while we ate Joyce's apple and bacon salad.
"During World War II your Uncle Tommy brought his
band to an R.A.F. camp in England where my mother
was stationed. She was a W.A.A.F, part of the Women's
Auxiliary Air Force, the women's arm of the Royal Air
Force. She worked for the Commander of the air station
typing up air crews reports and correspondence between
squadrons and Fighter Command. Mum typed up notes for
the D-Day invasion eighteen months before it happened,
but she didn't know it at the time."

"She must have been awfully young," Joyce commented.
Along with Camille, Joyce had drooled over snapshots of
my family on vacation in the south of France and Italy my
mother had sent.

I nodded. "About my age, eighteen or nineteen."

Julie wanted to know why my mother had joined the
armed forces. "Was it mandatory?"

I shook my head. "My mother lied about her age when
she signed up but by the time they found out she was
of legal age, seventeen. She begged her widowed mother
to sign the papers because she knew the Air Force was
where the exciting action would be. Besides, mum said
the W.A.A.F.'s had the most stylish uniforms and at the
beginning of the war they used really nice material, too."

Joyce and Julie burst out laughing. I regaled them with a few more tales of my mother's exploits in her war-related youth with the flyboys from Canada and Australia, Poland and Czechoslovakia, the Free French squadrons, and later, the Americans, who she'd apparently enjoyed the most.

"They used to send over Jeeps from their base and pick us up after work," my mother had told me. She worked from 6:00 a.m. until 6:00 p.m. There was just enough time to run a comb through her hair after work, and off she and her girlfriends would go.

The Americans would feed everyone first, steak and fried chicken, plus other food the English girls hadn't seen since before the war. Then the band would start up and they'd jitterbug for the rest of the evening into the night: 20 W.A.A.F.'s to 200 airmen."

"Sounds like she had a good time, in spite of," Julie said.

I nodded. "Nobody was getting much sleep, mum said, but when the women started falling asleep at their desks, the Camp Commander confined them to barracks for two weeks."

Joyce and Julie howled with laughter. I didn't tell them that my mother had been engaged more than once, and that most of the pilots she'd known had died.

Camille came to pick me up on her way back from the market and running errands. Her mother was watching the kids.

"Can't stay long," she said accepting a quick drink while saying "Hi" to Julie, who was entertaining us with a story of being stuck in an elevator the week before with

Maximilian Schell, the Austrian-born actor, who'd won the Oscar for his role in *Judgment at Nuremburg.*

"He's *so* damn handsome," Julie gushed. "It was instant attraction on both sides. I swear we could have done it right there."

"And?" Joyce and Camille said in unison.

Julie sighed, stubbing out her cigarette. "Friggin elevator started up again."

I wanted to stay and hear more Hollywood gossip, but Camille and I both had appointments with Debbie's diet doctor, Dr. Elliot, who had new ideas about slimming. He thought people were too fat due to a chemical imbalance. After a few tests at the first office visit, he dispensed herbal pills. Camille was now getting so skinny that I wanted in on this latest thing, especially since you didn't have to actually cut back on food.

We'd just arrived home from the doctor's, who'd sat on the edge of his desk smoking a cigarette as he pinched my upper arm between his thumb and forefinger as one of the tests, when Camille got a phone call that made her scream. Dick had gone on a bender. All painting at the new house had come to a stop.

17

Dick Goes On a Bender; I Go To Disneyland

"*D*amn you, Daddy!" Camille slammed the phone down. "Why'd he have to do that *right now?*" she yelled, heading for the scotch decanter and pouring herself a healthy dose of J&B.

Honey and I listened to Camille rant and rave. Apparently, her father would go on a drunk every two or three years, then check into the sanitorium for a few weeks to dry out.

I had years of it," Honey said to me, looking distressed as she tried to console her daughter.

"Why *now?* We're only halfway through painting the new house, and we're already behind schedule." Camille sank into one of the highbacked armchairs, weeping. Little Doggie went to sit by her feet.

"I believe it's a sickness," Honey said. "Some sort of chemical imbalance, an illness they can't help. One day they'll acknowledge that about alcoholics."

I thought that was awfully understanding of her considering she was an ex-wife. Maybe there was something to this chemical imbalance idea. After all, I'd just come from the doctor and had a pocketbook full of herbal pills to try and correct mine. A wail came from Elizabeth in her crib upstairs.

"She's up from her afternoon nap, I'll go see to her," Honey said, glad of the diversion and abruptly leaving the room.

"Do you know what he did to my mother after they got a divorce?" Without waiting for a reply from me, Camille carried on with her rant. "She got a job and the day before she was due to start, he broke into the house while she was out and poured ink all over her clothes!"

Since it was cocktail hour I helped myself to a gin and tonic, then sat down on the sofa. Jerry was in Las Vegas for the day, seeing about a music arrangement job he could fit in between all his other composing jobs. Joyce had once mentioned to me that Jerry had expressed concern about Camille's drinking, that he didn't want her to become like her father. Jerry did not drink much himself. Of course, Joyce had been inebriated at the time she said this to me, but Joyce never held back her opinions and when she was drunk she said all kinds of things, some of which she apologized for later.

Camille slugged back the last of her scotch, stood up and wiped her eyes, then grabbed her keys and pocket book. Now she was really mad.

"Goddammit! I'm going over there and give him a piece of my mind before he has a chance to start sobering up!"

As she stomped out the front door, I had the feeling Dick was about to get a good telling off for a number of years of alcohol-induced benders.

Drama at the Fieldings didn't faze me that much on the surface; it was just an extended, amped up version of what I'd always experienced at home. I was used to my parents complaining about me and each other, and their constant friction and shouting. Whatever happened to upset Jerry and Camille on a daily basis didn't touch me *that* deeply or emotionally, or so I told myself most of the time. I felt bad for them, but I wasn't to blame. Camille had commented that I'd got "that British reserve" when I'd arrived, i.e. rather quiet and non-opinionated unless asked. I eventually ditched the latter, but I've always maintained that it's what a person has in reserve that you have to watch out for. I'd been in the country less than three months, but was rapidly finding hidden depths and ways of coping with mine.

Everyone felt sorry for Camille, so her friends and family pitched in even more by helping clean and, especially, paint. Her brother Brad said he'd help on weekends, and so did Donna his wife. Both of them worked regular Monday to Friday jobs and had a two-year-old at home, but Camille had laid down a mandate that we were having Christmas at the new place no matter what. Everyone enjoyed Camille's over-the-top Christmases, as well as genuinely wanting to help out in the current crises. Even Honey would put in a few hours of painting on some weekends. I thought that Americans worked very hard. Europeans prized their relaxation time and weren't so crazy about chasing the dollar.

Joyce was still on lay-off from her job as a colorist at Hanna Barbera Cartoons. People who worked in film and television were regularly on hiatus between shows and, thus, regularly on unemployment, Joyce was a standard on Camille's painting crew. Jerry's cousin, Nurse Cynthia, even pitched in when she wasn't on duty. Cynthia was a nice woman but couldn't help her "ward matron" manner. I'd nicknamed her "bossy-boots" ever since she'd showed disapproval and told me to put some clothes on when she saw me wearing my bikini right after I'd been playing with Elizabeth in her paddling pool. She often stayed overnight, attempting to soothe Camille's nerves with nursey-type advice when Claudia came home from the hospital, although she didn't have much to actually do with Claudia. The problem was, Cynthia got on Camille's nerves just by being there.

Cynthia had a habit of raiding the cookie jar every time she came around. Camille said she didn't mind that so much, but she did object to the trail of cookie crumbs Cynthia left all over the place that she, Essie or myself had to hoover up.

"She's sad," Camille explained to me after I'd complained about the crumbs everywhere, especially in places Little Doggie hadn't discovered. "Her fiancé died in a car crash."

I felt a moment's remorse for Jerry's cousin which started to dissipate when I learned the accident had happened several years before. But the more time Cynthia spent around the Fielding household, the faster she lightened up and became more flexible. Since we were all on diets, she even started losing a lot of weight, especially after Camille removed the cookie jar announcing she was economizing further on her household budget. That, and the fact that Cynthia got a new boyfriend Jerry christened Braunschweiger Dave after he met him.

There were no idle moments around the Fieldings. After a day of painting at the new house, or shopping for it, Camille and I would continue our crafts projects. We were now making beaded and embroidered felt napkin holders in holiday colors using some of those jeweled necklace beads Camille had bought at Save-On Drugs back in July, as well as creating a table centerpiece and making sparkly Christmas tree decorations. Claudia slept beside us in her carry-cot. She was never left alone in case she had a seizure, although she seemed to be doing much better with the medication and slept like a log most of the time. But, you just could never tell when she'd stop breathing. I was now sleeping on one of the twin beds in the spare room with Claudia on the other one next to me in case of an emergency during the night. I also was responsible for her middle-of-the-night and early morning bottle feedings. It was exhausting. Fortunately, there was an electric bottle warmer I kept on the nightstand; I just flipped the switch while I was still half-asleep.

"I need a day off," I told Camille. "Rita and Sharon are going to Disneyland, and I've been invited."

Camille nodded. "Okay."

★★★

None of the three of us had much money, but in those days admission and a ticket book for the rides was only $4.00. Parking was free. So were children under three if their parents held them on the rides. Children four to eleven were a reduced price, and so were Juniors, ages twelve through seventeen. As I waited in line at Admissions, wearing a striped t-shirt, shorts and flip-flops, my hair in a ponytail, I considered trying to pass myself off as sixteen-and-a-half. A Junior ticket book would only cost $2.50. Then I noticed the Disneyland tour guides, young women about my age wearing red plaid skirts and red knee socks standing in front of the bank of flowers planted in the shape of Micky Mouse's head. Evoking a hunting scene, they sported velvety horse-riding helmets and carried whips. Ostensibly these were used to point out things of interest or directions for people. But still. I purchased an adult ticket book.

Everything was fake, but so enjoyable, I wrote home, sending snaps of the life-size costumed characters that ambled through the park so that people could take photos with them. Snow White and her Seven Dwarfs skipped past us in Fantasyland as we headed for the Mad Hatter's Party with its spinning teacups, a ride for small children that everyone was really crazy about, especially teenagers. All the best rides were E-tickets, which we used up first on the Matterhorn rollercoaster ride, the Jungle Ride, and the Submarine Voyage which had long-haired young women posing as mermaids sitting on rocks in the lagoon and waving at everybody.

We endured Great Moments with Mr. Lincoln and the animated figure of the president giving a speech on democracy and the United States Constitution not only to step out of the heat, but because it was free and we'd used up all the tickets in our books. The actors in the chipmunk costumes and other Disney animals like the giant rabbit skipping along hand-in-hand with a very blonde Alice in Wonderland must be hot in their furry costumes I thought as we sat in the shade on a park bench eating a hot dog and drinking Coke for lunch. We'd really wanted

fried chicken dinners at the Southern-style restaurant on
Main Street, but they were too expensive for our limited
pockets. Sharon told us about Disneyland's special grad-
uation night for high school seniors when the park was
open from 11:00 pm. to 5:00 a.m. One of her classmates at
Santa Monica College had attended this past June. It had
cost $7.00 for unlimited rides and a chance to win a 1965
Ford Mustang. Rita and I looked at each other. Lucky kids!
There was no graduation celebration when I'd left school.
We'd all just walked out of the classroom at four o'clock.
I'd retrieved my bicycle from the bike rack shed and rode
home before my mother arrived and caught me wearing
her blue faux suede jacket over my school uniform. Still,
here I was, three years later, sitting in the middle of the
perfect capitalist's P.R. dream for the "young and young at
heart" and in spite of not having enough money for souvenirs, by the time we walked out of the exit gate, I was
very, very happy.

18

The Highs are Really High And The Lows Are Really Low

"I don't know what I'm doing,"

I was sitting in the passenger seat of Jerry's 1964 Ford Thunderbird at LAX, experiencing a moment of panic.

"You're going to San Francisco," he said in an even tone that instantly grounded me.

"Right!" I nodded, getting out and retrieving my suitcase. "Thanks for the lift."

It was November. I'd been In California for four months. Sometimes I got a little bored at the Fieldings on the rare occasions no one else happened to be around for several hours and I was left by myself with the children; sometimes I felt a little overwhelmed with new experiences flying in my face before I had time to absorb them.

Life on Reklaw Drive teetered up and down by the minute. The highs were really high and the lows were really low. Joyce was drinking more at cocktail hour, putting Dick's bender to shame, and Jerry had started using Camille's diet pills, not the herbal ones—she'd moved on to Dexedrine—to keep himself up at night so he could complete his composing jobs. Most days musicians, business associates, friends and family moved in and out of the house like it was a train station or a hotel.

The seven phones rang constantly and sometimes I felt like an answering service. Essie didn't like to answer the phone; she was afraid of getting the messages muddled, she said, so it was up to me to assume the role of receptionist if Jerry or Camille weren't around. Camille had told me she wasn't even sure that Essie could read and write, and didn't want to embarrass her by asking, so I didn't mind. Some days I almost felt like I was back at the office in London. At least Debbie didn't send over so much fan mail now to be answered.

The Fieldings were now going out to dinner at least three or four times a week. On the other nights, someone was usually coming to dinner at their house. We'd abandoned left-over night casseroles. I just heated up whatever was in the fridge when Jerry and Camille were out dining, and that took care of any left-overs. I didn't have the time or inclination to cook. If someone, i.e. Cynthia, was staying over (not likely unless a showbiz person was coming to dinner) she had to heat up her own left-overs. There was a sudden drop in her impromptu visits.

Camille's old dancing partner, 1950's actor and entertainer Dan Dailey, had popped into town for a few days. They were very fond of each other and I think his presence helped her recuperate from the postpartum depression that she hadn't had time to properly acknowledge and process. Dan was a lovely man, a cheerful Irish-American, with a sense of humor who made us all laugh, especially at cocktail hour.

"He'll be back in January, so we're gonna do Christmas twice," Camille told me enthusiastically after he left. "We'll do Christmas at Christmas, and then we'll do Christmas again in January."

Oh-Kay! "Do you think we'll be in the new place by then?" I hardly dared ask. The house-being-ready-and-moving dates kept getting changed and pushed back closer and closer to the holidays.

"Oh, yes, come hell or high water." Camille was determined.

I thought hell was the more likely description. I'd have to make an extra Christmas fruit cake for January, but it would probably taste better than the one in December since it would have an extra month to soak in alcohol. Camille heartily approved of the chocolate brandy ball recipe I'd brought from England, so I didn't mind making a double batch of those.

The night after Dan left, we were in the kitchen preparing crab-stuffed avocado appetizers because Jerry's business manager was bringing his girlfriend to dinner.

"She's an heiress," Camille confided. "But she's dying of cancer."

"Oh!" I was speechless. What could one say to that?

Sitting opposite the young, blonde woman in her pale blue linen dress during dinner, watching her smile and politely chat in her Southern drawl, I felt only sorrow and astonishment. She was just a few years older than me. Life could definitely not be fair. She had plenty of money to do anything she wanted in. I didn't have much money, but my options in life looked wider than hers, I realized. No one mentioned the word "cancer" at the dinner table; it would have been impolite and intrusive. And personal discussions amongst strangers at a dinner party just wasn't done.

Camille came back from painting the new house one day and found me sitting in the armchair feeding Claudia her bottle. Thirteen-month-old Elizabeth had climbed up next to me and was looking at her picture book. Little Doggie had tried to jump up, too, but there wasn't room for him so he was sitting on my feet. It hadn't taken Elizabeth long to get used to her new baby sister. At first she'd stared at her, then backed off in fright when Claudia opened her mouth to cry. When Jerry and Honey had hurriedly taken the baby back to the hospital after the seizures, Elizabeth had got up in the morning and made a beeline to the carry cot, looking for her. Now that Claudia had been back for a month, Elizabeth liked to look at her and would babble away to the sleeping, sedated baby. None of us could hazard a guess what she was talking about, but if we approached, Elizabeth would get between us and the baby.

"I think she's jealous of the attention Claudia gets," I wrote my mother. Surely, she was too young to be protecting her? Maybe she didn't want us to disappear her little sister again.

Camille watched me for a moment as she fixed herself a J&B, her arms streaked with white paint. "When we move, you're having complete control of the babies and the dog. You can do anything you want, as long as they're out of the way while Essie and myself, and everybody else, clean up and rearrange everything."

Fine with me. I was still sleeping in the spare bedroom with Claudia on the other twin bed so I could give her middle-of- the-night feedings, and take care of her if she had a seizure. Teenagers sleep like logs, so I hadn't been thrilled with that idea at first, but there wasn't much choice since the Fieldings couldn't afford to hire a proper nurse, and they couldn't send me back to England. Honey and Cynthia were long gone. They both had jobs and homes to attend to and it was decided that I could cope when Essie or Camille weren't around. Complete control sounded okay. There was a pool at the new house in a corner of the back garden, some way away from the house. I could invite my friends over and we wouldn't be bothering anyone.

"I owe you a lot of time off," Camille continued, plopping down exhaustedly on the couch with her scotch and lighting a cigarette. "Now might be a good time to take it before the holidays start. I wanted to be in the new place before Thanksgiving. Thanks to my father, that's not happening. But," she stabbed at the air in front of her with her cigarette, "...we WILL be moved before Christmas."

I nodded, putting Claudia up to my shoulder to burp her. She was doing much better and if she had a seizure, I could handle it without fear. "Yes, I need a break," I agreed.

I think Camille expected me to say I'd go and stay with Rita for a few days, hang out with the teenage neighbors across the street, sun myself by their pool, then go to the British pub in Santa Monica, *Ye Olde Mucky Duck*, to carouse with the Aussies and New Zealanders, all of whom seemed to be in the country illegally, but nevertheless had well-paying engineering jobs.

"Actually, my uncle's wife has relatives in the Bay area and I've been invited to spend some time up there," I told her. Camille took a long swallow of her scotch and was silent for a moment. "That sounds like a nice idea."

Now, here I was, sitting on the plane waiting for takeoff and pondering my life in America so far. I didn't see myself as a bit player in the Fielding's daily drama. I was floating through time and space with my own destiny. It didn't matter a damn if I knew what I was doing, or not. For the most part, I rose to the occasion and coped. At nineteen years old I had my personal create-your-own-adventure kit. As the plane taxied down the runway, my inner voice started humming "*San Francisco, open your golden gate....*"

19

Cal Berkeley And Walking Through History

$\mathcal{M}$r. and Mrs. Anderson met me at the airport. They knew all about young women and their longing for adventure. Their twenty-something daughter, Fern, was married to a ship's engineer. Fern lived aboard and sailed all over the world with him. Every few days the Andersons had a ship-to-shore conversation with her while I was there. The Andersons lived in a small California Spanish-style house in the Oakland Hills with a view of San Francisco Bay that encompassed not only the Golden Gate bridge, but Angel Island and Sausalito.

Freda Anderson took me shopping in Union Square the day after I arrived, where "we hit all the big shops and I spent loads of money," I wrote to my mother. Plus "we had lunch in a place that was there before the earthquake in 1906." Afterwards, we ambled along Fisherman's Wharf with my hands full of shopping bags including one from Macy's where I'd bought a purple linen suit. Mrs. Anderson bought sourdough bread from a waterfront stall loaded high with fresh loaves, explaining its historical place in the Gold Rush and San Francisco history. At another stall she bought fresh clams to fix in another local dish for that evening's dinner which turned out to be what I thought of as unnecessarily messy. She steamed the clams and served them in a thin tomato sauce over spaghetti. I copied how the Andersons pried clams out of their shells and then wrapped their forks around the strands of pasta with a spoon, but I still managed to splash flecks of red on the tablecloth and left red stains on my table napkin where I constantly had to wipe my fingers. My experience of Italian food only extended to scallops in a lemon sauce served over rice. I always ordered it at our favorite Italian restaurant when my mother and I had been to the theater in London. ("*Bye, 'Bye Birdie*" had been our last musical together.) I had never eaten spaghetti before the Andersons. Overall, it was not a satisfying meal. Mr. and Mrs. Anderson were quiet while they ate and did not engage in conversation at the table, much like mealtimes at home in England and very unlike dinner at the Fieldings where people engaged in heated political conversations along with Hollywood gossip. I loved the sourdough bread though and was relieved to learn it was socially acceptable to mop up the sauce on your plate with a chunk.

On Friday, Freda took me to see the University of California at Berkeley. We stood at the southern entrance at the end of Telegraph and I watched as hundreds of students streamed in and out of Sather Gate, strolling around Sproul Plaza, sitting in groups on the grass. Tears pricked my eyelids. This was where the energy was. This is where I would have liked to have been every day. American young people my age were so lucky to be able to go to college. They had opportunities that had not been available to me.

I'd been fifteen when my high school art teacher had taken me aside after class one day and asked me if I'd like to go to art college. It was like the sun coming out over my entire life; I felt he saw inside my secret soul. He told me he'd work with me to get my portfolio together in the coming year and put my name forward for an interview and scholarship, which meant I was a shoe-in for acceptance. Excitedly, I'd told my parents that night. My father immediately nixed the idea, saying I was too much of a Bohemian to start with, and he had me transferred to a typing class the next day. No matter how much I'd argued he'd argued back that I could always get a job as a secretary and support my husband if he found himself out of work. My mother was not on my side; she'd always worked as a shorthand typist and secretary, since he'd never been a stable provider.

"You can't always do what you want," she'd said. "I wanted to go to the Max Factor School in London and learn how to do makeup, but I had to leave high school after my mother was widowed."

I was not impressed with this logic. My mother had gone to a private, prestigious high school which she'd always maintained she'd hated and had been glad to leave because she loathed academia. I, on the other hand, was thrilled at the thought of it, and as Mrs. Anderson and I walked onto the grounds of the University of California, I was in my element.

This was where the current U.S. Secretary of Defense, Robert McNamara, had obtained his Bachelor of Arts degree. Jerry lambasted him every night when the Vietnam war news was shown on television, or when he read the *Los Angeles Times* at breakfast. Gregory Peck, the Hollywood actor, had obtained his B.A. here as well. This was where the Free Speech Movement about civil rights with some of the Freedom Riders, who'd registered African-American voters in the south, and anti-Vietnam war protesters were currently enrolled. Just a few months before they had used the roof of a police car as a speaker's podium surrounded by three thousand students as one of the graduate students, who'd been arrested for distributing leaflets against the U.S. government being involved in Vietnam, sat inside for thirty-two hours. This had led to the famous sit-ins at the University. I'd seen the photographs in the English newspapers and followed the stories. This is where it all took place, and would continue to do so. A delicious shiver went through my body. I was walking through history as it was happening.

What did kids my age in England have as protest? Long hair and short skirts. A crop of teenage musicians playing guitars to bouncy pop music. Still, I reasoned as we walked past tables protesting a variety of social concerns, it had been fun and become a larger movement, which had grown internationally. Some conservative young Americans were even burning the English records in mass demonstrations of their own against the new culture. The Beatles and the Rolling Stones were not to be sniffed at, even though Jerry constantly scoffed at their music. It was a different kind of revolution.

Freda and I spent most of the day at Berkeley walking around. There were thousands of students milling about on campus. It never occurred to me to wonder how many might actually be attending classes. We had lunch at the student café, and I picked up lots of leaflets and a copy of the student newspaper. A big football match between Berkeley and Stanford was being played the next day. I wanted one of the buttons that read: "Screw Stanford Blue," but they were sold out. There was also a big march against U.S. policy in Vietnam being held the next day, too, and lots of groups were busy making their placards to carry.

"I want to come to the demonstration," I told Mrs. Anderson, but she had other plans. We went shopping in Oakland. However, the anti-war demonstration went on so long we caught the tail end of it, and I was able to give Jerry and Camille a report when I got back to Reklaw Drive. They were duly impressed.

"There were hundreds of people everywhere," I told them. "Maybe thousands. I don't know since a lot of people were also sitting on the grass in groups at the university listening to a woman folk singer. Some students carried *Resist the Draft* and *Stop the War* signs with the ban the bomb motif. Some of the attendees looked like they may have been professors. There were lots of cops carrying truncheons and long sticks, but I didn't see anyone getting hit. It was very passionate and boisterous, but I wouldn't call it rowdy."

Rowdy had been the Mods gathering on Brighton beach the year before and the ensuing fights and scuffle with the police, which had also had the effect of making the British establishment sit up and take notice. But that hadn't been about justice or civil rights or war. It was about frustrated young people wanting change in society. People just weren't going to take it any more. They wanted change. Now.

Berkely excited me as well as making me a little bit scared. I'd never seen anything like it, never experienced that kind of energy before. But what really impressed me was that these young Americans felt free to express themselves in that way. They weren't afraid to speak up. Loudly. In fact, they thought it was their duty. There was a lot to be said for higher education in my mind.

The rest of my time with Mr. and Mrs. Anderson was jampacked. We did all the tourist things: riding cable cars, visiting Chinatown, walking in Golden Gate Park and watching surfers on Ocean Beach near Seal Rocks, then driving across the Golden Gate bridge in their big, black 1954 Oldsmobile to Sausalito and Muir Woods where we didn't encounter another soul as we strolled through the hushed silence of the majestic California Redwoods. I sent postcards home.

"Hang onto my correspondence," I instructed my mother. "I don't have time to keep a diary and life is moving too fast. I'd like to read about all the things I did when I get home again." I'd stopped mentioning that I was keeping her letters in my dresser drawer and would take them out to read from time to time when I felt momentarily homesick.

20

It Never Rains in California

"*I*'m sending you a parcel of shoes," my mother wrote in a blue airmail letter. "I bought them in that Italian shop in Bond Street, *Raouli*, but they're too small for me. It's no use trying to cripple myself. They're good black leather with a two-and-a-half-inch heel and strap and cost £4.9.6d. I had already worn them in Town when I bought them, so couldn't exchange them. Dad doesn't know I've bought them as he's hard up for cash at the moment (as usual), so when you write back to us, say 'Thank you Mummy for my shoes you sent. I still like them, and they still fit me.' Okay? Then I'll get the message. If you don't like them say, you've 'gone off them,' or something like that. But they are the latest in Italy: club toe, latest heel, etc., and are very 'with it.' In fact, the smart set in Town were all trying them on."

I was sitting in one of the window seats in the living room of the new house. Camille had picked me up from the Hollywood Greyhound Bus Station on Vine Street. I'd chosen to come back to Los Angeles from San Francisco by the California coastal route, a big mistake as it turned out, since torrential rains on the last day of my vacation had brought down rocks and debris that closed parts of the highway and shut out the scenery in a blanket of gray fog. The bus had been diverted through the San Joaquin Valley, a landscape of endless fallow fields and barren scrub in those days that reminded me more of the desert in a Western film without the benefit of cowboys galloping across the horizon. I'd slept most of the way back.

"November is our rainy season. Two weeks of dripping wet, and then we go back to sunshine for the rest of the year," Camille assured me again as she maneuvered her big black Ford Fairlane with the V8 engine up Outpost Drive into the Hollywood Hills.

It had already stopped raining in Los Angeles, but the sun hadn't come out yet. I looked out of the window at the city spread below me. It was blue, different shades of blue after the rain, and the air was clear. I could see all the way to the ocean and down to the Palos Verdes peninsula with the outline of Catalina Island in the distance.

"*Twenty-six miles across the sea,*" I hummed. "*Santa Catalina is a-waitin' for me-e, Santa Catalina the island of romance, romance, romance, romance....*" Maybe Rita and I could go there for spring vacation next March along with hundreds of college kids, I thought to myself, already planning my next escape.

Camille stepped into the sunken living room. She looked at the blue airmail letters on the window seat beside me, and the parcel my mother had sent with the shoes, along with some clothes I'd had to unpack from my too-heavy suitcase at Heathrow Airport the previous July. My mother had been mailing clothing parcels to me every few weeks ever since.

"God, I swear you get more mail than I do, and we haven't even moved in yet," Camille noted.

I'd given the new address to my mother in anticipation of the move, but it turned out I was merely jumping the gun as the date had been pushed back again.

"But, we're definitely moving in two weeks. December fifth," Camille told me. "I've booked the movers."

She'd had to drop off more paint at the house on Maravilla Drive after picking me up from the bus station. The house wasn't *quite* ready yet, read *nowhere* ready, but she'd mustered her brother and sister-in-law, and every other friend and family member she could, except Jerry, for the upcoming holiday weekend to finish painting and readying the place. Jerry was busy scoring a *Get Smart* episode for television. Camille's primary concern was getting his studio and all the music he was currently working on, as well as his grand piano, moved in smoothly without any interruption to his writing schedule. That was requiring a different set of movers entirely.

"Come on, let's go." Camille ushered me up and out the front door. "I have to take Essie to the bus, then we'll have a quick dinner. We can prep for tomorrow's Thanksgiving dinner after the babies are in bed."

She had invited all the family and friends over who would be helping her paint and clean. "I've got a thirty-five pound turkey, and a ham, so that should be enough to go round with the mashed potatoes and candied yams, plus the sides. We can do the stuffing tonight. My mother always makes two kinds of cranberry sauce, the cooked one and a raw one. She shreds the cranberries and grates orange peel into them, then sweetens the whole thing with orange juice."

"That sounds like a lot of work," I commented as we headed back along Mulholland Drive to Studio City."

"It is. That's why my mother's doing it," Camille responded. "She's the health nut. I don't have the patience. My Aunt Pat is doing a green bean dish and Joyce is bringing a salad of lettuce, with pineapple spears and sour cream. Donna insists on making her lemon and lime Jello mold with cottage cheese and sour cream."

"Jello? Is that the dessert?" I asked. "They usually serve it at children's parties back home."

Camille laughed. "No, it's not dessert. Cynthia's bringing that: pumpkin pie and whipped cream.

It sounded like a lot of food, and a lot of dishes to wash afterwards.

"I'm serving champagne, too," Camille said. "Get everyone in a good mood, ready to finish the painting."

I was looking forward to my first Thanksgiving in America.

It went on until 3:00 a.m. and was a preview of things to come for the month of December. Cocktails had started by 3:00 p.m. Jerry, who was never a whole person unless he was composing music every day, or thinking about it, left to work in his studio on Chandler Boulevard after breakfast, but was back again by four o'clock entertaining a steady stream of friends who dropped by. Camille's liquor supply became severely depleted. Her family were in and out of the kitchen as much to snack as to help with the dinner. The turkey took hours to cook, and the hors d' oeuvres of guacamole with chips and chopped chicken livers with rye bread rounds didn't last long enough. By 7:30 p.m. everyone was ravenous. And quite drunk. Camille opened a bag of frozen peas for another vegetable dish to supplement her Aunt Pat's green beans, Although I was inebriated on gin and tonic, Camille's mother, Honey, gave me a lesson in how to make gravy from scratch, one which I still use to this day. Camille whipped the potatoes with butter and half-and-half, which was a novelty to me. Where I came from mashed potatoes were just that: potatoes, mashed, with a fork instead of an electric mixer. And usually lumpy. Apart from the turkey and the peas, everything was a new taste and I enjoyed it all.

21

One Moving Day Is Not Enough

$\mathcal{T}$he weekend after Thanksgiving while everyone else was frantically putting final touches to the house on Maravilla Drive. I was taking phone messages and watching the babies while packing as many moving boxes as I could. Camille and I had started months before, as soon as she'd bought the house. Every time we went to the grocery store it had included forays behind the supermarket to scavenge for empty cardboard boxes next to the dumpster. There were now hundreds of them stacked in the basement. Essie had started complaining it was difficult to maneuver a path to the washer and dryer, and moved the iron and ironing board up to the kitchen so she had room to work. And yet, we were far from finished. Just as I thought we'd packed the last box, Camille would come up with even more household items.

"Where did all of this stuff come from?" I'd asked.

"Wedding presents," she'd replied.

I'd never seen such a glut of wedding presents like this before, but, then, this was Hollywood.

Towards the end of her pregnancy when Camille was tired and it had become more laborious for her to move around—and when she found out I was good at packing—Camille would sit in the wing chair and supervise.

"I have space in this box for something up to sixteen inches long but not more than two inches wide," I'd told her one afternoon.

She held up her hand. "And I have just the thing," she'd replied, bringing out an antique brass candle snuffer, the likes of which I'd only seen in churches before. As I wrapped it in the comics page from the *Los Angeles Times* I wondered if it might have come from the same church as the Black Madonna which Camille and Debbie had purchased in Spain. The Madonna never did get packed in a box; Camille carefully wrapped and placed her in a brown paper grocery bag, carrying the statue over to the new house, along with her purse, in much the same way the Madonna had arrived with Debbie back in July.

We were all in bed fast asleep when the movers arrived at 8:00 a.m. I threw on a dress I'd been wearing the day before and ran downstairs in my bare feet to answer the persistent doorbell. Three men stood on the top step: one young, one middle-aged, and one who looked rather old and frail. Camille had hired the only moving company who would work on a Sunday.

"Just a minute. Wait here," I said, shutting the door and running back upstairs to knock on Jerry and Camille's bedroom door.

"They weren't supposed to be until after ten," Camille screeched, running a comb through her hair as she puttered down the staircase in her bathroom flip-flops. "God, I need coffee."

"Me, too," I yawned, heading for the kitchen and measuring pre-ground Yuban into the Corningware coffee maker as quickly as possible. Apart from the weeks of monitoring and feeding Claudia at night (she now slept right through) I was so used to staying up late and getting up late that 8:00 a.m. seemed like the middle of the night. While the coffee perked I heated Claudia's bottle and laid out Elizabeth's breakfast. Little Doggie sat expectantly by her high chair, his little gray poodle ears automatically twitching at the sound of workmen's boots walking into the house and starting to move furniture.

"Can you pour me a cup of coffee while I feed the dog?" Camille rushed into the kitchen and stuck a can of dog food under the automatic can opener as she reached for Perrito's dish. "He better stay with you and the babies out of the way today, otherwise he might get trodden on."

"No worries," I told Camille pouring coffee and starting to sound like the Australians I was hanging out with at the *Mucky Duck* pub in Santa Monica.

Camille rushed out with her coffee mug to oversee the movers and I carried my coffee upstairs to see to the children, who were both wide awake in their cribs. Fifteen-month-old Elizabeth was pretending to read her picture book to three-month-old Claudia, who lay on her back, sucking her pacifier and listening attentively. "Up," Elizabeth cried, flinging aside the book and holding her arms out to me.

"Okay, kiddo," I said, imitating Jerry as I lifted her out and laid her on the changing table. "First we get you dressed, and then your sister." Claudia was a very quiet baby most of the time because she was doped up on

Phenobarbital and Dilantin. Elizabeth was good-natured like her mother and easy to manage, although she had a temper that would flare up at times. Overall, they were both very good and I was growing more fond of them every day.

By the time we maneuvered past the moving men and down to the kitchen, Jerry was fixing his morning cup of tea and toasted English muffin, which he ate standing up by the sink.

"I'm driving down to Watts to pick up Essie and take us both to the new place," he told Camille, who'd rushed in for a coffee refill. "The piano tuner said he could come by this afternoon, so hopefully I'll have a few more things sorted out and be able get some work done tonight. I'm looking forward to just walking downstairs to my office."

"Me, too," said Camille, giving him a peck on the cheek before opening the back door so she could take Perrito out for his morning pee while she drank her second cup of coffee.

She and Jerry had already spent several days putting his new workspace on the lower floor in order after it had been sound-proofed. All his music arrangements and compositions, anything to do with his life in show business since Groucho Marx had hired him at age eighteen and eventually brought him to Hollywood, had been organized and filed in a huge closet, almost the size of another room, adjacent his office.

★★★

The move was far from over by 7:00 p.m. I'd helped carry boxes down to the moving van while the babies took their afternoon naps, but there were still stacks of them in the basement. I'd been amazed at the older man, bent over double, as he carried the refrigerator, strapped to his back, down all those stone steps by himself. I'd never seen anything like it. Wasn't the dolly for moving large items? He'd assured me that was the easiest way to get it down the steps—exhausting, but not impossible if the weight was distributed evenly. I still thought it was a bit much to move kitchen appliances that way, and so did Camille, but who were we to tell the movers how to do their job?

However, when they said it was quitting time, Camille put her foot down. The men said the move was supposed to take one day, not two. Camille retrieved the paperwork and got on the phone to their boss who had written up the contract, pointing out it stipulated moving all household contents, not how long it would take. An argument ensued with the movers claiming going up and down all the steps had taken extra time and so they were unable to complete the job in one day. No one had mentioned hilly terrain to them. Camille stood her ground. Too bad their boss that not factored that in when he'd written up the estimate in her living room. In the end, it was agreed the movers would make one more run to take our beds over to the new house, and then they'd return to finish the job the next day. I wasn't surprised at this turn of events; it was chaos, as usual.

"The young one wants to ask you out on a date," Camille told me as we drove along Mulholland Drive after picking up hamburgers from Bob's Big Boy in Burbank for dinner. The babies were asleep on the back seat. "He's about your age, quite handsome, too," she added.

I was shocked. "He's married," I said. "And he has a nine-month-old baby."

"When did he tell you that?"

"When we were moving boxes."

I didn't date married men. In my book you were either married or you weren't. If this guy was only twenty-one his whole situation smacked of messy and complicated to me, not to mention unhappiness and deceit. I'd seen enough of that with my father and his secret girlfriends. Plus, several years before, my uncle had left his wife and two children for another woman, which had scandalized my grandmother, who went by the Victorian playbook.

"I will not have that woman in my house," she'd stated, meaning the new wife. And she never had. I loved my grandmother, so I'd taken my original cue from her. Since coming to live in America, five months before, however, I'd revised this a bit since standards seemed to be a little different here. Separated and almost divorced *might* be okay, I conceded, just as long as I wasn't the excuse for it. And this twenty-one-year-old mover didn't fit that category for a date.

22

Am I Really Losing My Marbles?

*A*s soon as we'd moved Jerry started having what I called his nightly constitutional, and what the rest of the household called taking the dog for a walk before dinner. For Jerry, it was also about scoping out who lived in the neighborhood.

"Suspected staunch Republicans at the Colonial with the high hedge," he announced the first night, already planning at the back of his mind to let the air out of their car tires the following Halloween. "And the last house on Oporto Drive lets the neighbors bring their own lawn chairs and watch concerts at the Hollywood Bowl during the summer," he informed us. "Their garden is directly above it and overlooks the whole place. And the guy who lives on the corner of our street is an executive at Capitol Records."

Jerry had recorded an album for Capitol soon after I'd arrived. Since I represented the teenage population in the household he would bring home what I called "pop-ish" tracks and would want to know which ones I thought were the hippest and the not-so hip. I privately thought none of them would appeal to my generation whatsoever, and tried to tell him that I wasn't qualified to judge young

America's taste, but he insisted I choose one. So I did. I don't know if it ended up on his *Hollywood Brass* album when it was released. When Jerry played it for Camille and me I couldn't tell. It was so unlike the music I listened to, the rock and roll he hated.

"Yeah, Phil's married to a young woman from Omaha," Jerry continued, helping himself to chicken wings and Spanish rice, a staple in Camille's culinary repertoire when there wasn't any company for dinner. Since Phil dealt with young musicians, their paths had never crossed before, but now he and Jerry were on a first-name basis a few days after we'd moved in.

"They have an au pair from Germany who takes care of his two little girls," Jerry told me as Camille poured us all a glass of red wine. "I said she should come on over and meet you sometime since you're about the same age."

Karin turned up the next morning at 11:00 a.m. with her two and three-year-old charges in tow.

★★★

Camille and I had gone downtown after dinner to the trainyards a few evenings before to buy a Christmas tree. Camille needed one at least fifteen feet but under twenty she'd maintained, one that wouldn't be dwarfed by the living room's cathedral ceiling. Jerry had disappeared into his office muttering something derogatory about "Hanukkah bushes," and Essie, who now had her own bedroom and bathroom down on the third floor for when she was in residence, put the babies to bed while Camille and I headed east across the endless web of train tracks to tramp past dozens of box cars filled with evergreens newly arrived from Washington state and Oregon. I'd breathed in the heavenly smell of blue spruce and scotch pine, balsam and noble firs in the cool night air as Camille haggled for the one she wanted—an over-sixteen foot tall Douglas fir, which would end up being almost seventeen feet once they'd hammered the base on. I'd previously thought there was only one sort of Christmas tree, not some with skinny branches you could see through, or trees with dense branches you practically had to lay the ornaments on rather than hang them, and definitely not trees sprayed with white flocking. We'd had sad-looking Christmas trees for years during my childhood, ones with skimpy branches, usually not more than three feet high, standing on a side table with the presents arranged around the base. In the past few years they'd been improving, though. The branches were still skimpy but the trees stood on the carpet and were up to five feet tall. Still, I didn't think they'd ever approached the likes of this behemoth from a northern forest which Camille was purchasing.

"It's cheaper to buy a tree down here at the trainyards where they come in fresh every day," Camille explained. She was still economizing; the old house still hadn't sold yet and the Fieldings were still paying two mortgages, so Camille was using some of her own money for Christmas. "Besides, you can't buy one this big on a regular lot," she added, jotting down the tree dealer's name and phone number in her little notebook for future reference as he tied the Douglas fir to the roof of her car.

"Now we can have our first annual Christmas Tree Decorating party!" she'd announced with a big smile on the drive back from the trainyards. "Next Saturday."

"That's less than a week away!" I'd replied.

"I know it's short notice, but my family will come, and Joyce and my other friends, so I just have to call some of Jerry's friends and associates when we get back from Olvera Street tomorrow."

I looked at her quizzically. Olvera Street? The oldest street in Los Angeles? For Christmas ornaments? "I thought it was all Mexican imports, clothes and things." And Mexican food, too. Yum. (I'd immediately acclimated to that when I'd first tried it.)

"Yeah, they should really have some good Christmas stuff," Camille said. "Plus, there's a discount warehouse for party supplies in the nearby garment district we can swing by afterwards."

That made perfect sense—Camille-style.

★★★

The piney smell of sap and evergreen wafted out from the living room into the entrance hall as I invited Karin and the two little girls in. Karin said she couldn't stay long as her young ones were due for their morning nap, but agreed to come and say a brief hello to Jerry and Camille. Karin couldn't help glancing over as we walked past the living room; the tree filled one of the big arched windows, stretched up to the rafters and several feet out into the room.

"We don't have *der Tannenbaum*," she commented, nodding at her small charges. "Their household's Jewish."

"So's this one," I replied. "Jerry's Jewish, but Camille's not, and Christmas is her thing so he goes along with it." *Because he wants her to be happy.* And Camille was very happy now we were moved. The house wasn't completely ship-shape; there was still lots to do, but it looked all right and would pass muster for the holidays. A few new pieces of furniture that Camille had ordered, like the avocado green velvet loveseat added to the living room (avocado green being the fashionable color *du jour*), and the new Spanishy-décor dining room table and twelve chairs, had been delivered and installed. Any lack of décor in the huge rooms was circumvented by the huge windows offering sweeping views of the city sprawled out below that people were immediately drawn to. Besides, space was necessary for people to stand around in small groups and talk, Camille maintained.

Karin and the two little girls hovered just inside the kitchen door as I made introductions. Essie was making Jerry's breakfast while he scanned the *Los Angeles Times* in between answering the phone. Camille was feeding Little Doggie while the coffee perked. Elizabeth was sitting in her high chair guzzling milk from her sippy cup and alternately humming a few baby-song notes to herself. She stopped at the sight of the two little girls in their matching cats and bonnets. The three of them stared at each other. Three-month-old Claudia was asleep after downing her medicine and half of her morning formula.

Camille invited Karin to sit down and asked if she'd like a cup of coffee, but Karin explained she couldn't stay as her eyes swiveled around taking in the scene, just as Little Doggie started choking on his breakfast and throwing up on the kitchen floor. Later, Karin would tell me that she was astonished at how late we got up each day, and that Camille and I were still in stylized bathrobes which doubled for morning wear every time she came by. Her music-related household was a lot different from mine, she confided.

Meanwhile, proving that her social skills were on alert the minute she opened her eyes, in that brief introductory visit Camille managed to find out that Karin came from Hamburg, was twenty-one years old, and that her father had died on the Russian front during World War II when she was four months old, causing Jerry to later remark to Camille and myself how amazing it was that every German he'd met in the last twenty years had merely been a lowly foot soldier in Hitler's army on the Russian front. No-one, it seemed, had served on the western front, and definitely not against the Americans.

Karin's two little charges stayed mute, holding onto her skirt while they stared at Elizabeth and Claudia snoozing away in her baby recliner on the kitchen counter.

As I walked Karin and her charges out to the front gate, suggesting "next time stay longer and the kids can ride on the little merry-go-round," and nodding towards the home-made wooden carousel with four horses someone had constructed on the brick patio years before, all four of us were energized by our new contact and the prospect of new friends.

"It was really nice to meet you," I added, silently admiring her short razor-cut blonde hair and European Mod-style clothes, so different from American girls, and so much more like the taste and style I was used to. "I'm delighted you came by."

"Same for me," Karen replied, smiling enthusiastically. "It's nice to know there's someone my own age who's moved into the neighborhood."

The night before the party I was desperately trying to finish sewing the t-shirt style dress I was hastily making for the holidays. After Olvera Street and the party supplies warehouse, Camille and I had discovered a fabric warehouse across the street, which wowed us with its selection of the latest materials. We'd immediately decided that despite the hundreds of unpacked moving boxes stashed in the basement, the upcoming Christmas Tree Decorating Party, and all the presents to be wrapped for Christmas Day, some yet unbought, we had enough time in the evenings to sew new outfits. Mine was a reddish-pink glittery material that looked very festive and was all the rage. Camille was sewing evening pajamas in silvery white glitter for herself. All evening, we'd taken turns on her sewing machine, which she'd used for over fifteen years to make all her dance costumes, a machine well used to glitter. Just as I finished sewing the back seam on my dress, the machine broke down.

"Dammit! Now, I definitely won't be wearing this tomorrow night."

Camille was hemming the trouser legs on her outfit by hand. "Oh, not again! Guess it'll have to join the typewriter in the repair shop on Monday."

I'd planned on wearing the dress with several strands of long black beads I'd bought in San Francisco, but now resigned myself to not wearing my outfit until Christmas day at the earliest, maybe not until New Year's.

"Rita hates the material, anyway" I said, "even though I told her it was the latest fashion and very hip."

Rita and Sharon had come up to Hollywood the evening before to see the Steve McQueen film currently playing at the Paramount Theater, *The Cincinnati Kid.* They'd stopped by to collect me and deliver my Christmas present early (a sexy nightdress with three layers of see-through nylon they felt would suit my future lifestyle.) They were also curious about the new house.

"What'd they think?" Camille asked me as she hemmed away.

"Since they'd christened Reklaw Drive 'the castle,' they were speechless over this place," I told her.

She'd laughed when I fetched the nightie to show her. "Put it away for your trousseau," she suggested.

Camille's head swiveled. "Where are the scissors?"

I shrugged.

"Oh, never mind." She knotted the sewing thread and bit it off with her teeth. "A little press with the iron, and I'm all ready for tomorrow."

We were sitting in the small room off her bedroom, boxes and Christmas wrapping paper stacked up around the sewing table. The windows faced west and made the room sunny in the late afternoon, but now the lights of Los Angeles twinkled far below us all the way to the ocean, a dark stripe on the horizon where the vast Pacific met the night sky.

"It's almost 1:00 a.m. I think I'll go to my bedroom and finish writing to my mother before I go to sleep," I told Camille. "D'you have a pen I can borrow?"

The typewriter's up the creek again, I continued writing to my mother once I was in my room, using the 14ct. gold pen Camille had lent me, a gift from Debbie that she never used. I'd started typing the letter on flimsy copy paper earlier in the week, but had put it aside when the portable gave out. I was temporarily out of the blue airmails and we hadn't had time to go by the post office.

The kids were fast asleep: Elizabeth in her cot in the pink bedroom, Claudia in her cot in the little blue alcove off my room, so I could be close by in case she had a seizure. They'd lessened since she'd started the medicine, but we still had to keep her close to us at all times so that we could keep an eye on her.

The weather's 90 degrees here during the day, I wrote, *but it gets cold at night. The sunsets at this time of the year are fantastic. I sit in the living room as the sky turns mauve streaked with gold, pink and coral. The other night we were driving back from the old house where we'd gone to pick the tangerines. On the west side of Mulholland Drive the sky was a bright orange and pink over the city, while on the San Fernando Valley side the sky was pink, mauve and blue turning the mountains purple. We passed by what I've christened the mushroom house, which must belong to an architect. This long concrete stalk rises up from the ridge that has to contain an elevator otherwise how would they get up to the living quarters on top with all those windows and their 360-degree view? I just hope the power never goes out on them because then they'll be stuck.*

Camille mailed you a parcel last week; it's a gift from her, Jerry and the kids. The Hollywood Ranch Market had stacks of figs, dates and nuts: Brazil nuts, pecans, walnuts, pistachios, you name it.

Brazil nuts were my mother's favorite, and I'd never seen pistachios in England. My father always bought dates and figs at Christmas which came from the Middle East; they reminded him of his time there serving in the RAF at the end of World War II.

I've also booked a telephone call to you on Christmas Day. It has to go through New York. "Let's see," the operator told me, "that's 10:00 a.m. your time, 1:00 p.m. our time, and 6:00 p.m. their time!" So I'll be talking to you between 10:00 to 11 a.m. my time which will be between 6:00 to 7:00 p.m. your time. I'll barely be starting my Christmas Day and you'll almost be finishing yours."

I went on to mention the dress I was making. *Can't say I'm absolutely mad over the material, but, my dear, if it's in fashion then one just has to come round, doesn't one?!* I finished up by telling my mother what was happening the next day. *Camille doesn't have time to decorate the tree so she decided to throw a party and let others do it. Her family will be here (but not her father and stepmother; he's still being punished for going on a bender and letting her down). Otherwise, we have no idea who'll turn up. Everything Camille does takes a lot of work, but she makes it as enjoyable as she can.*

P.S. She's concerned that I've lost my marbles since I got here.

23

The Christmas Tree Decorating Party: I Accidentally Set Myself On Fire

"You're on fire."

The Christmas Tree Decorating Party had been in full swing for several hours. I was standing at the kitchen stove absent-mindedly stirring the brandy sauce I was making for one of the desserts, a walnut mince tart, and gossiping with Leonard, Jerry's new business manager, who was washing dishes at the kitchen sink. Jerry dried. More people had turned up than anticipated.

"You're on fire, kiddo," Jerry repeated.

I turned back quickly to what I was doing. Sure enough, my blouse sleeve was in flames around the wrist. Shoot.

"Excuse me." I quickly turned the gas off, walked over to the sink and plunged my arm into the dishwater as Leonard stood aside. Dammit, I liked that Edwardian-style blouse with its long sleeves trimmed in lace. Still, I reasoned to myself, maybe it would work with short sleeves. I inspected my arm. No harm done. It didn't even feel sore. Thank goodness I was drunk.

"We're through here." Jerry picked up a stack of clean plates and shook his head as in 'maybe you should stop drinking while you're cooking,' as he and Leonard walked towards the dining room, both of them snickering.

When I came back downstairs from changing my blouse and stepped into the living-room, the first thing I saw was a Santa pinata hanging from an abandoned picture hook between two antique Spanish church candelabra on the mantlepiece. Jerry and Leonard stood in front of the fireplace, cocktails in their hands, snickering again. *Well, we know who stuck that up there.* I wasn't the only one who'd been drinking.

The sound of a vacuum cleaner startled me. Amongst the party-goers, a middle-aged woman with short, reddish-brown hair, dressed in a blue polo neck shirt and black skirt was hoovering up huge clumps of tinsel from the floor. Nobody took the slightest bit of notice, and nobody stopped her.

"Who the hell is that?" I asked Camille as she passed by me with a fresh supply of guacamole and chips.

"Signe Hasso," Camille confided *sotto voce.* "She was very popular in the 1940's when she made a lot of films. Now she does TV."

I nodded like I understood. I didn't know who many of the people Jerry and Camille entertained were or what they did. Out of earshot, Camille would always fill me in and give me a brief bio, plus any latest gossip, so I didn't feel so out of it.

The living-room was crowded. Camille's Christmas Tree Decorating/Housewarming party was a smash hit, smashed being the operative word. By now, I'd been in the country five months and a Swedish actress vacuuming the floor in the middle of a party didn't seem so strange to me. Over breakfast the next morning, Camille would tell us the last thing she remembered about the evening was being helped up her to bedroom by Signe, then waking up in a strange nightdress she swore she'd never seen before and didn't know she owned.

Meanwhile, the Christmas tree, which stood in front of one of the enormous arched living-room windows, looked as if a lot of the ornaments had been thrown on. The tinsel definitely had, hence the many clumps on the floor which had missed their mark. I walked over to inspect the sagging branches. The entire back half of the tree facing the window, and part of the sides, were entirely devoid of ornamentation. A little redecoration was in order. I hopped up onto the window seat and started rearranging glass bulbs and untangling handfuls of tinsel, hanging single strands along branches.

"What *are* you doing back there?" Actor Farley Granger, who'd shot to fame after appearing in Alfred Hitchcock's *Strangers on a Train*. slipped the ornament in his hand onto an empty branch. His other hand held a lighted cigarette.

"Decorating for Hollywood," I replied, eyeing the cigarette warily and inclining my head towards the view far down below outside the window.

He laughed. I liked Farley. He was handsome and he was funny.

"You know, before I went to England, I thought all the English were gay," he teased, helping redistribute the tinsel.

"That's because they are," I bantered back. *In your world, anyway.*

He laughed again, and we both looked up as Richard Dawson entered the living-room in a tuxedo.

"He's not," Farley commented as we watched the British-born actor, one of the stars of *Hogan's Heroes,* walk over to give Camille a kiss on the cheek and shake hands with Leonard as Jerry introduced them.

"That show's a big hit," Farley said. "I'm glad for Jerry. D'you watch it?"

"No," I replied, not wanting any comment of mine to get back to Jerry, especially since he always worked so hard at any composing job he took on.

"A comedy about a group of prisoners in a Nazi World War II camp?" I'd turned to Camille puzzled after we'd watched the initial episode when Jerry was in New York. I was appalled and couldn't see the humor in it at all.

"It's a parody," she'd explained. "And the Nazis are all played by Jews. One of the actors even spent several years in a real prisoner of war camp."

"You're kidding?"

"Uh-uh. And the actor playing the Nazi guard escaped from Germany after Hitler came to power. A lot of his family died in the camps."

That remark left me speechless.

When I'd first met Richard Dawson the show hadn't been discussed, we'd just chatted about World War II as the English were wont to do a mere twenty years after hostilities ended, it still being fresh in the mind. Like mine, Dick's family had lived on the south coast. His father had been in the Home Guard, he'd told me. One night, they'd spied some Germans trying to slip ashore in a small boat under cover of darkness. A switch was thrown at the local sewage plant and instead of sewage flowing far out into the ocean, oil was sent down the pipeline and the sea set afire, thwarting that particular landing. Still, Hollywood Jewish humor was beyond me; I was too young and unsophisticated. But I was catching up. I liked the Santa Claus piñata dangling above the mantel.

Farley went over to join his boyfriend, Bob Calhoun who was talking to Camille's mother and current boyfriend. Honey and her pal were about to leave for a dinner dance, along with Aunt Pat and her boyfriend.

"I swear those two women have a bigger social life than I do, and they're twice my age." Joyce had come to check up on how the tree looked, although how she could see much of anything through her glazed eyeballs astonished me. Joyce had been steadily drinking vodka tonics for several hours.

She grabbed my arm. "Oh God, Cynthia's coming this way. Quick, let's go into the library. You need a drink," she added sternly.

If that meant avoiding Jerry's cousin, yes, I did. Cynthia was a nice girl, I'd mentioned diplomatically in a letter to my mother. But, in truth she grated on my nerves. On everyone else's, too, I'd come to discover. But, family was family, and Camille's family was polite to everybody, so I took my cue on behavior from them. I was polite to Cynthia, but I did my best to avoid her. *Now she'd lost a few pounds from dieting, she thinks she's Sophia Loren,* I'd written to my mother.

"You really did a great job helping Camille paint," I told Joyce as she fixed drinks for us in the little cocktail nook off of the library.

"Well, honey, she is my oldest friend," Joyce replied, liberally pouring vodka into glasses. "We all felt obliged to pitch and help in after Dick went on his bender. Even Cynthia was a big help. Camille tried to have us all work in different rooms, but it was really a challenge when we were all scrubbing the floor tiles in the dining-room with those damn toothbrushes. Donna and Cynthia gossiped non-stop."

"Who're you talking about?" said a voice behind me.

"Oh, hi, Donna, need a refresher?" Joyce stuck a cocktail in my hand, and reached for Camille's sister-in-law's empty glass.

"We're talking about Cynthia." I turned and smiled at Donna.

I liked her. She was a sweet, unassuming mid-westerner who had married Camille's brother Brad. Camille and Jerry had a running joke about Donna's pear-shaped anatomy and short legs that I thought was true, but unfair. However, Joyce was right; Donna did tend to talk non-stop once she got going. If only she would stop wearing skin-tight trousers.

Cynthia's honking laugh could be heard out in the hall.

"Oh, God, is she coming this way?" Joyce added an extra shot of vodka to her glass and just a splash of tonic.

"She's on her way out to meet her boyfriend," Donna informed us. "She told me he's quite a bit older than her, but very tall."

"Is that Dave the Braunschweiger?" I said.

"Aletheia, you're so bad," Donna giggled. "That's not how Cynthia described him."

"Well, that's what Jerry calls him," I protested. "He *is* tall, that's true. He also belts his trousers super tight so his middle bulges above and below it, hence the name."

"You only look sweet and innocent behind that British accent, but we know better, don't we, Joyce?" Donna said.

"Yeah, that's why she fits into this household." Joyce plopped down in one of the two leather armchairs Camille's former dancing partner, Dan Daily, had given her from his Encino ranch house since he'd recently gotten a divorce and had to move.

"Jerry always has such pithy comments about everyone, and he never spares Cynthia behind her back. Must say I agree with him this time, though. I need a cigarette," Joyce continued.

"Me, too." Donna settled herself in the other armchair and propped her feet up on the matching leather footstool. "Damn, these chairs are comfy." They helped themselves to cigarettes from the silver box on the little table between them, and lit up.

Camille's parties fell into two categories of guests: mostly family in the late afternoon and evening morphing into more friends and business associates as the night wore on. When I walked out of the library to see if Camille needed help with anything, she caught my arm. We stood in the entrance hall looking towards the sunken living-room where a couple were talking to Jerry.

"Darren McGavin and Kathie Brown." Camille was *sotto voce* again as she inclined her head in their direction.

"Huh?" The names were lost on me.

"They're actors. He co-starred with Katherine Hepburn in *Summertime* and Frank Sinatra in *The Man with the Golden Arm*. She's done a lot of TV: *Gunsmoke, Bonanza.* They met on the set of *The Virginian*."

I'd watched a lot of TV, but I still didn't recognize them.

Camille wasn't finished updating their bios. "He's divorcing his wife. She's his new girlfriend. Look at that mink coat draped over her shoulder. Early Christmas present," she concluded before swanning off to give some people a brief tour of the house.

I sat down on the tiled bench that ran alongside the staircase and took a sip of my drink. The front door had been left open since people were coming and going every few minutes. Most people stopped by for a cocktail before they went on to their next engagement. It was the holidays and there were lots of parties, a good time for business as well as pleasure. You could be seen without looking as if you were trying to line up your next job or begging for one as you did the rounds. Since it was also the Fieldings' housewarming party friends and acquaintances had dropped in for a look-see. I could hear Camille's voice coming from upstairs talking about some previous occupants: Max Reinhardt, the director who'd built the house in 1928, and Janet Gaynor, who'd been the first actress to win an Academy Award. Camille was in her element.

I could also hear Joyce and Donna's conversation coming through the open library door.

"How's your mom doing?" Joyce's voice was slurred.

"Not good, I'm afraid," came the reply. "The cancer's spread."

"Oh, Donna, I am so sorry." Joyce had nursed her own mother through cancer until she died Camille had told me.

"She and Dad are flying out from Illinois this week." Donna's voice had a catch in it. "It'll probably be her last Christmas."

"Oh, honey, that's too bad."

"Camille's invited us for Christmas dinner." There was a moment's silence. "Will you be here, Joyce?"

"No, I'm going to my brother's in Palm Springs. He and his wife have two little girls. I don't get to see my nieces that often."

They continued on chatting about their respective families as I sat there in a sad silence, interrupted by a woman wearing bright green cocktail pajamas in the same sparkly material as Camille's. Her blonde hair was scraped up into a ponytail and she weaved a little as she came through the front door.

She had a broad smile and raised her arm in a salute. "Halloo-oo!"

"Elsa," Jerry came out from the living-room to greet her. "Where's your husband?"

"Dunnoo-oo," she replied. "Aww, look at your tree."

Jerry steadied her arm as Elsa walked down the steps into the sunken living room. "I've brought an ornament for it."

I'd stood up and started following them. Jerry introduced us. "This is Elsa, who lives next-door but one."

"Lovely to meet you," I said graciously." Even through my haze of vodka tonic I could clearly see Elsa had a red nose and the whites of her eyes were pink.

"You're the Brit!"

I admitted I was. Over Elsa's shoulder, I could see Jerry was now showing Dick Dawson out. He winked and gave me a little wave as he left, mouthing *Happy Christmas*.

Elsa had staggered over to the tree and was now trying to hang her ornament. She missed, and it dropped out of sight. "You should come to my Christmas Eve Party. The priests from Blessed Sacrament down on Sunset Boulevard will be there." Elsa began fumbling in the greenery.

"Let me help you." I hastily bent to retrieve the bauble before she brought the whole thing down, then pointed out a convenient spot to hang it. Elsa's arm wavered, so I helped gently direct it to the branch.

"Are you Jewish?" she asked.

""No, Church of England."

"We should go to Midnight Mass!" Elsa dismissed 400 years of ecclesiastic reformation in an instant.

"Church of England is protestant."

"But it used to be Catholic. The priests won't mind. They're Irish."

★★★

"I'm not going. I still have too many presents to wrap." Camille was getting frantic. It was after a late dinner Christmas eve and the house was finally quiet. Jerry had gone down to his studio, now permanently nicknamed "the Dungeon," to work, and the babies were asleep. In spite of diligently spending her evenings wrapping presents ever since we'd moved in, Camille still had a stack of gifts and rolls of Christmas paper and ribbon spread out on the dining-room table.

"Why don't you take advantage of the free giftwrap service," I'd suggested when we'd been shopping at *The Broadway Department Store* one afternoon. "The line's too long, and it's important that a lot of my gifts have the personal touch of a hand-wrapped present," she'd replied with emphasis. Especially, the close business friend gifts, I observed. Debbie Reynolds had come by Christmas eve afternoon carrying an armload of presents. Camille had spent a very long time wrapping Debbie's gifts. You could barely see the boxes underneath their flourishes of bows, bells, and bits of greenery complete with teeny-weeny ornaments and gewgaws. She'd just finished when the front doorbell rang, and while she ushered in Debbie and her young son, Todd, to admire the Christmas tree and the panoramic view from the living-room window, I hastily shoved the wrapping paraphernalia out of sight. As Camille showed her friend around the rest of the house, I entertained Todd by giving him a Winston Churchill commemorative stamp from my mother's latest letter for his stamp collection.

People had kept stopping by early Christmas eve for a drink before they went on to other functions. Mitzi Gaynor and her husband had dropped in for cocktails, along with a lot of writers Jerry had known from New York, including Bill Manhoff, who'd written a successful Broadway play, *The Owl and the Pussycat,* the previous year. TV writer Syd Zelinka was a favorite of mine. He was so warm, good natured, and funny! He'd been a writer on *The Phil Silvers Show,* also known as *Sergeant Bilko* in the 1950's, a show that my family had loved and watched religiously every week.

★★★

"I'll just have a quick drink at Elsa's party," I assured Camille as I walked out the door at 10:00 p.m.

By 11:00 p.m. I was being escorted to church with a very drunk South African folk singer named Simon hanging on one arm, and an equally drunk Elsa wearing the gardener's old raincoat over her glittery green evening pajamas, hanging onto my other arm. We staggered up the steps of Blessed Sacrament suppressing giggles, and sat in a second-row pew. The Jesuit priests had hurriedly left the party fifteen minutes before us when they realized it was time to go to work. *At least they don't look inebriated*, I noticed, although their faces looked very ruddy in the candlelight.

Simon and Elsa, fueled by a scotch-infused enthusiasm, tried to out-do each other every time the congregation sung a Christmas carol. Simon had a lovely voice, but Elsa was slightly off-key. You couldn't help but notice this as she sung louder than anyone else and was getting pointed looks by some of the congregation sitting nearby. I started giggling. So did Father McGinty, who was having a hard time trying not to laugh up at the altar. I focused on the Italian Renaissance architecture to calm myself, making a mental note to mention that Bing Crosby had married his first wife in this church when I next wrote to my mother.

24

Contemplating Life While Sitting On A Rotting Diving Board

January 1st, 1966, sitting at the end of the diving-board suspended over the pool, I contemplated my life. I was very hungover. Camille had said there would be lots of partying after we moved, and she wasn't exaggerating.

After midnight mass on Christmas Eve I'd declined to return to Elsa's, and arrived back at 2201 Maravilla Drive to find Camille sitting alone on the library floor trying to follow the written directions on how to put a doll buggy together. She had a screw driver in one hand and a glass of scotch in the other. Jerry was still working downstairs in the Dungeon aka his office/studio.

"You're back early. Dull party?"

"Uh-uh," I replied. "Lots of drunken priests. I ended up at church with a South African folk singer."

"Elsa's parties are certainly different!"

"Yeah, I've never been drunk in a Catholic church before."

Camille downed a slug of scotch. "I've been sitting here for two goddamn hours and if I don't figure this out Dana won't have a present tomorrow!" Dana was her two-and-a-half year-old niece, Brad and Donna's daughter.

"Can I help?" I offered. She'd already taken it apart once after placing the hood and the handle at the wrong end.

"Fix yourself a drink, then you read me the directions and I'll attach the parts together."

Forty-five minutes later, we were still trying to figure out how to attach the wheels to the chassis. The front doorbell rang.

"Come in!" Camille yelled, past caring who it might be at that hour.

Farley Granger and Bob Calhoun walked into the library. Camille fixed them drinks and explained our predicament.

"No worries," they both assured us and went about fixing the problem after presenting Camille with a little Christmas gift.

"There!" The guys stood up and admired their hand-iwork. Camille was ecstatic. Farley gave the buggy a little push and it sailed across the library floor, collapsing grad-ually as it went. The wheels fell off as it hit the bookcase.

We burst out laughing. Camille and I sat in the two leather armchairs as Bob and Farley attempted to reas-semble the doll buggy, so it wouldn't be a dangerous toy. And they succeeded. Finally. We celebrated with another round of drinks until Jerry came up from the Dungeon at 3:00 a.m. Then it was scotch and soda nightcaps and more chit-chat before bed.

Christmas morning I'd spoken my parents while I was lying in bed with a sore throat, although I didn't tell them about that. I'd opened my presents from them at 4:00 a.m. on Christmas eve so I could thank them for their gifts. After I hung up the phone, I realized how homesick I was when my mother said it had been snowing and the lane where they lived looked so picturesque with the hedgerows and tree branches dusted with white. Outside my bedroom window the sun was blazing and it was at least eighty-five degrees. In the past week everyone in the household had taken turns coming down with the flu, but nonetheless kept going with the help of aspirin and other medication. Now it was my turn. I felt rotten. I gargled with salt water and took two aspirin, dressed the children and went down to the kitchen. Camille was standing by the stove in her dressing-gown making stuffing for the turkey. Jerry was getting his own breakfast.

"What time is your family coming?" he asked her.

"Three o'clock."

He nodded to himself and checked his watch. None of us had had enough sleep, but there was time to get a few hours of work in for him, and maybe a short nap before everyone arrived. Elizabeth and Claudia were wide awake and had already developed the habit of entertaining each other while they waited for their breakfast. Elizabeth would sing and babble alternately to Little Doggie and her sister, and Claudia would gaze at her and smile while listening, waving her arms and legs, which would encourage Elizabeth to continue with her performance. We were all amused, although I think Little Doggie was just waiting for a piece of toasted bagel to fall onto the kitchen floor from the high chair.

"Are you sick?" Jerry was looking at me as he fixed his morning cup of tea. "You're glassy-eyed."

Camille whipped her head around and stopped caramelizing the onions.

"Yeah," I croaked. "But I'll be all right. I took a couple of aspirin."

That satisfied Camille. She turned back to the onions. Jerry took another Lipton teabag out of the box in the drawer and dunked it into a mug of hot water for me. "You'll need honey in that as well."

Camille reached into the cupboard and pulled out the jar of honey, then cut a lemon in half for me. "This, too."

I hadn't the heart to tell them I hated Lipton tea and that's why I never drank it in America. I was a confirmed coffee-holic, and had been since I was eleven years old. I'd always hated my mother's brewed tea also, which was so strong I swore it would burn holes in the furniture if someone spilled a drop on the upholstery.

Christmas Day passed in a blur. I put my hair up, wore the glittery cerise-colored dress I'd somehow miraculously found time to finish sewing, threw the strands of jet beads I'd bought in San Francisco around my neck and plastered on a LOT of makeup as I nursed my sore throat with scotch and soda for the rest of the day. I swore later in a letter to my family there were at least five hundred presents piled up under the Christmas tree.

Camille and Jerry gave me a crepe dress in the latest colors and style, which I was thrilled with. Claudia gave me two bangles, one gold, one of tiny pearls, bless her little three-month-old heart, and Elizabeth gave me a photo of herself and paid for part of the phone call to my parents. Santa also brought me a fancy pink robe that screamed Hollywood. Donna and Brad gave me some Avon body lotion because I'd been complaining about the Los Angeles climate drying up my skin so much, and Jerry's cousin

Cynthia gifted me with a perfume and cologne set, *My Sin* by Lanvin, which she chose because she snidely thought the title appropriate for me.

Dinner was similar to Thanksgiving, full of over-consumption, the massive helpings of food compared to English meals encouraged over-eating. Because I was having such a good time cooking up American recipes, Camille put me in charge of the sweets and desserts. In addition to the pumpkin pies and fruitcake, I'd made a Baba au Rum, and bowls of candy filled with rum balls, brandy balls, Divinity and fudge. It didn't matter how many people turned up, there was plenty of food for everyone. And drink. Camille's family went home after dessert at 10 p.m., but the front door was left open as people kept arriving.

I would later write to my mother that the Fieldings' place was like a crowded pub. Jimmy Dorsey's daughter, Julie, arrived with her sixteen-year-old son, Billy, who'd lived in Rome for years. I wrote that he was a really nice boy and a cut above American teenagers of his age. Since I was also still a teenager, albeit slightly older, I felt eminently qualified to pass judgment on this. Dan Daily, who said he'd be dropping by in January, actually turned up early and spent the holidays in Los Angeles. Camille was thrilled, and so was Joyce. They loved Dan, and after I met him, so did I. He was a lovely man, always smiling and full of good humor. I never saw him in a bad mood.

After opening her presents on Christmas Day, Camille spent most of the time in her little cocktail niche off of the library, filling drink orders for people who hung around the entrance chatting with each other and looking at all the framed photographs Camille had plastered over the non-bookcase wall. Some, like the ones of Debbie and Dan, I'd seen in the hallway lining the wall between my bedroom and the kitchen at the old house when I first arrived. But, now that she had more room, Camille had dug out photos previously in storage: James Stewart, Olivia de Havilland, Ann Sheridan, Vic Damone and Dick Powell amongst others beamed down on us. The black-and-white photo of a four-year-old Camille chatting to Carol Lombard at her studio dressing-table was up there, as well as one of an adult Camille with Rita Hayworth. Doris Day, one of my childhood favorites, smiled down on us, too. Camille had told me one of her dancing jobs had been dubbing Doris's dance steps in some of her 1950's musicals. Realization had dawned: When I'd been sitting in an English cinema hearing Doris tapping away in her song and dance sequences, I'd probably been listening to Camille tapping away in a Hollywood sound booth. Suddenly, I felt more aligned with my destiny. Everything was connected in some strange way.

"You couldn't hear the dance steps while they were filming," Camille had told me. "So they'd have a dancer copy them in the studio later and add the recording to the film soundtrack."

As she made drinks and answered questions about the photos, Camille jotted down each refill in a little notebook, courtesy of Jerry's business manager, Leonard. Even her OB/GYN doctor dropped by, complementing how she looked in her white silk evening pajamas now she'd lost the pregnancy weight. By 4:00 a.m. Jerry was playing some of his albums for the guests at full blast on the built-in living-room stereo. At 6:00 a.m. I went to bed.

There were nine trash cans at the Fieldings. The day after Christmas, three of them were filled with scotch bottles, one with soda water and tonic bottles, and one with Christmas paper wrapping, in spite of Honey saving a pile of it to be ironed and re-used the following year. Camille's mother came by before we were up to start washing dishes. There were so many cluttering up the kitchen on Christmas night, Camille had started shoving them onto the back porch so she didn't have to look at them. She'd added "buy a dishwasher" to her to-do/fix-it list, but it was way, way down on the list of items needing attention.

"I felt so bad for you both," Honey told us from the kitchen sink as we stumbled down to breakfast at noon. "I couldn't bear the thought of all that work facing you first thing in the morning, along with all the rest of the clean-up." Indeed, the dining room was a mess, and so was the living room and library. It was going to take us three days to clean it all up.

"Mother, you're a saint," Camille said, giving her a thank-you kiss on the cheek. I wished Honey were my mother, who would never have thought of such a thing as washing someone else's dishes. She always managed to get someone else to do the clearing up after a meal at our house, usually me.

Jerry insisted on driving me to an emergency appointment he'd made with his ENT doctor in Beverly Hills. It turned out I had a bad strep throat that was swollen and starting to close, but after fixing me up with some strong antibiotics that worked like a charm, I quickly started feeling better. This was just as well as Jerry brought home a surprise overnight guest late the following evening, whisk-ing her hurriedly in the front door.

"She's hiding out from the FBI and the mob," Camille confided as Jerry showed his surprise guest into the living room. "She's been ordered to testify before a Grand Jury tomorrow. She doesn't feel safe in her hotel room, so she called Jerry, who knows her from the old days. Nobody must know she was here."

The petite, dark-haired woman was very pretty, and seemed fragile standing there in the most beautiful ranch mink coat I'd seen yet; a ranch mink even better than Camille's, which she'd let me wear for a Christmas photo to send home to my family.

I nodded confidentially, glad of the 10-foot high sturdy wooden gates set in the 10-foot high stucco wall that secluded the house from the street. The woman was a singer, part of a famous sister act popular in the late forties and fifties, Jerry said as he introduced us, which meant nothing to me, but I smiled politely as if I understood. This was Hollywood and I'd become adept at faking it, which I hoped came off as being diplomatic. I was always polite to everyone, even if they were the girlfriend of a well-known gangster. Nevertheless, on my way to bed, I checked that the solid wooden front door was securely locked, as well as the scrolled iron and thick mesh screen door.

Jerry knew such interesting people.

She was gone before I got up the next morning, but she stayed safe. Jerry was recording down at the studios on Sunset Boulevard that day. Since Essie was back at work after the Christmas break Camille and I went down there to join him. We sat in the sound booth for hours and it took days for my ears to recover. People who were famous in the music world kept coming in and out; the coffee tables in the lobby were full of empty liquor bottles and overflowing ashtrays. It was another party of sorts. The son of comedian Jerry Lewis had his own rock and roll band, Gary Lewis and the Playboys, and they were recording next door.

The next couple of days passed pretty normally, with just a few people dropping in for drinks in the late afternoon, and then on New Year's Eve Camille had another party. This one had a Mexican food theme: enchiladas, tacos, ceviche, tamale pie casserole, and the usual guacamole and chips.

Pamela, an English woman who'd worked for Otto Preminger before marrying a drummer Jerry sometimes employed, observed me digging into an enchilada at 2:00 a.m. and was surprised I liked it. She said it usually took English people awhile to get used to the taste, the spices were so different.

"Not me," I said, helping myself to a taco. "I think it's delicious."

Camille had had Pamela over to vet me soon after I arrived, and I'd passed her test, Camille told me later. Guess I now passed her culinary meter, too.

I went to bed at 7:00 a.m. on the first day in January, but the kids woke me up at 10:00. I staggered down to the kitchen. All the other guests had gone home, except Dan Daily who had fallen asleep on one of the sofas. He recommended leftovers for breakfast.

"They taste better the next day," he said as we sat in the Captains' chairs around the kitchen table consuming gallons of coffee. Camille told me I'd missed a spectacular sunrise as she retrieved remains of the tamale pie casserole and Black Bottom chocolate pie from the refrigerator, a crème pie that Dan had brought from the *Brown Derby* restaurant for the party which I hadn't had a chance to taste. After I'd finished eating, and pronounced it my most delicious breakfast ever, Dan laughed and said it was the best cure for a hangover he knew of.

Now, here I was two or three hours later, sitting on the diving board feeling crappy as I ruminated about the holiday season.

"Aletheia, look over here." Camille brought me back to the present moment by the swimming pool. She was standing at the top of the steps leading down from the top terrace and had her new Polaroid camera in hand, one of her Christmas presents from Jerry, and it was aimed at me. "Take off your sunglasses."

"The sun's too bright," I whined. "And I'm not wearing any eye makeup."

"Your mother won't mind," Camille assured me. "She'll just notice your bikini and the sunhat."

"I feel bloated."

"Don't we all," Camille replied, clicking away. "We'll go back to the diet doctor next week. Right now, we have to start dismantling the tree and pack those 350 ornaments and 81 feet of Christmas lights away, which is going to take a while. We're having a late dinner party the night after tomorrow. Jose Greco, who's regarded as the world's greatest Spanish dancer, and his flamenco ballet troupe are in town. He and his prima ballerina, Nana Lorca are coming over, plus his business manager and a few others,

although I hope he doesn't bring the gypsies. Great flamenco dancers, but they set fire to their hotel room in
New York when they decided it was too cold and they
needed to warm themselves up. Can you believe they built
a fire in the middle of their room? They're real gypsies;
they live in caves back home."

I sincerely hoped they'd find Los Angeles warm enough
for them.

"Mitzi Gaynor and her husband are coming to dinner,
too."

I liked Mitzi. I'd admired the actress after seeing the
movie *South Pacific* several years before so it was interesting
to meet her and eat dinner at the same table. Mitzi seemed
unpretentious and down to earth. She'd helped clear the
dishes after a prior dinner party, carrying them into the
kitchen, and noticing some people had not touched the
butter pats on their bread and butter plate. "Oh, save the
precious butter," she'd said, and meant it.

In the land of plenty this had surprised me, but like a
lot of stars who'd grown up during the Depression years
prior to World War II, she was grounded in the value of a
penny and the value of hard work to get what you wanted
in life. She'd lived in the same house in Beverly Hills for
years, and Camille told me one bedroom was devoted to
her theatrical costumes.

Even though I was meeting people who were famous
in show business, I never asked questions about their work
or discussed roles they'd played on the silver screen or
television, and I never asked for an autograph. I felt it
would be gauche of me; plus, Jerry and Camille might not
approve, although we never discussed it. I also didn't want

to appear naive or starstruck. I was trying to fit in. And I needed to feel that I belonged, even though I was an outsider. It seemed to be working. Camille had sent my family a Christmas card, along with the fruit and nuts gift, and my mother reported back to me that she'd written on it: "Aletheia is a joy."

Camille finished snapping photos of me just as Cynthia appeared at the top of the stone steps with Claudia in her arms. and Elizabeth in tow. Jerry joined them with his eldest daughters who looked excited. When I'd first met them, Georgia, the twelve-year-old had been dying to know if I knew the Beatles, and very disappointed when I said I didn't; I'd only seen them in concert and at The Regent dance hall in Brighton.

"Dan's left," Jerry announced. "He has a rehearsal for *The Odd* Couple at the Huntington Hartford Theater down on Vine Street. We're going to the zoo." He looked at me. "All of us."

Okay, time to get off the diving board (a good thing since it might be rotten in places, according to the pool people, who turned out to be right a few weeks later when Camille finally had it removed. Not only did it have advanced rotting at the end of the board anchored by crumbling cement into the retaining wall, but a black widow spider's nest in it, too). I dipped my toe in the water. Too cold for a swim, anyway, since the heating pump was broken, another low priority on Camille's to-do and fix-it list. It had been generally agreed that after the maintenance people were through we'd wait for the sun to warm the water up to a suitable swimming temperature. I slipped on my sandals and walked up the steps to join the others.

What the heck. I'd just throw a dress over my bikini. No one would notice.

There was a unanimous "no way" vote on actually walking around the Griffith Park Zoo when we got there, so we took the elephant train, a series of elephant-shaped box cars mercifully roofed with faux banana leaves to shield us from the hot sun as we drove round and looked at the animals in their cave-like cages. I felt like I was in the jungle. The zoo was small and quaint, but soon to close as a larger one was being built in a different area of the Park with better accommodation for the animals.

Jerry's older daughters had very different personalities. The twelve-year-old was much more outgoing than her nine-year-old sister, who was usually sullen and often looked as if she'd smelled something unpleasant when she was around Camille, no doubt due to her mother's influence. She wanted her father to herself, which, in turn, made Elizabeth jealous. Jerry was a loving father to all four of his daughters and would pick up the babies and play with them every day before going back down to the Dungeon to work. When he was with the older two he gave them his undivided attention. On this particular afternoon, with Elizabeth sitting on Camille's lap, Claudia sitting on mine, and Jerry and Cynthia on either side of the older girls as we rode around the zoo, no-one was whining or crying because all attention was on the animals, some of which I'd never seen before. I wrote later to my family that this was probably because Los Angeles was a warmer climate for them than the chill of England.

I was starting to feel numb from the lack of sleep, so after the party for Jose Greco, I made myself go to bed by midnight for a few days, and cut back on the alcohol. It was impossible to cut it out entirely as people kept dropping by at cocktail hour. Not willing to be unsociable, I'd managed to limit myself to one drink per day. The house had become an informal party central, just as Camille had promised. Jerry's studio downstairs might be his work place, but it was hard to see how it was his sanctuary as far as show business people went. Friends from New York would drop by when they were in town to discuss work/ gossip about people they both knew/see the new house/ catch up on the family. Ditto for those who lived in Los Angeles. Camille's family and friends were a constant, too. She was in her element.

Jerry and Camille liked having the children around no matter who was visiting, and people liked seeing them. Elizabeth had a favorite toy, a plastic slice of Swiss cheese on wheels that Santa had brought. She'd run up and down the entrance hall and around the dining room pulling it behind her. The faster she went, the faster the mice kept popping up and down through the Swiss cheese holes. It made a terrible racket on the bare Saltillo tiles. Fortunately, she couldn't run around the library; it was too small, had a carpet, and was usually full of people lounging around in chairs with their drinks.

Of all the people constantly coming in and out of the house—producers, directors, actors, musicians—the writers seemed to be the quietest. Camille would say to me in reverent *sotto voce* tones after one entered the house: *He's a writer.* I'd glance over at the man sitting in the library or on the living room couch looking like a picture of misery and think: *Who would want to be a writer; they're so glum.*

Syd Zelinka was an exception, but then he wrote comedy. And he was much older than the others.

"Are most writers wretched-looking?" I asked when there were just the three of us for dinner one night,

"What? What do you mean?" Jerry stopped eating.

"Well, most of the writers I've met so far complain about their bosses at the studios when they open their mouths to say something."

"That's because the bosses are screwing them over," Jerry responded. "Besides, writers usually have a different story going on in their heads that they're trying to work out in words and pictures. Plus, they think they're more intelligent than the people hiring and paying them," he added. "Oftentimes they're also writing something other than what they really want to be writing," he finished up.

Okay, so they needed to pay the rent, I surmised, thinking that actors were more interesting especially when they got drunk, even if they did talk about themselves all the time. Anyone in earshot was fodder for an audience to an actor.

Jerry was always complaining about actors. *Untalented.* But then he'd show contempt for other music composers, too. At the mention of Andre Previn's name, he'd snort derisively. I put it down to the fact they were all competing for the same jobs, which wasn't really true as everyone seemed to have their own particular musical style. The competition was that *their* style was the right one for a particular project.

"I think all you creative types just like to complain," I said. "It gives you a feeling of solidarity."

Camille always joked that her husband walked around with his own little personal dark cloud above his head, and I felt emboldened to speak up.

Jerry turned back to his food and grunted. "Just you wait a few years. You'll find out."

25

Mother Reads My Letters In The Restroom

Living in Los Angeles was almost like a vacation; almost, but not quite. The children were easy: they got up, they laid down for naps, I dressed them, threw their cute clothes in the washer and dryer once or twice a week, and fed them. Sometimes they cried, but they didn't require much conversation. Elizabeth babbled a lot, but all you had to do was smile at her and she was satisfied you were paying attention. Camille was more responsible for Elizabeth, and I was more responsible for Claudia. When she was around, Essie was always a big help in her quiet way, and occasionally Cynthia helped, too, if she felt like it.

Cynthia had dropped by the night before Christmas Eve and found Camille and me standing on the window seats gazing out of the arched living-room windows with binoculars.

"Looking at the bright lights of L.A?" she'd quipped, stepping down into the living-room and coming over to join us.

"Nah," Camille replied. "I just wanna see Omar Sharif. *Dr. Zhivago's* premiering at Grauman's Chinese Theater

205

tonight, but we're too far away, with too many trees in the way, darn it."

Giant studio spotlights down on Hollywood Boulevard were beaming in crisscross patterns across the sky for the premiere.

"Let me have a look." Cynthia stepped up next to Camille, who handed her the binoculars. "You can see the red carpet!" Cynthia was overjoyed.

"Only partially," Camille sighed, stepping off the window seat.

Cynthia enjoyed being Jerry's cousin, and had started coming by as often as she could to scope out celebrities. Camille and I suspected that Dave the Braunschweiger boyfriend was no longer an item.

After breakfast, I'd take Claudia and Elizabeth out to the front garden for playtime. One benefit of living on a hill was the light breeze that blew when it was stiflingly hot down on the flat area of Los Angeles, and although we could see the layer of smog laying over the city like a blanket, it didn't seem so bad up amongst the trees. When I first arrived in Los Angeles, my eyes had teared up and smarted from the smog, but I had acclimated. They were no longer red, and I didn't sneeze as much.

Claudia was sitting up now and giggled a lot. We'd found out she was allergic to milk after switching her around on several kinds for four months. She was doing much better on her concentrated soy formula. Claudia was a strong baby and the seizures didn't seem to have damaged her in any way, although she still had one now and again, especially if she caught a bug and got sick; that triggered convulsions. She mainly cried when she was in pain and not feeling well. When she caught the stomach flu the doctor recommended a tea enema. Claudia remained still and quiet while Camille and I administered it. although perhaps the fact that we were being very un-Nurse Cynthia-like and trying not to laugh about new and varied uses for a cup of tea had something to do with it. Big sister Elizabeth always amused and entertained Claudia to no end. Sitting in the playpen she'd watch Elizabeth ride on the merry-go-round while I sat on the little park bench and wrote letters to my family and friends.

I had a lot of catching up to do with my correspondence. Letters were arriving from family and friends telling me about their Christmas.

The friend who worked in New York had visited her family in England for the holidays, but couldn't wait to get back to the U.S.A., she wrote in a quick note.

My Great Aunt Em in Canada wrote in an old-fashioned loopy scrawl that she hoped I'd settled into my new life by now and made some friends. "Be sure and go to church. You will meet some nice people there who are friendly." I thought of Elsa the drunken neighbor and Simon, her folk-singer friend. We'd all been three sheets to the wind on Christmas Eve, along with the priests from Blessed Sacrament, who'd had to scramble to get to work on time and dispense Midnight Mass. *Oh dear!* Aunt Em had enjoyed watching the Rose Bowl Parade on television on New Year's Day and wanted to know if I'd watched it. *No, I think I was falling into bed around the time the parade was just getting started.*

Avril had finished traveling around the Continent, and wrote she was back in London. She'd had the latest short haircut at *Vidal Sassoo*n's and could afford *Mary Quant* makeup. Due to her now-fluent French she'd been able to work at the Galleries Lafayette London for the Christmas rush helping celebrities like the model, Jean Shrimpton, and several members of the Rolling Stones with their seasonal shopping. Avril was about to start a new job working for the assistant editor at a magazine, although one of her boyfriends was emigrating to South Africa. She thought she might go with him, instead. "What do you think? It would only cost £15 and there was no obligation to stay." But then a few lines later, she "might go back to Paris" where she'd left the love of her life. Avril's letters were always peppered with so many different boyfriends I decided to wait a couple of weeks before responding. The situation might remedy itself.

"By the way," my mother reported in her latest letter, "now Avril was back in England everyone said she looked like she was on drugs. Her heavy eye makeup didn't help." Also, a girl in the office (my mother had gone to work there after I'd left for America) had a crush on Tommy Steele, the British pop star who'd appeared in the Gene Kelly show that Jerry had worked on in New York. Would I ask Jerry to get Tommy's autograph for her? *No, I would not.* My mother was still visiting my friends and lending them my letters to read, as well as doing pseudo open mic readings of them in the woman's restroom at the office—without the mic. Apparently, it was a popular place to gather for a ten-minute break in the afternoons. Was she trying to steal my life, I wondered, but concluded, no, she was just bored with hers. She'd been saying that she'd come and visit me from the day I arrived, and now she'd found a cheap flight with an Anglo-American club. Could I pay them the fare and she'd pay me back later? *What? No, I could not!*

I wrote back saying I might just have enough money for a one-way ticket to Honolulu when my contract was up with the Fieldings, and planned on living on the beach until I got a job.

Oh, don't do that, dear, she advised me in her reply. The friend of a girl who worked in the office had just moved back to England after living in Honolulu, and said it was a rat race. My mother did not want me "going from the frying pan into the fire," i.e., end up on an island in the middle of the Pacific ocean without a job, a place to live, or any money. I got the message, but was annoyed that she might be telling me what to do anyway.

Since I was under twenty-one, which was adult legal age in those days, I was not responsible for anything, although no-one was really responsible for me. Even though life was interesting, I felt stuck in many ways living on a promontory at the end of a cul-de-sac in the Hollywood Hills. When I'd first arrived in California, Camille had said she'd teach me to drive. That hadn't happened yet because there hadn't been time. *And there never will* be, I realized. Camille was always way too busy. My airfare was almost paid off. That would free up some money to pay for driving lessons. I'd seen an advertisement in the *Los Angeles Times* for the Hollywood Driving School. I was impatient to get my driver's license so I had more mobility. Camille had said she'd sign for my driver's permit in place of a parent and I could use her car. She didn't mind. She wanted me to pass my driving test, too, so I could run some of the errands, and we'd all have more flexibility. After all, I was living in her home. But if I left there, got another job with more money, moved into an apartment, or even went to Honolulu, she would withdraw custody and my driving license would be taken away. I could reapply for it when I was twenty-one, if I was still living in the U.S.A. I could even buy my own car, if I could afford one, but it would have to be in Jerry or Camille's name and co-signed by them. And I couldn't really rent my own apartment even if I wanted to; that would have to be in someone's name who was over twenty-one, too. I sat on the patio and thought: *I'm old enough to be almost seven thousand miles from home, but not old enough to stand on my own two feet. Old enough to care for babies, one of them sick and requiring strong medication and life-saving methods if she has a seizure, but not old enough to be responsible in the eyes of the law.* It sucked.

Camille took me out and about as much as possible. Jerry was the musical director for a show business industry event one evening; Camille invited me along as she said it might be interesting. I wore a long green velvet skirt I'd made with slits up the side and a lace blouse. Camille had given me an enormous fake diamond ring as a gag gift in my Christmas stocking, so I wore that, too. Charlton Heston, the actor from *Ben Hur*, smiled a me from across the room and inclined his head.

"He thinks you're a starlet," Camille had giggled.

"He's one of my mother's heartthrobs," I told Camille, flattered to be noticed but not enough to smile back. I was astonished he'd noticed me in the throng. Everyone was there to work the room, except me.

We were sitting at a table with some of Jerry and Camille's friends, all of them at least a minimum of twenty years older than myself. One of the wives corralled Camille out of my earshot and accused her of corrupting me. "She was a sweet and innocent young girl when she arrived. Now look at her; she's wearing an evening skirt with slits up the side and drinking scotch!"

Camille explained that I arrived in Los Angeles no stranger to scotch. "She worked in London and there was a bar in her office building. Aletheia often frequented it at lunchtime. She says alcohol helps with her monthly cramps. Her mother thinks it's medicinal."

Later, when we arrived home, Camille told me about the encounter. When we finished laughing, Camille asked me: "Do *you* think I've corrupted you?"

I shook my head, *No*. Jerry and Camille had been very kind to me since I entered their home. Certainly, I came from a different world than the one I found myself in now, but the world was not a monastery. It was a school, and I was learning fast. The world was full of as many realities as there were people. The life of doctors was not the same as the one of a college English major or a musician. Each one interpreted the world from a different point of view and used different codes and signs in their language to describe human experience. And what was life? Something we made up every day with a combination of hard work and fantasy. I was bedazzled by the glamor around me, but I wasn't starstruck. Glamour was a veneer on really hard work in show business. Even young and innocent little me could see that.

"I think that woman's got subliminal worries about her own family," Camille finally decided. "Her niece, Sally, is an actress. She's making a pilot for TV about a teenage girl who's crazy about boys and surfing. It's based on a novel and a film from the 1950's, *Gidget*. Her niece is the same age as you," Camille concluded.

I nodded affirmatively. That made sense, even though I didn't know what the word "subliminal" meant.

A Really Important Party For A Really Terrible TV Show

$\mathcal{T}$he new year marched on toward Spring. The Gene Kelly show that had caused so much angst for Jerry the previous Fall when he'd been traveling back and forth to New York finally aired on CBS. Jerry and Camille held a party for executives and industry business people just prior to the television air date, which turned out to be a good thing. If it had been on the actual air date and the party had included watching the special, everyone would have been lying through their teeth as they congratulated each other on a job well done. Jerry had said it was awful while it was in production. He blamed Gene Kelly, left it off of his resume, and never mentioned it again. However, entertaining CBS executives was important. Camille, Essie and I cooked for the party of seventy-five.

"Are you kidding?" I said to Camille as she plonked down a mountain of fresh grapes on the kitchen table that had to be peeled for the Waldorf salad. "Peel me a grape, or in this case, nine hundred million pounds of them! No one'll notice if they're peeled or not, and what's more, they're not gonna care."

"It's what the recipe calls for," Camille replied trying to remain calm. She was already nervous about entertaining top industry executives from New York.

Essie chuckled as quietly as she could over by the stove, and kept it up as I stood at the kitchen table shredding grape skins and complaining about the insanity of it all. In the end, Camille capitulated.

"Oh, all right, you've made me feel guilty." She moved over to help, but more to shut me up. Essie, out of sheer loyalty to Camille, peeled a few grapes, too.

At the party, I thought the executives a pretty cold and hard-nosed bunch who stood around chatting to each other more than anything else. The household ended up eating leftover Waldorf salad for the next few days until it started to ferment and we had to throw it out. Camille lamented the waste of food as I did privately, but wisely kept my mouth shut as I thought of all those who didn't have enough to eat. Essie, as usual, made no comments, but remained stoic. In her neighborhood, chicken necks for dinner were a luxury.

Essie's son, Roy Lee, joined the army. Camille had employed him as much as she could, but the old house still hadn't sold, so the fix-it/to-do list was put on hold. Jobs for were not yet forthcoming for young black men in Watts after the riots; the army was the best Roy Lee could do. Essie was in despair, worried that he'd be sent to Vietnam. But Roy Lee was not as idiotic as everyone thought he was. He'd calculated the odds of a young black man who lived in an American ghetto in 1966, and joined up before he could be called up. They gave him a gun and taught him how to shoot it. Alas, Roy Lee was not as good a marksman as the army wanted him to be. They did send him to Vietnam, however, where he became a cook—just as his mother had been while he was growing up in Texas. He peeled potatoes, stayed safe and eventually returned with some new skills he hadn't had before. At a time when many Vietnam vets of all races came home to unemployment, Roy Lee went to work at a steady job as a short order cook in a restaurant.

Camille told me I shouldn't miss seeing Jose Greco's flamenco ballet now that the show had opened in Hollywood, especially the Horsemen dance where he and two male dancers would sweep onto the stage in one coordinated flying leap, clicking their Spanish boot heels and cracking horsewhips through the air. As a dancer, Camille thought it was brilliant. She got in a large supply of Beefeater's gin especially for Jose's business manager, John Nonnenbacher, who liked to drop by in the afternoons for early cocktails and be really drunk by showtime. He gave me tickets to Jose's show, and Dan Daily gave me two tickets to a matinee of *The Odd Couple* at the Huntington Hartford Theater after it opened. I'd passed my driving test without any difficulty, or cheating, and invited Karin. At the last minute, her employer wouldn't give her the afternoon off to see Dan's play.

"You missed the fun," I told Karin the next morning as we sat on the patio while her two little charges enjoyed a ride on the little merry-go-round with Elizabeth. "There were drinks backstage with some of the cast afterwards."

Karin thought I'd landed a wonderful job with the Fieldings. It wasn't as conventional as hers. Mrs. Skaff, her employer, was very strict. Karin was always nervous about spending too much time at the Fieldings when she was supposed to be taking the two little girls for a morning walk before lunchtime.

"But they love playing with Elizabeth," I'd reasoned. "They're only a year or two older than she is."

Apparently, Mrs. Skaff didn't approve. There was far too much traffic, partying and noise coming from the Fieldings' end of the cul-de-sac. Phil's young and pretty wife was always pleasant to me, but she seemed very uptight. Privately, I thought she was unhappy.

"They're getting a divorce," Karin informed me one day. "Her husband's moved out."

Well, that explained a lot.

"I'm leaving soon," Karin told me. "I've given my notice."

"Oh, no!" I was dismayed. We'd enjoyed a friendship since I moved in and often went out together on her day off, sometimes to the movies, sometimes with Karin's friends. One of them, Edith, another young German, was a nanny for film and television actress, Nina Foch, who was divorced with a young son. They were temporarily living at an apartment hotel just off the Sunset Strip opposite the side entrance to the Playboy Club, while their house in Beverly Hills was being redecorated. Karin, who'd said she was done with au pair jobs and being treated as a mother surrogate, wanted to visit Edith before she left Los Angeles. We went over there one afternoon and swam in the pool before going to dinner at Hamburger Hamlet on the Strip..

Karin told Edith I had an unusual job and was very lucky to have Jerry and Camille as my employers; Camille usually gave me time off when I requested it. I maintained we were both reasonable and flexible, didn't try and take advantage of each other, and we both hated snobs. As a result, we had a good working relationship that suited us, even though Claudia would now cry if her mother was holding her when I left the room. When I returned, Claudia would whine until I picked her up, causing Camille to say, "She doesn't know who the hell I am." Elizabeth, on the other hand, was a mommy's girl and would often mope when her mother wasn't around no matter how much I played with her.

I wrote to my mother that Edith lived with her little charge in one apartment, while the mother lived down the hall in another. When Edith was off on the weekends and the mother was working, she would leave the child with his mother's friends.

I'd begun noticing how very young children who were left with the help for most of the time cried for their mothers and ran towards them seeking attention when said mothers finally appeared. Elizabeth did that, especially if Camille had been out all day, but the general family consensus was that Elizabeth was spoilt anyway. Even Camille admitted it, although she was a very good mother and both she and Jerry lavished attention on their daughters. Jerry always played with the babies, picking them up and swinging them, rubbing noses, and listening to their baby babble although he drew the line at playing with their toys. I personally didn't see what was wrong with a bit of spoiling for very young children; they deserved it. They also deserved a lot of attention. I came to the opinion that not enough people got enough of the right kind of attention when they were very young.

I knew all too well how difficult it was for busy and working mothers, like my mother and most English women after World War II who'd taken jobs because there was a shortage of men, not to mention a lack of money. Not many of us children had had nannies. Women had always been in a no-win situation, no matter which way they'd turned.

My mother had mentioned in her latest letter that the agency I'd used to obtain my job was now running advertisements in the newspaper that a person had to be over twenty-one to apply. The immigration rules, which were always changing, had changed again, too. Robert Kennedy had sponsored a bill limiting the import of European women to work in American households because they wanted those jobs to be available for Americans. It had passed and effectively canceled once and for all indentured servitude—the way a lot of people had come to America for two hundred years. At least legally.

"So it seems you were lucky to get out there at all," my mother added.

She was always writing how lucky I was and how she envied me "out there in the sunshine."

Sometimes my mother included clippings from the local or national newspapers with her letters so I could feel more at home. This time it was the story of Rusty, the golden cocker spaniel, who'd been stabbed to death by two youths defending his mistress at her tobacconist's shop. He'd been awarded a silver medal for bravery by the *Daily Mirror* National Pets Club. My mother never cared for pets and we hadn't had any, apart from two canaries named Bubble and Squeak for a brief time. Did she really think the enclosed article was a positive plug for life in mid-century England? Hardly. I put this choice of a newspaper tidbit down to the effect of the cold and miserable wet weather she was always complaining about and the dark afternoons of an English winter. Glancing down at Little Doggie sitting contentedly by my feet as he watched Elizabeth play on the merry-go-round, I wondered what sort of a protector and rescue dog he'd be if Camille or the kids were in danger. For the life of me, I couldn't imagine him with a medal.

To cheer my mother up, I wrote back and told her that Jerry had been scoring the music for a new television series, *Run Buddy, Run*, which was a take-off on *The Fugitive*, a popular television series that we'd also watched in England. The star, Jack Sheldon, was a trumpeter as well as an actor, who often "played with the boys who usually play for Jerry," I added. Camille and I had spent all day at Warner Brothers studios, breaking for lunch in the canteen where we gaped at actors such as Geraldine Page, while we shared a roast beef sandwich because it was so huge, and because we were back on our diets.

My mother liked to hear about the food Americans ate, so if I didn't want to mention some of the goings-on at the Fieldings, like the gangster's girlfriend spending the night, I'd write about meals and party food. I'd even sent my family a big slice of a Christmas cake I'd made, pointing out the difference between English and American fruit cake. Americans used whole dried fruits; the English used more raisins and decorated with marzipan and royal icing. My mother had enjoyed knowing that. She hated cooking, which is why I'd started experimenting in the kitchen when I was nine years old. Her mother had been a great cook, which may have been the reason she avoided it. I remember standing on a wooden chair at the kitchen stove as a very small child watching my grandmother make parsley sauce, telling me it was important that the parsley be chopped as fine as you could get it, while I stared at the scars on her fingers. Or it may have had something to do with the fact that when my mother was a young woman during World War II ingredients just weren't available since food was severely rationed for years. The nation suffered a loss that had never been mentioned: a whole generation had never learned to cook food properly.

27

Sam Pekinpah Salutes Hollywood

Before Karin left, Camille arranged a small birthday dinner for me and invited her, along with Rita and Sharon. The breakfast room was an intimate little nook off of the dining-room and Camille set the table there with her best china and silverware. She cooked chicken with a mushroom wine sauce, and surprised me with a beautiful birthday cake decorated like a present with ribbons of frosting and twenty candles. She dared me to blow them out all at once, which I did, spinning the cake plate. Camille rolled her eyes muttering, "These smart kids. Hmmph!" and left to join everyone else eating in the kitchen. I was touched by all the trouble she'd gone to for my first birthday away from home.

Avril wrote and asked me how I felt now I'd left my teenage years behind. *A little older, not sure about wiser, but my view of life had certainly expanded.* She was still in London with no further mention of South Africa, or the guy she may have gone there with at one time. I'd now become her regular *Agony Aunt* while she mulled over various romances with: (a) druggie Vic, (b) good-friend Bob, (c) wanna-be-more-than-a-good-friend Paul, (d) good-looking Len, and (e) Austin-Healy-owner and party-goer John who worked in the same small office as she did, which is why she was writing to me since she couldn't discuss him with her friends there. She was still in love with Jean-Louis in Paris, however, but I could tell that affair was falling by the wayside. Really, I wondered, how did she find time for all these men, and how did she manage to keep their names straight? My dates with guys I usually encountered at *The Mucky Duck* were always casual and never as exciting as the company I found myself in at The Fieldings.

Camille gave me an extra day off that birthday week along with my other presents. I'd made contact with friends of a friend from work in England, Florrie and Mick, an older couple who were working for record producer Phil Spector as housekeeper and butler. They invited me along on a drive to Santa Barbara, and turned up for our excursion in a Pepto-Bismol pink car. Even for Los Angeles I thought it was outrageous, and tried not to feel self-conscious while people driving alongside stared as we drove up Highway 1.

"It was his mother's," Mick explained. "He's given it to us to use while we work for him so we can get out and about."

I focused on the ocean view and tried not to feel that I was trapped inside a neon bubble as Mick regaled me with wild tales of all the rock and roll stars and parties at the house. Apparently, Spector liked to film his sexual exploits by having cameras in the bedroom ceiling. "Wanna see what we did last night?" he'd say to Mick out of Florrie's earshot. Florrie tut-tutted at hearing this, and we rode along in silence the rest of the way to Santa Barbara.

It wasn't my first visit to the town; I'd driven there with my driving instructor when I was taking lessons. I'd realized it was a pitch for an expensive lesson since the driving school charged by the hour, and a bonus ploy for him when he suggested it, but I thought it would be good idea for a safe bit of fast-driving practice since I'd be spending a lot of time in the future zipping along the Santa Monica freeway between my house and Rita's. Plus, the instructor said he'd take me out to lunch. We'd walked along the beach and enjoyed a great seafood lunch at a restaurant on the wharf which probably ended up costing him a good part of his bonus; but, the excursion gave me great confidence in my driving ability.

Mick and Florrie nixed the beach and wharf as it was foggy and opted for looking around the shops on State Street and eating at Woolworth's lunch counter, another first for me. I didn't mind, it was a new experience, but one I didn't think I'd opt for in future. On the way back to Los Angeles we'd stopped at their son and daughter-in-law's apartment for a cup of tea and a quiet after-dinner visit.

I was feeling refreshed and restored when I walked through the front door at Maravilla Drive, only to be confronted by raucous laughter and loud voices coming from a dinner party in the dining-room. I peeped in. The French windows to one of the flimsy wrought-iron balconies were open, and very drunk film director, Sam Peckinpah, was teetering dangerously against the railing as he pissed over the edge toward the bright lights far below, shouting at the top of his lungs: "Here's to you, Hollywood!"

"He's got a reputation as a bad boy," Camille nervously explained as she carried dirty dishes into the kitchen where

I was getting a drink of water before going up to my room. Jerry had coaxed the director back into the dining room before disaster struck and those probably loose and rusty screws pulled away from the stucco wall, plunging Sam onto the terrace below and to his possible death. "The studio took away his last film, *Major Dundee*, and someone else made a mess of the editing and ruined it, so he's very upset," she added.

I reflected upon what Jerry had said about creative people and negotiating the minefield that was show business, business being the operative word. It wasn't show-art. Creativity was a fragile commodity, yet a person had to be tough like granite, too. I marveled at how the two opposites rubbed up against each other; that was where the sparks flew.

"Sam's here to discuss the music for a television drama he's going to be directing, *Noon Wine*," Camille explained. "The producer's taking a chance on him because he's brilliant."

I glanced into the dining room again as I went upstairs. Jerry and Sam were now deep in conversation. No one knew it then, but it was the start of a long and contentious working relationship that would earn Jerry an Academy Award nomination several years later for *The Wild Bunch*.

Hiding A Bengal Tiger
In The Living Room

*N*ow that I was able to drive, I could do some of Camille's errands so she could spend more time at home with the kids. I was driving along Hollywood Boulevard one afternoon after grocery shopping at the Hollywood Ranch Market, when a silver-gray Aston Martin pulled up alongside me at a traffic light. Actor Buddy Ebsen of the *Beverly Hillbillies* TV show fame was in the driver's seat. He gave me a quick smile before driving off as the light changed, and I made a mental note to mention him in my next letter home. My family had always watched that television show on a Sunday night. Before I drove off myself, I noticed a cute little shoe boutique to my right, so I pulled over for a quick window-shop. They didn't have anything I was interested in, but the Hollywood Wax Museum was next door. Camille had been good about showing me some touristy things like the footprints outside Grauman's Chinese Theater, but she'd nixed the wax museum. Inside, I listened to waxwork President Kennedy giving snippets of his famous speeches, then fought my way past the tourist crowd practically swooning in front of the waxwork

Beatles. The Fab Four were ensconced behind glass so people couldn't grab at them for souvenirs.

On the five-minute drive up into the hills afterwards I reflected on whether Americans really were more mad than the Brits. A lot of Americans I'd met seemed to think the British were a more rational people. Hardly. My mother's letter this week had included a couple of typed pages on beheadings in Henry VIIIth's reign with the last words of Sir Thomas Moore and Lady Jane Grey at their executions. Why? What on earth had prompted that? Did she need to remind me of the heritage I'd left behind? Even the English had moved on from five hundred years ago. Upon reflection, I didn't think Hollywood was that abnormal.

Now we were into spring, my mother was fervently angling to spend her summer vacation in California, without her husband or my brother. Rita's mother had a relative who lived in Sant Ana, and she was coming out to visit Rita. My mother was not about to let that one go by unchallenged. She didn't need to see any film stars, she wrote. "I don't care two hoots for Disneyland or anything else for that matter...the main reason for my coming out there is TO SEE YOU." She then went on about "motherlove" and "now my Mother is gone, how I must have hurt her when I was very young and away in the WAAFs." Oh, and by the way, she'd met a woman who'd been to Honolulu and said it was nothing special, that it looked just like Los Angeles.

I was feeling pressured, torn between indecision about exactly what I was going to do when my year was up with the Fieldings, and my mother demanding I decide right now and let her know since she was making plans. It was too much for me; I'd have to discuss it with Camille. Before we arrived in America, Rita and I had talked about going down to Mexico when our year was up and writing poetry on the beach. Or, getting a car and driving to New York via the southern states before sailing back to England. Camille nixed the driving across country train of thought when I'd mentioned it, saying young girls traveling alone through the south was a bad idea: "They're funny about things down there."

After the Wax Museum I walked into a quiet house, in spite of the fact that Joyce had dropped by to see Camille bringing realtor Bette's sister, Barbara, along, and cocktail hour had started early. Essie was resting in her room and watching her afternoon soap opera, the babies were still napping in their bedrooms, and Jerry was out discussing a television commercial with Ray Charles they were to collaborate on the following week. My chat with Camille would have to wait.

I poked my head into the living room to say hello, then stopped dead when I saw what Camille and her friends were staring at. A Bengal tiger rug lay sprawled across the hardwood floor. When had that arrived? I'd only been gone a couple of hours.

"Leonard brought it," Camille explained. "It needs a home for a little while. Somewhere where no one knows where it is."

Somewhere outside of the authorities' view, I thought. Party central had just become the hideout in the hills. Again. My mind went back a few weeks when a 1950's chanteuse and Jerry's old friend had spent the night so neither the mob nor the FBI knew where she was on the day before her Grand Jury testimony.

I went into the library and fixed myself a drink after dropping off the grocery bags in the kitchen. When I stepped down into the living room, Joyce was rearranging the once-magnificent animal that had long ago roamed a far-off jungle. It now stretched out in front of the fireplace, its massive head with open jaws and snarling teeth pointed toward the windows overlooking Hollywood. "Endangered species" was not a watchword in everyday vocabulary then, and the Endangered Species Act was years away.

"Slightly to the left," Camille directed from the couch.

Joyce made the adjustment, then petted it. "Poor kitty," she said, her voice slurred from several gin and tonics.

"It's very old," Camille explained to me. "An antique from Victorian times."

"Are you sure it's not motheaten?" I sipped my G&T.

"Leonard assured me not," Camille responded, unfolding herself from the couch for a closer look.

"I think it's sticking it's tongue out at us," I remarked.

From there things went downhill fast. We refilled our drinks and what had once been a wild beast became a giant striped feline in front of the hearth as we inspected and contemplated the decidedly non-Spanish themed addition to Camille's antique-filled living-room.

"Where's my camera?" she finally said.

The rest of cocktail hour became a photo shoot. Camille wrapped the tail around her neck and peeked out provocatively from behind stripes as Joyce took a photo. Barbara lay full-out in a goddess pose across the animal's flattened back, and I stood in a big white hunter pose with my hands on my hips and one foot on its head mugging for the camera. At the back of our minds we knew we were appalling, but we couldn't help ourselves. When would we ever be this close to such an animal again? There was nothing we could do to save the long-dead creature. It had hung on a trophy wall or been a rug on someone's floor for a very long time before now taking up residence in the Hollywood Hills.

Jerry was speechless when he saw it; he just shook his head and went down to the Dungeon muttering derogatory comments under his breath about colonialism, and about his business manager, Leonard. Essie refused to vacuum the living-room, and neither Elizabeth nor Little Doggie would go near that end of the room, although I did manage to snap a photo of six-month-old Claudia sitting on the tiger's head, propped up from behind by Camille splayed across the entire length of the rug, The tiger stayed for several months and took on its own persona. Mostly, though, people seemed to think there was nothing unusual about having an endangered species, albeit a silent one, sprawled out on the floor. Then one day it disappeared as suddenly as it had arrived, and Leonard became vague about its whereabouts.

It was hard to find a moment alone with Camille to broach the subject of my mother. There was always something going on, people popping in and out and huge problems to be solved. Jerry was still in court with his ex-wife explaining why he owed her money and couldn't afford to give her all the alimony, medical and private school expenses, plus thirty percent of his gross income, of which paying orchestrators, arrangers, studio costs, copiers, and so on took fifty percent to begin with. The house on Reklaw Drive finally had a buyer and it went into a long escrow, much to Camille's relief. The lot next door (which had been a wedding present from Dan Dailey) and the house belonged to her, as did the Maravilla Drive house and the furniture. She told me to keep my fingers crossed for escrow to close; money was super tight now. Camille didn't mind so much that the ex-wife's house, with swimming pool, were already paid for by Jerry, or the generous alimony, but she got furious when the woman laughed out loud and said, "Oh, shit!" to her friend in court while Jerry was explaining to the judge that Claudia had to be watched twenty-four hours day because of the seizures. He produced a letter from the doctor stating this, to justify my employment. It was also mentioned that the hospital was still owed thousands of dollars for her care.

At a time when career options for women were limited, I realized many women, even at my young age, made a career out of marrying several times and collecting alimony and/or child support as a survival mechanism so they could have a comfortable lifestyle. I thought it made the way of life I'd left behind look very uncomplicated by comparison. No wonder Jerry had heart problems.

Cynthia came to dinner which delayed another opportunity to talk to Camille as Cynthia wanted a chat of her own. I put the children to bed then decided to take care of a little chore since I was going to visit Rita the following evening. Plus, we were out of ice cream. While I was at it, I could sweeten up Camille before our discussion about my mother. I grabbed Camille's car keys and drove down the hill to the supermarket on the corner of Sunset and La Brea, formerly the site of the Charlie Chaplin family home, and right next to the old Charlie Chaplin studios which now belonged to trumpeter, Herb Alpert as the future home of A & M Records. Hovering over the ice cream freezer case I asked myself, black walnut or Dutch chocolate? I couldn't decide. I threw both cartons into the basket, as well as a box of frozen chocolate eclairs. Then I added another one for Rita and myself for the following evening.

When I got back to the house, Jerry had gone down to the Dungeon to work. Camille, Cynthia and I had a feast. None of us cared about our diets at that moment, or tomorrow's sugar hangover. Cynthia left before midnight, and I broached the subject of my mother wanting to visit as Camille and I did the dishes.

Camille shrugged. "You'll still be with us in July, so before you go, if you go, she can stay here. You've got a double bed in your room; she can sleep with you." In light of all her other problems, to Camille this one was a no-brainer.

"What if she comes after July, though, like August or September?"

"So stay an extra month or two, then you can decide what you really want to do."

Well, that was easy, Problem solved. Too bad if I had reservations about it.

"I'd love to meet your mother, and I'm sure Jerry would, too. This place is like a hotel, anyway. One more visitor won't make much difference."

True. Someone was always coming to dinner or staying the night, or staying overnight after dinner if they were too drunk to drive back down the hill. I sat up in bed and wrote a letter telling my mother she could go ahead and book a flight, that Camille had kindly offered to let her stay here.

For the next few months my mother drove me crazy writing about flight arrangements and trying to find the cheapest one, while I tried not to worry about Jerry's now-serious consideration about accepting the job in Denmark for a period of two years so he could outwit his ex-wife. The job was still on the table after all these months, and the producer had made a special trip to let him know that it would remain there for a while, she'd told him over dinner one night.

My mother's mood had improved now she was actively working on coming to America; plus, it was springtime. She ditched enclosing snippets about stabbings and beheadings, and any murders in general. Now, she enclosed a local newspaper clipping about one of my friends coming second in her firm's beauty contest, stating Janice would have come first if she hadn't been wearing a mini-skirt.

The next letter contained an article from *The Daily Mirror* about Duke Ellington's jazz orchestra playing his religious suite, *In the Beginning God*, in Coventry Cathedral. Mum enclosed a picture of the Duke conducting from the High Altar steps in front of artist Graham Sutherland's famous tapestry of Christ. The cathedral had been bombed during World War II leaving only the High Altar standing pockmarked with bullet holes. It had been rebuilt in a modern design around the ancient altar. My family had stopped by to see it once after visiting one of my father's brothers who lived nearby. I'd written an end of term paper for my junior college speech class on the tapestry, agreeing with many observers that Christ's eyes seem to follow a person wherever they walked in the Cathedral.

Meanwhile, I'd planned another little getaway of my own. Rita had nixed the idea of Catalina Island for Spring break; she and Sharon wanted to go to Palm Springs. Okay by me. Rita booked us into the Holiday Inn on North Indian Avenue for a few days. We shared a ground floor room which I thought was very nice, but Sharon said it was just all right, that we could have done better. Really, Americans were so spoiled. It wasn't as if we'd be actually be sleeping in the room, anyway, I pointed out. I, for one, intended to work on my tan by sleeping in a beach recliner by the pool during the day and partying at night.

After setting up a mini bar in the bathroom we went out to dinner and walked around the town where over 100,000 college students milled around in beach wear eyeing each other as they sat in trees and on mailboxes, and hung out of windows recruiting candidates for parties later that night. As we passed boys my age, I wondered how many of them were enrolled in college to escape the Vietnam war and avoid being drafted.

I loved the desert air. The temperature was almost a hundred degrees, but there wasn't any humidity so it didn't seem so hot as it would have been in Los Angeles. I thought snow on the surrounding mountains "rather novel" I wrote my mother on the motel notepaper. I also loved swimming in the hotel pool late at night and very early in the morning.

Rita had seen someone she fancied as we'd driven into town. A yellow convertible with six boys crammed into it had whizzed past us and pulled into a gas station.

"Go round the block and get some gas in that station," Rita commanded Sharon, who was driving.

"We don't need any," Sharon had replied, but did as she was told since Rita insisted.

No sooner had Sharon stopped beside a pump than the yellow car inhabitants swarmed our car. A short while later we had an invitation to a party later at the Monte Carlo hotel.

Unfortunately, since we weren't residents, the front door staff of the Monte Carlo wouldn't let us in. We walked around the building and got in through the back entrance. It seemed like combined frat house party was going on with hundreds of young people. The swimming pool was full of floating beer bottles and beer cans, as well as people who had been thrown in. After getting invited to three separate parties on the way, we eventually found the room we were looking for, but it was too crowded; we couldn't get in the door. We did manage to meet up with three of the guys from the yellow car, and promptly left for another party at a ranch, ending up back at the Holiday Inn just before sun-up. Sharon passed out before she remembered where she'd left her car. Rita entertained the boy she liked while I got the other two to drive me around town until we located Sharon's car in a parking lot.

The next few days were much of the same: drinking, partying, tanning and sleeping by the pool, and eating breakfast at two o-clock in the afternoon. Not that much different from my life at the Fieldings, I reflected, but with younger people and without babies. And no real stimulating intellectual conversation in spite of the fact that they were college boys. The guys were nice, but rather conventional, I decided. And their idea of circumventing any law was decidedly juvenile after what I'd already witnessed. I managed to get by socially, but where, oh where, did I *really* fit in, I wondered. I was ready to leave Palm Springs and so were Rita and Sharon. I felt I'd participated enough in Young America's rites of spring.

Camille was prepping for her Easter weekend, gardening and hosing off the pool patio when I got back. She'd invited friends and family over, and said I could invite Rita. Because Essie had trouble at home and was just coming in one day a week to do the laundry for a while, it was down to Camille and me to do the cooking. We discussed food. She made a ham and I baked French bread, which along with cheeses, salads and fruit, plus alcohol of course, constituted the pool-party food we set up on the credenza under the lanai by the end of the pool.

But there was another party to squeeze in first: Elizabeth had been invited to her first birthday party for a little boy who was turning two. Camille and I exchanged glances after we arrived at the Beverly Hills address: this was a production of the first order. Although Elizabeth was the youngest of the forty young attendees, she managed to conduct herself really well. The room was decorated like a circus tent, down to hand-painted faces on the walls which made it look like the children were sitting in an arena. Everyone had hats and balloons and were gifted with a children's book. Clowns did tricks and made animal balloons. There was a monkey who did acrobats, and a pony to ride in the side yard outside the French windows. I'd never seen a birthday cake that big; it must have measured two feet across with frolicking clowns and animals on top. Each child got either a clown or animal on their chunk of chocolate cake. After a couple of hours, the room was a mess, and so was the side yard courtesy of the little pony.

"We're not doing anything like this when Elizabeth turns two," Camille confided as we walked out the front door, me holding Claudia, who'd thoroughly enjoyed watching the other children as she sat on my knee, sans cake, clutching a little cloth book the party mother had given her.

I slipped out early Easter morning for the famed annual Sunrise Service at the Hollywood Bowl, carrying a lawn chair and a blanket, and headed for the next-street neighbor's backyard. Karin and I had walked over there some weeks before she'd left to introduce ourselves and receive permission to sit at the end of his property that overlooked the Bowl when a concert was on. Everyone in the neighborhood did it. That's how you got to meet your neighbors, most of whom worked in the movie business like Haskell Wexler, the documentary film maker.

"We had a thousand people trying to come and sit on our lawn for the Beatles concert last year," the neighbor had told us. "Most of them, of course, were not from the neighborhood. Fortunately, I'd hired ten security guards. Nobody had ever seen anything like it. There were people crawling all over these hills with cops chasing them," he laughed. "That in itself was entertaining, like watching some silent movie."

I was the only one in his yard at 5:00 a.m. that Easter Sunday and it was cold. Fortunately, I'd brought a flask of coffee, along with a flashlight. The neighbor didn't mind refreshments, as long as you didn't leave any mess behind. It really was like actually being at the Hollywood Bowl as the back seats were only several yards down the hill in front of me. I could have walked down and sat there, but I didn't. Those wooden benches looked hard and my little lawn chair was soft and comfy by comparison.

The sun was up when I staggered back to the Fieldings' a couple of hours later, and promptly fell into bed. No one else was up, including the children. The service had been long and boring. At breakfast, Jerry said I wouldn't have gone if it hadn't been a tourist thing. I denied this, saying of course I would, I'd always accompanied my mother to church at Easter. What I didn't say was that she'd made me. (Also, I'd liked one of the choirboys who I discovered was in my year at school.) In her latest letter, my mother had written, "Try and take your Holy Communion somewhere if you can, dear. If not, keep up your prayers." This was as close as it was gonna get in my books. In truth I'd only gone to witness the service at the Hollywood Bowl as it gave me something to write about that my family could relate to, cocktail hour at my parents' house being relegated to drinks at Christmas, or a pint in the pub.

My mother had just had emergency back surgery and was convalescing at a patient care facility at the quieter end of Brighton, i.e. a large Victorian house near the beach where the National Health Service sent patients to recuperate and free up much-needed hospital beds.

Camille was laid up herself a few days later. Little Doggie had got in-between her feet as she came down the stairs causing her to fall on the Saltillo tiles, break a blood vessel, and sprain the ligament in one foot. Her movements were now restricted, much to her annoyance, so it fell to me to do all the errands. Debbie Reynolds came over to discuss business with her while I went to the bank and deposited the checks, went to the drugstore and supermarket, the cleaners, the post office, and did a few other things like pick up different colored cotton thread for our latest sewing project.

Dan Dailey's girlfriend Carol, a friend of Camille's she'd initially recommended to him as a dancing partner replacement, had made a pattern from what she said was the best bikini ever. One size fit all, and looked fabulous to boot, so after making several new bikinis for herself, Carol passed the pattern on to Camille, who shared it with me. We were now busy sewing our new outfits for summer. My bikini was pale pink and white check with white Embroidery Anglaise trim. Camille's was tiny white polka dots on a black background. She suggested I also surprise my mother with one when she came for her visit later in the summer. I bought peach and white check material for mum.

Since shorter skirts were now the rage, I was busy hemming all my dresses and skirts, too. Camille didn't wear dresses or skirts unless they were long; her daily wear was different colored pants, or shorts in hot weather. American women wore trousers far more often than English women did, I'd observed. Camille made almost all of her own clothes, including the pants and matching or contrasting tops, and many of her evening dresses. Apart from sharing her typewriter and car, we also shared her sewing machine, which was in constant use when *it* wasn't in the repair shop. Thriftiness was always the order the day; at least that's what we aimed for. Basically, it translated to the fact you could stuff your closets with more clothes, have more choices, and not be seen wearing the same thing too often. I made a few of my own clothes and did alterations on some that I bought to supplement my wardrobe.

Honey had taken us to Downtown Los Angeles one day and introduced us to shopping at the Goodwill, a second-hand store. On a prior trip, Honey had spied a lined cedar chest that looked brand new and would make an elegant hideout for the kids' toys. While Camille mulled it over, trying to decide whether she could spend as much as $30.00 for a toy chest, with Honey assuring her what a bargain it was, and suggesting she could also use the chest to store extra blankets later on, I discovered the delights of fifteen cent blouses, twenty-five cent skirts and forty-five cent summer dresses crammed onto revolving racks. For less than $3.00 I acquired a whole new summer wardrobe. It pleased me immensely. I became addicted to the Goodwill, although I never bought shoes or sandals there as Camille warned me I might pick up some nasty disease or fungus that would rot my toenails.

29

April in Paris, But Not For Me

With legal access to Camille's car, I was buzzing all over Los Angeles. I'd go to Rita's in Mar Vista to visit and stay overnight with her if her employers and their family were out of town, or pick her up to stay with me overnight if Jerry and Camille had outside social engagements. We often went to the movies on the westside or in Hollywood, and although we were both on diets and were careful not to eat too much in the way of proper meals, from time to time our sweet tooths would get the better of us. We'd discovered ice-cream parlors: *Will Wright's* in West Hollywood and *Blum's* conveniently located near the corner of Wilshire Boulevard which we passed after exiting the Santa Monica freeway and driving up LA Brea Avenue towards the Hollywood Hills. I was particularly enamored of *Blum's* ice cream sundae called *Scheherazade* which consisted of coffee ice cream with caramel poured over it, raspberry sherbet topped with raspberry sauce, and the whole thing covered with a mountain of whipped cream, nuts, and a cherry on the top. Still, we managed to keep our weight down, usually by cutting out proper meals.

I'd dropped Rita off at her place on Windward Avenue one day and was driving up La Brea on my way back to the

Fieldings'. *Blum's* also had a mini sundae I was partial to: vanilla ice-cream with hot caramel poured over and topped with whipped cream and sliced almonds. It was a scorching hot afternoon, so I made a detour into their parking lot for a fifteen-minute break. When I finally walked into the house, Essie had gone home, the babies were asleep, Jerry was at the studios, and Joyce and Camille were crying in the living-room.

"Bette Elliot committed suicide," Camille sobbed after I'd asked what was wrong.

"What! Bette the realtor? Barbara's sister?"

Camille nodded as she reached for a fresh Kleenex to wipe her eyes. "I've known her since I was fourteen years old."

I was stunned. Not vibrant, chatty Bette, who'd been so enthusiastic about finding Camille her dream house? *Oh, no!*

"She had bad money troubles," Joyce explained, who had bad money troubles herself, exacerbated by buying cute and expensive clothes at *I.Magnin's* or *Robinson's* in Beverly Hills. Joyce didn't sew. "Bette couldn't face things any more. Plus, she was taking a lot of pills for all her ailments. One Sunday night, she just climbed into bed and swallowed them all."

"I'd just seen her the day before," Camille said. "They didn't find her for a week." She broke out in fresh tears.

I had tears myself. "How awful!"

"Yes, it is," Joyce said quietly. "The tenants upstairs were used to not seeing her for days. She'd go and visit her parents in Arizona, or her daughter up north at Mills College, so they didn't think anything of it. But the trash wasn't put out and the air conditioning had been running all week. The man from upstairs came down to see if he could turn it off. All the doors were locked, and he couldn't see in the windows; then he noticed one small one was open. When he went over to it he noticed this awful smell and thought, 'God, what has she left out in the kitchen and forgotten to put away before she left?' Then he started putting two and two together and called the police. They broke open the back door, but the smell was so terrible they had to air it out for a few hours before they could even go in."

Poor Bette!

Joyce swallowed the last of her drink. "They found her in bed with the electric blanket full on. The heat had speeded up the decaying process; she'd really cooked."

I felt like retching. *Poor Bette!*

"She's being buried tomorrow at Forest Lawn," Camille said, gathering her own and Joyce's cocktail glass for refills. "I'm going to the funeral, so I need you to hold down the fort here along with the kids."

I nodded. "Of course. How's Barbara doing?"

"Badly," Joyce said. "She had to identify the body."

After Bette's funeral, it was Mother's Day. Camille had invited her family over for dinner. As we fixed turkey with all of the trimmings for them, and I made a pineapple upside-down cake for dessert, I thought of Bette's nineteen-year-old college daughter signing all the documents she had to deal with as next of kin. Barbara had been reluctant to tell her that her mother committed suicide. The girl was my age. Although I'd never met her, I couldn't imagine what she must be going through.

"Can't Barbara just tell her that Bette had taken an overdose of her pills," I suggested to Camille as we cooked. "Then her daughter can choose to ask if it was suicide, or not." Somehow, I thought this might lessen the blow if the girl chose to ask the awkward question. Full realization could come later, when she could handle it better, perhaps, if she had a choice.

Camille just shook her head and shrugged her shoulders. "Maybe."

We put aside our sadness for Mother's Day, but it seemed as if news of Bette's death triggered a downhill slide of events that continued all week and into the next.

Elizabeth came down with a bad ear infection. The following day Jerry caught it. Cynthia got it next. Friday night I spent in my bathroom throwing up and was out of commission on Saturday. By then Claudia was vomiting and was having seizures. Saturday afternoon Elizabeth fell and put her tooth through her bottom lip. Sunday came and I stopped throwing up, but Cynthia started. By Sunday night Jerry had a queasy stomach and it was discovered that Little Doggie had been quietly vomiting all over the house. Camille was up all night with a terrible toothache and called the dentist first thing Monday morning to have two wisdom teeth pulled. After that, she was sidelined in agony for two days. In what can only be considered as unconscious sympathy, one of my fillings fell out causing another emergency call to Camille's dentist, where I was told I needed eleven fillings; x-rays also showed that one of my wisdom teeth had erupted half-way through my gums. Dental bills were about to put a serious dent in my effort to try and save money.

The following day Cynthia had a car crash. It wasn't her fault. A guy went to make a sudden lane change to exit the freeway, but put his car in reverse by mistake and smashed in the front of Cynthia's Volkswagen. Since it was rush hour, traffic on the freeway had actually stopped, but her car looked like a concertina anyway. To make matters worse, he didn't speak English and didn't have insurance. Cynthia wore a whiplash collar around her neck for quite a while.

Meanwhile, one of Jerry's older daughters was diagnosed with pneumonia, and he and Camille suffered another financial blow. Although the other house had sold and was in escrow, the man holding the second mortgage on it and the lot next door suddenly decided over the weekend that he didn't want to be paid off the few thousand dollars that the Fieldings still owed him; it would screw up his taxes as well as lose him interest. The Reklaw Drive house couldn't be sold, after all. He had a notice put on the front door by the county sheriff announcing it was up for auction.

"Rat Bastard!" Camile was so furious when she realized the guy could grab the money leaving her and Jerry with nothing, and they were both so fed up with having to make mortgage and tax payments on two houses for so long that, unbeknownst to anyone, Camille drove over to the old house and ripped the notice off the door before hiring a lawyer. When Jerry found out he walked around with his personal invisible black cloud hanging over his head, saying he'd probably be in jail by tomorrow; he couldn't pay his ex-wife all her alimony, plus he and Camille were hemorrhaging thousands of dollars.

By then everyone in the household had colds and Claudia was cutting her second tooth; she'd knocked the first one out by banging her mouth on the rim of the baby chariot. Minor annoyances like the phone ringing eighteen hours a day hardly registered. I put the one in my room under the bed with a pillow over it to muffle the noise. No one could sleep. We were "walking around like zombies," I wrote my mother. "Everyone has given up worrying about everything. You get to the stage where nothing matters."

I couldn't stand the atmosphere in the house any longer. I wished I could creep into a nice quiet bed in a hotel and sleep for days. After putting the kids down for their naps, I took my lunch outside and ate it down by the swimming pool while I did a quick review of my life and current mood. I was spiraling down into a bad state emotionally.

I'd been in the habit of watching a daily show on television entitled *Where the Action Is* that featured current popular singing groups. I didn't care for a lot of the American acts. Linda Ronstadt and her Stone Poneys were great, Bob Dylan was king, but I thought Sonny and Cher looked ridiculous in their striped pants and shaggy waistcoats, although I had to admit she had a great voice. Yesterday, the show had highlighted the Mindbenders singing their current hit outside the Albert Hall in London, as well as Marianne Faithfull, wrapped up in a winter coat performing her latest hit by the River Thames and the Tower of London. In spite of the fact that the black-and-white television screen kept slipping I hadn't been able to take my eyes off of it. I was getting bored with the sunshine. I was homesick.

I was also fed up with the see-saw life at the Fieldings. Every day there was some drama, theirs or someone else's, and it was starting to get to me. To compound matters, when Rita and I were in the *Mucky Duck* one evening, we'd found out we could be earning twice as much doing the same job. A new friend we'd met was about to start her third job this year. If she didn't like some element of her employment, or the employer, she switched to another one, Damn my mother for being so jealous of Rita's mother coming out for a visit, and damn Camille for being so nice and inviting her to stay. I couldn't leave. I felt trapped.

I heard voices approaching. Camille came down the terrace steps holding Claudia and leading Elizabeth by the hand. The house had three floors and lots of rooms. *Couldn't I even get away for some peace and quiet for ten minutes to eat lunch?* Apparently not. Camille was smiling. "We're going to Paris."

30

A New Dog For Jerry's Birthday

And Monte Carlo. But not all of us. Just Camille and Jerry, who'd accepted a quick job as music director on a television special featuring Grace Kelly and her princess life in Monaco. I understood part of his reasoning: the ex-wife couldn't haul him into court again if he was MIA and out of the country. Plus, it would be a little second honeymoon for him and Camille, not to mention a real break away from household problems. Still, a part of me felt irrationally jealous. After going home to Hamburg, Karin was now having a holiday in Spain. She'd sent me a postcard, which I'd added to the other postcards friends had been sending ever since I'd arrived in California and stuck around my dressing table mirror.

"You're spoilt," Rita pronounced when I drove over to visit her before the Fieldings left for France. We were across the street at Sharon's house taking turns helping type up homework and final papers for her classes while she took care of her maths homework. "Whatever happened to Denmark, anyway?"

"The producer wanted a two-year commitment. Jerry's being offered a lot of other work now and Camille didn't want to go for that long." I handed Sharon the final page

of a report. "You Americans get a lot of homework. Uggh!"
I grimaced, glad I was done with school and my one year at
the local Technical College learning shorthand, typing and
other boring office skills, although after my trip to the Bay
area and visiting Berkeley I'd enrolled in a beginner's con-
versational Spanish night class at Hollywood High School.
It was the best I could do to satisfy the academic part of me
at that moment, and did not require written homework.

It was also entertaining. Fifi D'Orsay, an actress from
the 1920's and 1930's, brought her white poodle to class and
held him in her arms, giving forth tidbits about her career
in her carefully cultivated pseudo-Parisian accent (Ooh
La La!) during the break to adoring elderly fans/students.
She also sat in the front row of the classroom demanding
attention from the teacher. Most of the students were at
least middle-aged, including a chatty Englishman. God, the
English seemed to be everywhere in California, but then I
suppose that was the heritage since we'd spread ourselves
over the planet and laid claim to two-thirds of it on and
off for about a hundred and fifty years.

When I wasn't listening to Fifi chirping away like she
just got off the European boat (she was born in Montreal),
from my seat at the back of the classroom I could hear the
Brit talking about his family and his son's new fiancée,
a "Chinese girl," that he and his wife were struggling to
accept, although "we're not prejudiced." Since my uncle's
wife had a brother with a Chinese-Malay wife who he'd
married while doing his Army National Service in that
part of the world, I was rather appalled listening to this
transplanted Englishman and his racial and class prejudice, but nobody else seemed to think there was anything

wrong with it. Nobody was interested in me or my opinion on anything anyway since I was, next to our teacher who was in her early thirties, by far the youngest person in the class. And you can learn a lot from listening.

Hmmpphh," Rita said, handing over a typed page to Sharon, and indicating we were all spoilt in that big house sitting on top of the mountain. As the only child of two older doting parents much closer to retirement age than mine, I thought she had a nerve calling me spoilt. Her mother had rarely let her see the vacuum cleaner, yet alone use it.

"Camille said you can visit to keep me company and stay over as much as you want. Essie goes home on Friday night and doesn't come back until Monday morning. Camille's mother is staying with me, but she works from nine until five so she'll be in and out, along with Brad and Donna on the weekends.

"What about bossy Cynthia?"

She'll be around, but she works, too, so I'll have a lot of time alone and can do what I want."

"As if you don't now," Sharon commented.

"Not always true," I countered.

Rita snickered. Really, couldn't they see that a bigger house came with bigger problems? Personally, I thought Rita's employers took advantage of her. She was left alone all day and took care of three children when they came home from school and during school holidays. Not only was she responsible for their nutrition, but also cleaning the house, laundry, and doing almost all of the cooking after commandeering Harold to take her grocery shopping.

Rita didn't drive; she didn't see the point since the family only had one car and Myra drove it to work. Harold used a company truck. Rita had just turned nineteen and ran the household.

Plus, there was something else I had to discuss with her out of everyone else's earshot. Myra had recently complained to me about Rita one afternoon while we sat in the den as I waited for Rita to change clothes before we went out. She had done things Myra did not like such as buying and preparing food for the family that Rita liked, not that Myra would have prepared. She was bossing around the children too much, acting like she was their mother. And, Myra felt Rita was starting to get a bit too heavy handed with her. I gathered she didn't want Rita around Harold, either. Myra felt she was being pushed out.

I'd listened to this tirade, speechless. Myra suffered famously dark moods, much worse and much deeper than anything I or anyone I knew could drum up. During the Watts riots she'd threatened to get out her little gun if "they" came up as far as Venice Boulevard. Coming from a country where even the policemen didn't have guns, except the special forces in London, it had alarmed me. She had a gun in the house? No, one had to be very careful with Myra, I thought. I just had to wait for the right moment with Rita to broach the subject of her job.

"Anyone feel like going to the movies?" After several hours, I'd done enough typing for Sharon, who bowed out of a night at the movie theater since she still had work to do.

Rita and I went to a double feature at the drive-in: *The Loved One* and a British farce with David Niven, *Where The*

Spies Are. I tried to bring up the subject of Rita's job with her during the interval, but she didn't want to spoil the evening by talking about it, she said.

As I took Rita home, Camille's car started making a grinding noise when I went to turn the steering wheel. I found an all-night garage open and the mechanic said it was the automatic transmission and power steering: the cap on the piston was leaking and the fluid had dripped out. He put some more in to get me home. After dropping Rita off, I drove very carefully on the freeway, under the speed limit for once. Steering the heavy car with its V8 engine up the mountain with all the twists and turns and steep drop-offs was more of a challenge. I could hardly turn the wheel and kept careening over to the wrong side of the narrow road. Luckily, I made it back safely and Camille had the man from her garage come and take it away for repairs the next morning. Like the typewriter and the sewing machine we shared, Camille's car was always breaking down and needed replacing, but that wasn't currently in the budget. Jerry had a 1964 Ford Thunderbird, but it didn't even occur to me to even ask if I could ever drive that, especially since he always had to go over to the studios at the last minute. Even Camille drove it infrequently.

It was fairly quiet while Jerry and Camille were away. I sat on the patio in the front yard or down by the pool and wrote letters by hand or typed them, or read the daily newspaper, as the babies played with their toys or napped in the playpen. They had very different personalities. Claudia was very good-natured and would let anyone hold her. Elizabeth was highly strung and getting more nervous with every day that passed. Camille and Jerry both blamed his mother for that. She'd come out from Pittsburgh to visit when Elizabeth was six weeks old, criticized everything Camille did as a new mother, and fussed over the baby so much that the child was a nervous wreck by the time she left. At three months old Elizabeth had to temporarily be put on phenobarbital, Camille had told me. The Fieldings agreed that the one good thing about the chaos and constant crises going on was that Jerry's mother couldn't visit.

Deep down Elizabeth was a wary child and wanted her mother all the time, although she tolerated Essie and myself as substitutes. Maybe it was because I'd buy her a new toy now and then to remind her we could be friends if she felt like it. Elizabeth especially liked the ball I'd recently bought her and enjoyed playing catch or kicking it around the lawn in the front garden. I'd also bought both children *Peter Rabbit* books for Christmas. Elizabeth liked books. She loved being read to and would bring a book over and say, "book." Then I'd have to read the story over and over again. Often, she would sit and look at a book by herself if Claudia was taking a nap. Elizabeth also liked 'writing.' If I was writing a letter to my family by hand (because the typewriter was always breaking down), Elizabeth would add a little scribble to a corner of the page. However, she did not want to learn to sew, even though Camille or myself were constantly making things. I'd made Karin a floppy sunhat before she'd left, then started on one for myself. If I wasn't reading the paper or writing a letter during playtime, I'd usually be sewing. For some reason, Elizabeth never interrupted this activity.

When the Fieldings came back from France, with Jerry muttering about 'the fat prince with the squeaky voice," the telephones started ringing non-stop again, and visitors dropped by, including an old friend of Jerry's who'd been a political prisoner in Czechoslovakia and now taught Russian at the University of Tucson in Arizona. His wife was from Manchester and had left England fifteen years ago because she couldn't stand the weather. We commiserated over that one. The weather was a safe harbor and staple topic of conversation for English people. Everyone could relate without controversy.

I'd only ever met a Russian once before. When I was fourteen a young woman had come to our school to observe current English schools and teaching methods for teens and young adults. Her clothes were really cool and she wore a stylish leather jacket. We all thought she was a Russian spy, which she might have been since the cold war was in full bloom during those days. We couldn't imagine why anyone from Russia would want to study English education. English private schools, aka public schools in that peculiarly quaint British way of labeling things, were for the rich and the aristocracy. Ordinary grade school education for the masses was considered inferior to that of children on the Continent, i.e., France, Germany, Switzerland, etc.; we didn't know about Spain and Italy. Surely, they had better schools in Russia, too. In our limited experience the really cool high schools were in America. They didn't have to wear uniforms

It was also Camille's birthday soon after they returned. She was thirty-five, but Jerry made the mistake of thinking she was thirty-six, said so out loud, and was very surprised when Camille screamed at him. Really, he was so absent-minded. I'd begged off working the afternoon before citing a dental appointment, but in reality I went to buy her a present: two skinny tops, one red, one orange, to compliment the tan she was working on. Her family came over for a pool party, and she got lots of presents constituting a new wardrobe of slacks and blouses for the coming year. I cooked dinner and made her a birthday cake soaked in rum, topped with fruit, then sprinkled with chopped walnuts and decorated with whipped cream. Camille said she didn't mind when I admitted to using up all the rum from her cocktail bar.

Little Doggie was having prostate trouble. He had me jumping up and down every two minutes: first letting him out of the house, then letting him again. Or, if I was outside with the children, he wanted me to let him in the house, then out again a minute later. Jerry had long since stopped taking an evening walk so Little Doggie took himself for walks. If the wooden gates were closed, I had to open them to let him out. I started leaving them open so he could get back in without me having to guess when he wanted back in. He was driving me crazy True, he was a sweet little thing, and affectionate, but in my eyes he was just too stupid to begin with; he did all the wrong things at the wrong time. Consequently, he was more of a bother than both kids put together. He also spent more time at his doctor than they spent at theirs. Little Doggie always had bad ears. After the serial vomiting episode, he'd come down with another earache. We were always waiting to see what he'd develop next.

Another thing that irked me about Perrito was the amount of time he spent at the beauty parlor. Why couldn't we just hose him off in the front yard with some of the kids' baby shampoo? I suggested. It would save a lot of money. But, no, he had to have a regular haircut and manicure at the dog groomers so he looked like a well-kept toy poodle. Apart from Jerry, who regularly went to the barbershop, the rest of us manicured ourselves. Camille bought me a bottle of blonde colorant so I could streak my hair, which was naturally dark brown. We'd agreed that some lighter highlights would accentuate my tan. I had to leave it on for two-and-a-half hours instead of the recommended ten minutes, but Camille assured me that the sun would help lighten it as she combed the solution through for me. And it did. Slightly.

Meanwhile, Claudia came down with roseola. She was fussing in her crib at 1:00 a.m. when I went to bed one night. After a couple of hours, I put her in my bed, where we both fell asleep at 5:00 a.m. She woke me up at 7:30 a.m. with a temperature of 104. Since it was never to get beyond 101 because that would trigger her convulsions, we were at the doctors by 9:30 a.m. By then she had the runs and I was wiping her poor little overheated body down with cold washcloths. Even with extra medication, her fever was up and down like a yo-yo for the next few days, but she didn't convulse, much to everyone's relief. A few days later, Elizabeth caught it. They both recovered, but then Elizabeth came down with a terrible cough. We had to keep the children apart so Claudia didn't catch it. Jerry had composed some arrangements for the singer Jack Jones and had to fly to Las Vegas for a couple of days. Camille had planned to go with him, but ended up taking care of Elizabeth while I dealt with Claudia.

Then it was Jerry's birthday. A photographer friend of Camille's had come to the house one afternoon when Jerry was out and taken candid photos of Camille and the children. The black-and-white pictures were stunning. Both Elizabeth and Claudia were very pretty little girls. People were always commenting that they could be doing modeling and film work, but Camille would not hear of it; she was not going to let her children go to work in the industry until they were old enough to decide on a career for themselves. Young as they were, I thought they could be earning a living, too, since they were so photogenic, but since Camille had worked on and off in show business from four years old, I realized she knew what she was talking about. Camille wanted her girls to have as normal a life as possible while they were growing up. She wanted to instill basic principles in her children that she had been instilled with as a young person so they could stand on their own two feet and cope with adult life one day.

Jerry came down to breakfast on his birthday morning to find several framed photographs beautifully wrapped in his place at the kitchen table, and a large cage on the kitchen floor with an Irish Setter puppy inside, courtesy of Leonard,

"You need a proper dog," he told Jerry, giving the evil eye to Perrito in Camille's arms. Leonard and I were on the same page regarding that dog.

Jerry was not happy with this birthday present and said so in no uncertain terms.

"His name's Sullivan," Leonard replied, waving aside Jerry's discontent.

"Not in a Jewish household it's not," Jerry countered. "His name's Solomon."

"He's an Irish dog, Jerry. You can't give him a Jewish name."

"Yes, I can. D'you really think this house needs more chaos, Leonard?"

"Don't think of it as chaos, Jerry. Think of it as your new exercise machine. The doctor's told you to take more walks."

"I take Little Doggie for walks."

"You haven't taken that poodle for a walk in months."

It was true. Weeks ago, Jerry had started taking a nap before dinner so he could stay up later at night and get his work done.

Jerry stared at the puppy. "Why is he in a cage?"

"Potty training,"

What? In the kitchen? This wasn't kosher in my mind. I caught Essie's eye; not in hers, either. The kids just stared at the cage. Camille and I were in the middle of potty training Elizabeth.

"Can we let him out to pet him?" Camille asked. I could tell she didn't like the idea of the little puppy stuck in a cage. She also didn't like the idea of yet another thing to take care of.

"No, he has to live in the crate," Leonard replied. "He won't soil his living space. When you let him out and take him outside to do his business, he quickly learns what's expected of him. Then you can pet him."

"As long as you put him straight back in the cage afterwards," Jerry stated.

"Exactly."

"What about feeding time?" Camille was already mentally adding extra dog biscuits and chew treats to her shopping list.

"You can let him out to eat."

I felt supremely sorry for newly-baptized Solomon, who stared out at us between the bars with his big puppy eyes, little tail wagging, as Elizabeth bent down and offered a toddler-talk greeting. He *was* cute with all that wiggly enthusiasm.

"Does he need to go out in the yard now?" Camille wanted to start the dog training ASAP; the crate took up a large space next to the refrigerator and we'd have to maneuver around it to get to nearby cupboards.

"Probably." Leonard produced a dog leash and handed it over to Solomon's new master. "Happy Birthday, Jerry."

While Essie prepared Jerry's breakfast, he walked Leonard out to the front gate with Solomon on his leash. Camille fed Little Doggie, and I fed the kids.

"Did it work?" Camille asked as Jerry came back in the kitchen ten minutes later with the puppy.

"He peed on every plant in sight," Jerry assured her, locking Solomon back in his crate. "And he'll probably kill every blade of grass on the front lawn by Labor Day."

We sat down to eat. Leonard had told us Solomon had been fed earlier. In the middle of breakfast, I looked over at Elizabeth and Claudia. What was that smell?

Then we looked down at the puppy. Solomon was busy pushing a dog turd through the bars of his cage onto the kitchen floor with his little front paw.

"Happy Birthday, Jerry." Camille burst out laughing.

"F---k Leonard," Jerry said, then started laughing, too, in spite of himself.

Essie and I couldn't contain our giggles. Even Elizabeth started smiling as she pointed at the puppy. Little Doggie wandered over for a sniff, but Camille shooed him away with the toe of her slipper.

Still snickering, Essie handed Jerry a paper towel. "Happy Birthday, Mr. Fielding."

31

The Norwegian Ghost Whisperer

Little Doggie didn't seem to mind Solomon, after all he wasn't Camille's pet, he was Jerry's dog. He tolerated the Irish setter, who soon realized in turn that he didn't have to curry favor with the little gray poodle. Plus, he grew bigger, fast, and towered over Perrito. Solomon liked his crate however, and was reluctant to give it up, even after his training was completed. The door was left open permanently to encourage him to leave, but he ignored it. He'd discovered a game he liked. Every time the doorbell rang both dogs started barking. Solomon would bolt out of his cage and would race Little Doggie to the front door, leaping over Claudia if she was crawling around on the floor. Chaos was here to stay. Camille had had enough of the crate in the kitchen. She tossed the cage out into no-man's land behind the garage.

Solomon did become Jerry's exercise machine, albeit intermittently. At first, Jerry would take him for a daily walk on his leash. Little Doggie was encouraged to tag along, and if he felt like it, he would. Over time this disintegrated into Little Doggie going walkies solo again as Jerry became busier with work. Camille had enough to do without exercising a dog, and I wasn't about to voluntarily add dog-training to my duties. Besides, Solomon liked laying around. When he wasn't exploring the front garden and peeing on everything, he was very content to snooze on the patio alongside Little Doggie while I wrote my letters and the children played or napped in the playpen. Solomon had two speeds: somnambulant or overly-energized, but, then, he was just a puppy we kept telling ourselves.

One day while Elizabeth was riding on the merry-go-round in the front yard, and I was supporting Claudia on one of the wooden horses so that she could share in the experience, the front gate opened and an elderly lady with a cane stepped into the garden. She had a nurse companion with her.

"Can I help you?" I called across the lawn, quickly picking Claudia up and helping Elizabeth down before walking across the lawn toward the two women.

The elderly one with the cane hesitated and stood stock still, gazing at the house.

"I used to live here," she said.

"Welcome back," I replied. "Let me go and tell the current owner that you're here."

"Camille!" I called walking into the house. "One of the previous owners has come to visit."

We walked back outside, but the women had already gone. Camille was disappointed. "I would love to have talked to her," she said.

"I think it was too much for the old lady," I replied. "She seemed to be rather distraught at seeing the place again."

"Still," Camille responded, "I'd love to have met her, at least."

Me, too. The unknown mystery woman turned out to be an interesting former occupant because of what the Norwegian ghost whisperer later told Camille.

A few weeks after we'd moved into the house, when the Christmas parties were over and there was a brief lull in visitors, Jerry, Camille and I were just finishing dinner in the breakfast-room one evening. The breakfast room was a cozy little nook off of the large and imposing dining-room, where we ate when no-one else was around. Admittedly, I'd had a glass or two of red wine, but I couldn't contain myself.

"I can't stand it anymore!" I burst out. Jerry and Camille both looked at me, concern on their faces. "There's someone standing over there by the far windows."

Camille's head whipped around to the darkened dining-room, its shadows lit only by reflection of the bright city lights from far below.

Startled, Jerry stopped trying to light his cigarette and craned his head. "Where?"

"At the other end of the room, by the chairs at the end of the dining-table."

The Fieldings both stared into the void for a brief moment.

"There's no-one there," Jerry said flatly.

Camille turned back to face me, an interested look on her face. "What does he look like?"

"I can't see his face, but I think he's wearing a tuxedo."

Jerry stared at me, the look on his face conveying *has she lost her marbles?* A conversation ensued between Camille and me where we chatted about the possibility of the house being haunted. I told her Elizabeth had babbled to me once or twice about the man she'd seen in her bedroom.

"In fact," I told Camille, "I think she talks to him when she's in her crib. I go in to check. but there's never anyone there, and the French windows to the balcony are always shut tight and locked. She never seems scared or frightened." I shrugged. "She even pointed to him once, but I couldn't see anything. Even though I have the impression he might have been wearing a suit and a hat," I added.

"Is *he*," Camille inclined her head over her shoulder towards the dining-room without taking her eyes off of my face, "still there?"

"No, he's gone now."

"So, maybe we have a ghost," Camille stated with relish.

Jerry stared at her speechless, then looked at me, then back to her. "You're both nuts," he declared, hardly believing the turn the after-dinner conversation had taken. "You come from a family of Christian Scientists, Camille. Do you really believe in ghosts?"

Camille gave a fluttery little laugh indicating that it might not be beyond the bounds of possibility. A lot of show business people were superstitious. Jerry was definitely not one of them. He stood up from the table.

"I'm going back to work," he said, shaking his head and muttering, "ghosts, my eye," as he walked down the hallway to the door that led downstairs to his office.

"And while we're on the subject," I said to Camille as we washed and dried the dishes later, "I don't like the energy below the patio, down in that far corner of the garden away from the pool, on that terrace where that big date palm is. It's creepy."

"I don't like it, either," she admitted. "Nobody does. Roy Lee didn't like helping my father clear the brush away in that area, that's why it's still more overgrown than the rest of the property."

I didn't mention that I wasn't too keen on looking down on the pool at night from the big picture window in the dining-room, either, especially when the pool lights were on. I sensed a man's fully-clothed body floating over the drain in the deep end, but I'd decided it was a figment of my imagination, even though I never liked swimming over that part of the pool during the day, and tried to avoid it. I didn't go swimming at night, but neither did anyone else. Because the steps and terraces were made of rocks they looked very pretty but were uneven. Camille deemed them unsafe unless it was broad daylight and you could clearly see where you were walking. She didn't want any broken ankles from anyone heading for a late night swim.

The possibility of the house being haunted became a much more exciting conversation piece at parties than the tiger rug had ever been.

"Is the ghost here tonight?" the actress, Paula Prentiss, asked me, looking round expectantly one evening when Jerry and Camille hosted a party for Dan during the run of *The Odd Couple.*

She and her husband had just walked through the front door and I was taken off-guard. I had to admit I hadn't seen it yet. She was very friendly and full of questions, but her husband, Richard Benjamin, had the same kind of look Jerry wore on his face, a definite non-believer. Without actually saying "you're both nuts," he drew her away.

Word got around. A short time after the old lady's brief appearance by the garden gate, someone mentioned to Camille that a very famous Norwegian psychic was currently in town who specialized in ghosts. Was she interested in an introduction? Of course she was; Camille was beside herself with curiosity. I felt apprehensive; this had gotten out of hand. People were asking me all sorts of questions I didn't know how to answer. I wish I'd never opened my mouth, but I was also curious. Besides, it wasn't my house, and this was Camille's show now.

I was upstairs putting the babies down for their afternoon naps when the Norwegian arrived. As I descended the staircase into the entrance hall an extremely tall, gray-haired woman, who'd look like one of Wagner's Valkyries if she'd had long braids instead of short hair, stood in the entrance hall watching me with a hard, penetrating look that I had to admit to myself was a little scary. Was it my imagination or did the entrance hall seem darker and gloomier than normal?

Jerry was pointedly absent. Camille could do what she liked, but he wasn't going to join in in this chicanery, as he'd put it earlier.

The ghost whisperer was accompanied by a couple of acquaintances, one of whom we found out was a reporter a couple of weeks later when we opened the Sunday edition of the *Los Angeles Times.* The Norwegian headlined an article on the paranormal in Hollywood. Her face was on the front cover of the *Times'* Sunday magazine and there was extensive coverage inside. Camille's excitement was cut short when she found out her house was not actually mentioned, but we both were impressed at how famous the woman was in international circles which verified her authenticity.

After introductions, Camille asked me to tell the ghost-whisperer what I'd seen in the dining-room, which I did as quickly as I could then made myself absent, since the woman never asked any questions, just stared at me. Or through me, I couldn't tell.

At dinner that night, Camille couldn't wait to tell me and Jerry about her afternoon. Apparently, there were three ghosts living with us. One was Camille's maternal grandfather, a man who'd loved parties and was very happy to turn up uninvited. Camille was thrilled to know this, although I don't think she ever mentioned it to her grandmother, Mrs. Reed.

"He's the one Elizbeth babbles to," Camille reported. "He's friendly."

Jerry rolled his eyes, and patted his shirt pocket to make sure his pack of cigarettes was there.

"It's nice to know she has a guardian angel, anyway," Camille finished up. "Young children often do, you know," she told Jerry. "And they can see things we can't."

"Uh-huh," Jerry leaned forward and lit his cigarette from one of the candles on the dinner table.

There was a malevolent entity down by the date palm in that area of the garden no one wanted to visit, Camille let us know. The psychic had given Camille a secret exercise she could perform to get rid of it. Camille had to go down there by herself three times for it to work. After she'd completed her ritual, the atmosphere did seem to be a lot lighter in that area of the garden, but people still avoided it, including me. The pool was in the opposite direction for one thing.

The third ghost was the husband of the old lady with the walking stick who'd turned up at the house, but left before Camille could meet her. Apparently, he'd hidden some money in the house, but couldn't remember where. This revelation led to some interesting cocktail hours for a while.

Even Jerry's interest had been tweaked at this news. "Let me know if the money turns up," he told Camille, Joyce and me, but eventually we got bored with poking around and not finding anything, so we forgot about it since life in the Fielding household moved on at a fast pace.

32

I'm Just A Fly On The Wall

My mother had finally gone back to work six weeks after her back operation, and now her letters were full of travel plans. Her return flight would land her back at Gatwick Airport at 9:00 a.m. on a Monday, she wrote.

"You're cutting it a bit fine, aren't you?" I replied. She was due in the office by 9:00 a.m. I advised her to consider possible delays. Newspaper and television reports were warning of possible riots that would "make last August's goings-on look like a kindergarten party." *Life* magazine cited five major cities that would see major demonstrations. "Trouble is," I wrote, "the men at the top don't take any notice until something happens, then they call people riff-raff." The racial situation was very tense. Voters had voted NO to a new hospital for the Watts area, which was not going down with the residents there very well at all. They didn't "even have an old one," I wrote mum. Also, an airline strike was looming, I warned. My mother paid no attention to that. She was going through her wardrobe and asking my opinion on which clothes she should bring. I nixed an all-white outfit she was planning to travel in because "it will get dirty on the plane."

I doubted the Fielding home was much of a place for recuperation, but my mother insisted the doctor had said her trip would do her the world of good, and her boss at work had said the same thing. "Everyone's encouraging me to go," she wrote.

My mother had done such a great PR job passing around my letters that I was getting correspondence from people who wanted me to get them jobs. I referred them all to Jackie and her mother over at *Continental Domestics* in Studio City, who I talked to from time to time. One day she telephoned me. There was a young English woman from Liverpool Jackie had placed with a prominent talent agent and his family in Beverly Hills, but Brenda was unhappy. She'd been here five weeks and was terribly homesick. Would I go over and talk to her? Take her out on her afternoon off, show her some sights? Cheer her up?

Rita's mother had already arrived for her visit. I'd gone to the airport as part of the welcoming party. Myra and Harold had not gone, but said Rita's mother, Dolly, could stay at their house part of the time when she wasn't visiting a relative down in Orange County. On this particular afternoon, Sharon, Rita and I had planned to show Dolly the oldest street in Los Angeles, Olvera Street, which was full of shops and colorful stalls selling imported Mexican goods. It was a tourist trap with an organ grinder and a monkey, as well as men and women in traditional costumes performing *folklorico* dances to a mariachi band, but Angelenos also liked to visit and shop there, including Camille and myself. And the food was good. We'd also planned to visit Chinatown just across Sunset Boulevard from Olvera Street.

I drove over to Beverly Hills to collect the unhappy au pair to take her with us. It immediately became obvious to me that things were wrong on both sides, I later told Jackie. The employers were snobbish and the au pair couldn't accept that life was different in Los Angeles. She brought along John Lennon's recently published book, *In His Own Write,* a slim little best-seller filled with the Beatle's witticisms and line drawings, which she clung to as if it was her lifeline to Liverpool while she grumbled to me. Brenda hated Los Angeles and wasn't interested in sight-seeing. I was sympathetic at first; we all suffered bouts of homesickness from time to time. However, after an afternoon of constant complaining I was more than ready to drive this twenty-one-year-old in her print dress that reminded me of my grandmother back to Beverly Hills. I felt sorry for her; she was a fish out of water, but I held out little hope for any adjustment to California in the foreseeable future.

I was fortunate to live in Jerry and Camille's household. They were hard-working people grappling with adversities amongst the glitter of their lives, but they had a decent core at the center of their being. Camille's whole family were just plainly nice people, gracious, warm and welcoming. They gave me a positive view of Americans and America, a view where everyone was equal as a human being and deserved to be treated with respect. Not all Americans were like that, I realized. When I'd taken a short walk around the neighborhood one afternoon I'd encountered a man trimming his hedge who told me he'd seen white nannies in Hyde Park pushing prams with black babies in them when he'd visited London. He'd been shocked.

"Can you imagine that? *White* women as servants to *black* children!"

I was shocked at his shock. I'd never thought about this sort of thing before; In my mind he didn't understand. "They're children of diplomats," I explained. "Children of royals and high-ranking officers from African countries in the British Commonwealth stationed in London. They need someone to take care of the children while they're working and carrying out official duties."

I was used to the sight of nannies taking their multi-cultural charges for a walk in any central London park. People of that stature needed the best of highly well-trained, local staff, most of whom were white at that point in time, I tried to tell him. He didn't get it. He shook his head and insisted that "it was wrong." Travel had not broadened his mind. He didn't realize status and money were not limited to whites only out there in the big, wide world. His brand of class system was new to me.

I'd also been used to the sight of foreign students from all nations studying at British colleges and universities; they usually came from wealthier families in their own country in those days. Hospitals were full of nurses in training from African countries with the intention that they would take their skills back to their own developing nations, although many of them stayed. Britain was short on nurses. Too many emigrated in the 1950's and 1960's to Canada or Australia where the need was great, the opportunities were wider, and the money was good. It was a restless world. People were on the move, But, then they always had been.

The next time I heard from the agency, Jackie told me that Brenda had gone home. Jackie also said an old school chum of mine, Marion, had applied for employment. Oh, and by the way, Rita had decided to change her job.

In the meantime, Rita was busy entertaining her mother. Sharon was now on summer break from Santa Monica College, and driving them around. After visiting The Farmer's Market, a collection of quaint little shops in West Hollywood that locals as well as tourists frequented, they drove up into the hills to show Dolly where I lived. Camille generously invited them to dinner and fixed beef stroganoff with strawberry shortcake for dessert. Jerry was out, so she took the children up to her bedroom while we had our little dinner party in the breakfast room. After the babies were in bed, she came down and joined us in the library where we all sat and talked for the rest of the evening.

Rita had a relative who'd married a Canadian during World War II. Eventually, they'd moved to the United States and were now raising two teenage daughters down in Santa Ana. I'd driven Rita down to visit them before. If it wasn't too hot, we'd all sit in the back garden under the orange trees, chat about England, eat barbecued hamburgers at a picnic table on the patio, and go shopping at more affordable stores than the ones I frequented with Camille. If the heat was overwhelming, we'd sit and chat in the air-conditioned living-room. While Dolly was visiting, either Sharon or myself would drive Rita down to Orange County when her mother was staying there, or bring Dolly up to Mar Vista to stay with Rita for a few days at a time.

I'd written to my mother that she wouldn't hear from me for a while as Rita and I had planned a little treat for Rita's mother and ourselves. We were going to Arizona for the Southwest All-Indian Powwow over the long July 4th holiday weekend. This was the gathering of Native Americans that Camille had mentioned soon after I'd arrived, the one she suggested I should try and see before I left after my year's contract was up. I'd been lucky enough to get tickets for the ceremonial dances on the Saturday night, and the Indian rodeo the following afternoon. Usually, they sold out by January.

"Tribes come from all over the States for this," I told my family, "although mainly they get the ones from the West." I was familiarizing myself with tribal names in a book I'd bought: Arapahoe, Ute, Shoshone, Navajo, Hopi and many others. We'd also take in a visit to the Grand Canyon while we were over that way.

My mother wrote back that she was "dead jealous."

We didn't tell Dolly about the powwow before we got to the Los Angeles train station. It was a surprise, she'd been told. When she heard the train ran all the way to Chicago, Dolly asked where we were actually going.

"Flagstaff," Rita told her.

"Where's that?" her mother asked, mystified.

"Canada," I teased as we settled into our seats for the overnight journey. Dolly was a good sport.

It was very hot in Arizona, but after checking into our hotel, we found a shady spot outside *Moore's Drug* corner store from which to watch the parade in downtown Flagstaff. People sat their children on top of parked cars lining the route for a good view as the baton twirlers in their short purple dresses decorated with long white fringe and wearing beaded headbands twirled their way down Main Street, their socks and tennis shoes blindingly white in the bright sun. "Miss Indian Princess 1966" led the American and Arizona flagbearers on horseback. Her escorts in their fringed and beaded buckskin dresses and carrying embroidered shawls followed behind in a dark red Cadillac convertible.

"She must be sweating in that long-sleeved velveteen blouse," Rita remarked as the Princess in traditional Navajo dress trotted by on her sorrel pony, her beaded crown perched high on her head.

"Not to mention her long satin skirt and knee-high moccasins," I responded. "But she's wearing fabulous turquoise and silver jewelry. Look at that concho belt." I turned to Dolly. "She's probably wearing family heirlooms." I was glad I'd done some homework.

Navajo women also wore the reverse: long, tiered silk velvet skirts paired with satin or cotton long-sleeved blouses, mostly in dark colors of red, blue or purple. Long hair was pulled back in a bun and secured by a beaded or silver and turquoise comb. If they didn't have a concho belt they wore a sash around their waist. The men wore as much jewelry as the women: silver concho belts, silver and turquoise buckles, bracelets, wristwatch bands, rings and necklaces, some of it sand-cast, along with silver buttons on their shirts. I thought the intricate beadwork on jewelry, earrings and headbands absolutely stunning, and cast my mind's eye back to Camille and I beading dinner napkin holders and jeweled tree ornaments last Christmas. She was one-fourth Cherokee via her long-dead paternal

Grandmother Sue, who she had never met. There was no beading tradition passed down in her family line, or any connection to native tradition on that side of the family at all. Camille's experience with beading came from making her costumes when she was a dancer.

There was a lot of music, singing and dancing along this parade route. The Zuni Pueblo Tribal Band, all men dressed in white trousers and bright blue shirts, followed two young women carrying their tribal flag. The White River tribe's marching band, again, all men—they didn't have women in the marching bands—wore long-sleeved red shirts over black trousers secured with concho belts shining as bright in the noon-day sun as their brass instruments. Their war bonnets, the elaborate feathered headdresses, signaled to everyone the band members were important people, maybe even chiefs for all I knew. From Parker, Arizona, the Colorado River Indian Band wore white pants and long-sleeved dark blue shirts adorned with silver and turquoise jewelry, and cloth headbands.

Teenage Indian girls dressed in white and beaded buck-skin ceremonial dresses, and a group of Zuni children, "pony riders" on their wooden hobby horses, wearing white cotton shirts and pants, led the Rain Dancers, women with white buckskin leggings balancing clay pots on their heads decorated with geometric designs. Taos tribe Buffalo Dancers preceded the Cochiti tribe, whose medicine man carried a large bunch of white sage for cleansing and bless-ing. And then came the Apache Devil Dancers terrifying to me in black hoods and painted upper torsos, somehow balancing elaborate wooden headdresses to drive off any evil as the young braves leapt and twirled in their yellow buckskin kilts and knee-high moccasins, a wooden sword in each outstretched hand. The Kiowa had a large contingent of wonderful Hoop Dancers.

"Look at all those feathers!" Dolly remarked.

The Kiowa braves incorporated more turquoise and bright pink into their feathered bustle costumes along with the traditional red, yellow, white and black symbolizing the four colors of mankind. They wore intricately beaded breastplates of what looked like porcupine quills, which I later found out were referred to as hairpipe breastplates, although there was nothing hairy-looking about them, and had a variety of bird feathers sticking out of beaded headbands: falcon, hawk, crow, owl, eagle. The man selling bright- colored balloons in the crowd was no match for this dazzling parade. Everyone was loaded with jewelry. Most tribal members wore intricate silver squash blossom necklaces, ropes of shell beads and multi-stranded turquoise or coral heishi beads around their necks. Navajo tribesmen carried Eagle feather fans, and so did the women. Apart from the Apaches, most younger men wore short hair; it was largely the older men who wore braids or shoulder-length hair, while some young Hopi women wound their long hair into elaborate butterfly whorls at each side of their heads.

Bringing up the rear came a procession of Native-American cowboys and rodeo riders on horseback, many riding tandem with young children in front, along with families in covered wagons, some of the women even holding papooses. At a powwow everyone's invited, so the crowd fell in behind and followed along to the fairgrounds. We followed too, stopping off first for an ice cream soda at the drugstore counter because we were now very hot and thirsty from standing under that bright blue Arizona sky. The three of us also had nosebleeds from the dry air and altitude.

At the fairgrounds we bypassed traders with their wares spread out on blankets and headed straight for a lunch of Indian fry bread and chili, another new taste experience, although Dolly was not as keen as Rita and myself. All afternoon we sat on covered bleacher seats fanning ourselves with our programs and drinking copious amounts of ice-cold soda in paper cups as we sweated in the heat and watched the rodeo: steer wrestling aka bull dogging, saddle bronc riding, team roping, bareback bronc riding, barrel racing, calf-roping, and cowgirls performing fancy tricks on galloping horses. In a desperate effort to quench my thirst I even drank root beer, a soda I disliked as it tasted too medicinal. Dolly said she felt like she was in a wild west film.

The sun went down and the ceremonial dancing began. We'd stepped away briefly for dinner, hamburgers at a nearby café, but were back in time to witness the gathering of the tribes in the darkened arena, which didn't have much electric lighting on the field itself. Fires had been lit in braziers throughout, which in our limited experience the three of us thought added more of an air of authenticity to everything. There were many, many more dancers than we'd actually seen in the parade. Tribal groups were highlighted by the announcer as each one entered and performed their specialty, but the men and women who'd preceded them never stopped dancing. The earth was covered in twirling figures stomping and stepping, imitating animals and birds as feathers flew in multi-colored patterns of movement. Armbands, cuffs and garters covered with silver bells jangled, and fringed buckskin swayed with the rhythm of the dancers as drummers beat time and the singers' voices rose and fell under the rising moon.

We went to bed thrilled, but exhausted.

Next morning the three of us took a Greyhound bus to the Grand Canyon. I wore a headscarf tied behind my ears in an effort to protect myself from the merciless sun, but soon surrendered it to Dolly. She sat on the wall at the canyon rim walkway looking like the quintessential Englishwoman of the mid-sixties in a sleeveless summer dress and sandals, her hair an immaculate bouffant with an upward flip just below her ears, a style just a tad out of date in my mind, but acceptable for a middle-aged woman. Dolly never complained, but she was hot, very hot, even in the shade of the ponderosa pines. We gazed at the magnificent pink, purple and sandstone-colored view before us and watched a string of horse-riders slowly pick their way down to the valley floor far below, where the Colorado river threaded through steep canyon walls like a thin green ribbon. Rita and I looked at each other and shook our heads: Uh-uh, we were not doing that. One of us was sure to fall off our horse and plunge over the steep trailside in a fit of vertigo. Besides, we were saving our money for shopping.

The Indian Cultural Center had a modern gift shop that offered air-conditioned respite from the heat outside. We admired hand-woven blankets lining the walls, clay pottery and baskets woven from native plants: bear grass, devil's claw and yucca, amongst others. I had bought some small souvenirs from traders' blankets the day before, including a miniature hand-beaded $3.00 buffalo head with bone horns, which to me, symbolized our weekend. I later learned it was actually for a bolo tie, but I'd already planned to wear it as a brooch by sticking a safety pin through the cloth lining at the back. My finances didn't run to a squash blossom necklace, or any other kind of necklace, but I could afford $5.00 for a little silver ring with a traditional sunburst pattern of turquoise petals that reminded me of a flower.

At the gift shop I fell in love with the Kachinas, Hopi and Zuni wooden dolls that represented various spirits and invisible forces that protected humans. I had just enough money left for a machine-tooled one, the hand-carved kind were out of my price range. Since I was a traveler, I chose a Kachina painted in colors for the six directions: yellow for the north, red for the south, white for east, turquoise for west, black for up and gray for down. My little protector had a plume of feathers on its head which eventually fell off, but I kept it for many, many years.

A drumbeat outside the Cultural Center signaled dancing, I snapped a new roll of film into Cynthia's camera. She'd insisted that I borrow her 35mm Canon since it was far superior to my little Kodak Instamatic. The San Juan tribe was showcasing a Deer Dance for the tourists, antlers on their heads, long animal bones in each hand to imitate the deer running on all fours.

A group of Hopi women Rain Dancers entered next, a matrilineal Pueblo tribe from Black Mesa, Arizona whose name was a contraction of *Hopitu*, "those who are peaceful," the master of ceremonies informed us; his headdress of red, turquoise, yellow and white plumes was punctuated by eagle feathers. The women wore woven white aprons over their dark cloth skirts, leggings of white buckskin strips over white moccasins and carried clay pots on their heads.

Then came the Hoop Dancers, whirling and twirling their bodies through intricate movements with several hoops all at once, and finally, a lone Eagle dancer.

"Do you think those are real eagle wings?" Rita asked as we watched the young man bend and swoop with an expanse of eagle feathers on outstretched arms from his shoulder blades to his fingertips as he danced the eagle's life cycle from birth to death.

"Actual whole wings? I doubt it," I replied. "Since it's a costume they probably gather the eagle feathers and sew them onto cloth or leather for dancing."

I'd read in the Cultural Center eagle feathers were considered sacred and it was a privilege to wear them. The eagle moved between heaven and earth. A dance was performed when there was a need for divine intervention, like a prayer for rain, since it was believed that the eagle had the power to control rain and thunder. The master of ceremonies informed us the dance was performed for numerous reasons, including friendship, and that the dancer's feathers should never touch the ground as he swooped down low on bended knees.

That night I dreamt of flying on the back of an eagle above a deep rift valley not unlike the Grand Canyon. Then I saw an image of myself at four years old crouching under the eagle's protective outstretched wing. I woke up thinking about the bald eagle as a symbol of the U.S.A., and wondered why I'd really chosen to come to America. After all, I'd had choices, even to go and join Avril in Switzerland. "Follow your bliss" had not yet entered the American vernacular, and I wasn't consciously aware of letting instinct lead me. I was just out in the world having an adventure; but destiny's a strange thing.

★★★

We left Arizona at night on the *Super Chief,* nicknamed "The Train of the Stars" by the Atchison, Topeka & Santa Fe railroad because it had carried celebrities between Chicago and Los Angeles since the 1930s, although we didn't see any on our journey because nowadays they all flew. Sharon and her handsome friend, Bob, met us when we arrived in Los Angeles the next morning. Sharon had met Bob in one of her Economics and Business classes at Santa Monica College and was trying to make him her boyfriend. Myra had previously confided in me that was a hopeless task since he was gay. After a while, Sharon realized he was not husband material and gave up, even though he was from a wealthy family.

When I got back to Maravilla Drive several letters were waiting for me, one from my mother who wrote that Avril had been to visit them "and talked incessantly." There was also a letter from Avril, who complained she hadn't heard from me "for ages and ages." She mentioned her visit to Sussex for the weekend "for a rest" at her mother's, and seeing my parents, as well as hers in two sentences, then went back to two pages of reporting on the usual subjects: boyfriends, money (always a lack of), work, entertainment and clothes, although not necessarily in that order. She was in financial difficulties and bouncing checks, including her rent, which is why she was now sleeping on various friends' sofas. She'd found it necessary to add a second job as a waitress at a very 'in' restaurant during the evenings, and as a result, had "met quite a few dishy characters." She was now hobnobbing at "some of the better places in London," like "Dolly's, or Birdland or Fanny's Bistro, etc. etc." This was all in aid of helping her not think about John, who was seeing other women. In spite of going out and having "lot of men" she was hooked into him and thought she might "have to leave the country or do something desperate."

But not as desperate as our friend Antonina, who went by the nickname of Tosia, Avril continued. She'd "been in hospital on account of drugs, couldn't see anyone for nearly three weeks, and now had to go out of London on a rest cure to Wiltshire for about two months, poor thing. Still, perhaps when she comes out we will go away again to France or something."

France was Avril's default dream place to run away to. She enclosed the rest home's address so I could write to Tosia, then went on to mention another friend of ours, Deidre, who had gone to live in Canada.

Everyone always seemed to be on the move in those days, but somehow we kept in touch with each other no matter which country we were in, or for how long, or whose place we were camping out at. Not everybody had access to a phone, the internet would not exist for decades and international phone calls were prohibitively expensive, yet we were able to easily find and communicate with each other, give or take a few weeks. Addresses would change frequently, sometimes every other week for certain people, yet letters would always find the intended recipient. Avril once wrote to me from Alhambra in Spain on Christmas Day. She was eating oranges from the tree outside her window for Christmas Dinner and told me she'd probably be in Morocco soon, so send my reply letter care of the British Embassy there.

It seemed my friends were divided into two camps: the ones who traveled and/or emigrated and the ones who stayed at home, got engaged while they were still in their teens, and were set to get married by the time they were twenty-one. Britain was a nation of immigrants over hundreds of years, or conquerors who had assimilated with tribes already there, depending how you wanted to look at it. We were a nation of mongrels; I myself identified as a Viking with a bit of the Victorian thrown in. Since we were an island people, when the tribe got too big and the land too crowded, in the name of sustainability it was necessary for some to move on, emigrate to places elsewhere. It had been the way of the world for tens of thousands of years. Moving on. That's how land got populated and countries were formed. The earth never stood still, and neither did its inhabitants. Walking in the world was a way of being in the world, belonging to the world. Home was where you were, even though the heart may remain in a place from where and what you had left behind. Immigrants could never feel fully whole. They were always divided into two parts: the new part that was here in the now, and the old part the culture and place a person had come from. And there was no escaping that old part; it followed the person like a shadow.

After arriving back in Los Angeles, I was ruminating about this over a gin and tonic at cocktail hour. I'd already told Camille and Joyce about Arizona, and now their talk had turned to local gossip and politics while I listened with half an ear. Camille was telling Joyce about her recent visit to David Jones, the elegant and exclusive florist's shop on Sunset Boulevard, where she'd gone to order a flower arrangement for Debbie.

"David told me he'd just got back from delivering flowers to Nancy Reagan, who was in the middle of her exercise routine. 'We have to get in shape,' she'd told him without interrupting her set of side leg raises and lateral bends. 'We're running for governor.'"

"You're kidding," Joyce replied with a groan, "I thought Pat Brown was running for re-election."

"He is. Ronnie's switched parties." Camille exhaled a stream of smoke and stubbed out her cigarette in the ashtray. "He told Mitzi weeks ago at a dinner party that he'd become a Republican. Jerry says Nancy's stepfather and his John Birch Society friends are backing him for candidate in the election."

"What're you talking about? Jerry had come up from the Dungeon and stood in the doorway.

"Ronald Reagan's run for governor of California," Camille replied.

Politics and the dirty deeds of show business were at the top of Jerry's favorite subjects. "He's running on a law and order platform, citing the Watts riots and the UC Berkeley student protests. Says he's gonna 'clean up the mess at Berkeley.' Gonna try and kill the Free Speech Movement is more like it, but what can we expect from a bad actor and his right-wing ultra-conservative backers over in Glendale." Jerry snorted in derision, leaning against the stucco archway at the top of the steps leading into the sunken living-room.

'Oh, those fascists." Joyce never minced words, especially after a few drinks. "Well, what do we expect? Julie says Reagan aligned himself with mob-connected unions to root out communists in Hollywood and sold out the Screen Actors Guild to the mafia when he became Guild President."

"Yeah, Gene Kelly nominated him, but since he also nominated himself it may have been a bit of a shock when Reagan won," Jerry said. "I just hope the people of California aren't so stupid as to vote for a third-rate actor."

We all knew how Jerry felt about actors, who he thought inferior to writers and musicians. We all knew how he felt about Gene Kelly, too, whom he'd worked with the previous fall on the *New York* show. Even though I knew nothing about politics or Hollywood history, I was constantly being reminded by conversations between Jerry and his friends of the grudges and bitterness that people who'd been blacklisted still carried. Those who'd been betrayed would never forget. Or forgive. Hollywood was divided into two camps: those who'd ratted out friends and colleagues, and those who did not. Careers had been wrecked. Jerry, like many others, had taken the Fifth Amendment and refused to name names. Ever since, he'd worked hard at building his career back up like one of his mentors, Dalton Trumbo, and with Camille's support he was succeeding. Her father, Dick Williams, had been in the middle of the union strikes when he'd been working at Warner Brothers in the 1930s, although from what Camille and her mother said, he'd usually decamped to the nearest bar with actress Ann Sheridan, later a Hollywood pinup and 'oomph girl.'"

I felt like a fly on the wall listening to all this, problems and chit-chat of a different generation, a shared history of people in a different place and time from myself. They all seemed to know so much about everything that at times it was intimidating. But it was always interesting. America gave me information that I had no basis for, nothing to build upon, except what I'd read about in the newspapers and seen in films. Now I was actually living in America, I had to learn quickly, absorb the lessons it offered, and decide where I stood, whether I wanted to or not. Maybe I should have taken the job in Sweden, or Switzerland, I sometimes thought, but then I'd have continued to pal around with Avril, which, upon reflection, had its own dangers. No, I was in the right place, at least for a while. No matter what was going on, and in spite of all the chaos, I felt safe with Jerry and Camille. Right in the eye of the storm.

At the same time, I'd also observed that a lot of Americans had a naivete about them, an immaturity that liked things sugar-coated. I'd got a whiff of it at Disneyland, that search for a mythological perfection, a veneer over reality that became cemented in my thinking about America on a later trip to Knot's Berry Farm. The surety that past was perfection, a wistful longing and insistence for life to be clean. But was it fair to dismiss that as an American attitude so easily? What about the rest of humanity? It was so much easier to blame someone else's naiveté than look at one's own. Did Europeans look at life the same way deep in their hearts, the horrors of war laying on top, clouding that search for perfection and cleanliness, everything nicely packaged up and tied with a bow instead of messy and fragmented? Did I? What was reality anyway? An experience? Someone else's opinion that we swallowed in lieu of our own thinking things through? Did higher education exist in order to countermand that, help us think for ourselves, or was it life's hard lessons, or a combination of both? Humanity has an inbuilt button that defaults to laziness which manifests in a lack of self-examination and we're all guilty of it at some point in our lives, I realized.

I took another sip of gin and tonic and turned my mind off. Sometimes, life was just too much to contemplate. And who cared anyway? I was underage and my opinion didn't count.

Later that evening, when Joyce had gone home, Jerry had gone back to the Dungeon to work, and the children were in bed, I started laughing as Camille and I washed and dried the dishes.

"What's so funny?" she wanted to know.

"I just thought of everyone at home; the problems they're having. Like finding somewhere to live, trying to make ends meet with the food bills, etc., and here I am bouncing from day to day, living in the lap of luxury and thinking about where shall I go next? Or, how do I pay for the new dress I want?"

"You also have a couple of other things going on like paying off the huge dental and optician's bills for that contact lens you lost," Camille reminded me.

"Yeah, but they don't rank as so important in my mind, especially if I don't think about them," I said.

She shook her head. "Youth! Enjoy it while you can."

Later in bed, I started a letter to my mother. "Well that's life I suppose. To each his own and make the most of things while you have them 'cause the picture may change all too soon." I ruminated on, "how quickly the present becomes the past, and how people are so busy with things they never stop to look over the day they have just spent and really examine it. Everything kind of merges together and forms a pattern so you only remember the outstanding things. Every day I try to remember to look at everything I see and kind of bottle it up in my memory, remembering the relatively small things like the sun shone brighter on Monday than it did on Sunday, but it's just impossible. Those thoughts get lost in amongst the other, and you just remember that June was hotter than May." I finished up with a disclaimer: "Don't I think of some peculiar things at times?" Then I turned off the bedside lamp and went to sleep.

33

Mother Comes Calling Whether We Want Her To Or Not

*I*n no time at all, Rita's mother's vacation was over. After two-and-a-half weeks, she looked worn out. Rita had taken her mother to Las Vegas for another long week-end. If it wasn't for the salvation of air conditioning, the three-digit heat would have done her in, Dolly commented afterwards. The airline strike was on and it took Sharon and Rita several days on the phone to rebook and then rebook again Dolly's flights back to England, but in the end they managed to get all the flights coordinated before the final dash to the airport.

Almost as soon as she'd left, my mother arrived. Camille and I met her at the crowded and chaotic airport where packs of soldiers were gathering for various flights *en route* to a final troop flight to Vietnam. My mother looked dazed. She'd been ill on the flight over the Atlantic, the young woman who'd been sitting in the seat next to her told me, and then again on the turbulent flight from New York to Los Angeles. Getting on that flight at Kennedy Airport had been a nightmare as the airline strike was still on and my mother discovered her American Airline ticket was only stand-by. She panicked when she found out some Americans had been waiting for two days for a flight to Los Angeles, and pleaded with the desk attendant at the Astro-Jet counter, who finally gave her and the young woman two first-class seats on their evening flight. They had ten minutes to collect their luggage, organize a porter and get to the gate. My mother had paid attention to my letter and not worn her white suit, but she carried a white raincoat over one arm and held a white hat in one hand. The other hand held her handbag.

I introduced her to Camille who made polite conversation as we walked out to the car. "I know you must be tired, Betty, but I just have to make a quick stop at the market and pick up a few groceries on the way home. It's my friend Joyce's birthday tomorrow and she's coming over for a little pool party."

My mother had been discreetly checking her wristwatch. *Grocery shopping at 10 o'clock at night?* She had never been in a supermarket in her life. My mother considered them vulgar, full of housewives who left their babies in prams outside the front entrance while they shopped. She preferred smaller, individual shops, the butcher, the baker, and so on, but would send my father out to the supermarket armed with a list of groceries on a Saturday afternoon while she went to a matinee at the movies or a play at the *Theater Royal* in Brighton. Tired as she was after the long journey, however, my mother perked up at the idea of a pool party, albeit a very small one, as Camille assured her.

"We thought you'd like to spend a day resting after your journey," I chimed in. "Resting and sunbathing by the pool."

My mother agreed that sounded like a good idea. She loved to sunbathe and had planned on getting a good tan while she was in California. She'd already admired mine, along with the weight loss and my tight jeans.

When we got back to the house, and after admonishing the dogs to calm down and lie down, Camille made a beeline to the kitchen refrigerator for a beer and asked my mother if she wanted anything to drink.

"A cup of tea would be nice," my mother responded as we placed her things down on the bench in the hallway. "I'm parched after that flight." She ignored the dogs.

My mother's head had been on a swivel ever since we'd walked through the front door. *Two refrigerators!* she mouthed to me as we sat down at the round kitchen table, a favorite place to gather for many visitors and a frequently crowded room at any time of the day or night. A few days before, the actress Shirley Jones had spent a whole evening having an impromptu business meeting there with Jerry and Leonard, Camille mouthing to me, "her husband's an ass#*le," from over by the refrigerator as she reached for another bottle of wine.

"You have a lovely home," my mother told Camille as she sipped her tea, and Camille and I sipped our bottles of Michelob.

"Thank you, Betty," Camille responded demurely. She loved to hear that from people. "It's my dream house."

I listened to the rap I'd heard many times before as she went on to talk about the house, how Max Reinhardt, the German director had built it after he came to work in Hollywood; how Janet Gaynor, famous in the 1920s and 1930s who'd won the first Academy Award for Best Actress, and played the title role in the original *A Star Is Born* movie had once lived here. Camille had the pedigree down pat.

My mother no longer seemed outwardly tired from her flight. I remembered the movie magazines she was always reading when I was a small child. *Photoplay* had been her favorite. Now she was here, right in the middle of the town where all those stories had originated.

"Another cup of tea, mum? Another beer, Camille?" I stood up, and after putting the kettle on, stuck my head in the refrigerator, looking for suitable leftovers to snack on with our second round of beers.

"What's this?" I pulled out a small Tupperware container.

"Ceviche," Camille said. "Leftover from last night when Sam Peckinpah brought his new wife over."

I remembered thinking how attractive Sam's Mexican actress wife, Bego, was when they'd arrived. When I heard he was coming over, I'd opted to have a tray in my bedroom so I could watch *Peyton Place* as I ate my dinner and keep an eye on the kids. He might behave if he was with a new wife; or, he might not. One could never tell with Sam. He could explode at any moment, which kept everyone on their toes. You could never tell with alcoholics, Honey had once reminded me.

I put the ceviche and some crackers on the kitchen table. "Help yourself, Betty," Camille said.

"Oh, no thank you, Camille." My mother patted her stomach, reminding us she'd just spent several hours high in the skies vomiting her way across America. She liked fish, but only boiled or battered. Ceviche was way off of her radar.

"Oh, it's cooked, Betty," Camille advised her. "The acid in the lime juice cooks it."

My mother looked skeptical as Camille got up to answer a phone call. She looked on disapprovingly as I dipped another cracker into the "raw" fish. I'd already exclaimed the delights of beef tartare in a letter home.

"You'll get worms," my mother admonished.

Camille had placed a beautiful flower arrangement with "Welcome Betty" beside my bed, and I'd added a bottle of brandy embellished with a pink bow, and a glass tied with a red bow beside it since my mother didn't drink alcohol, only brandy "for medicinal purposes" (usually while she was cooking the Sunday dinner). My mother loved her new bikini. She'd taken note of my habit putting on swimming togs under a dress when I got up in the morning, preparation ahead of time for a visit to the pool later, and did the same thing. Elizabeth had been intrigued to see another person sleeping in my bed. I'd been telling her for several days that Betty was coming to visit, and shown her a photograph. She stared at mum all through breakfast, watching her father and my mother both drink cups of tea while Camille and I chugged down a pot of coffee from the Corningware. Then, she burst out with a "Hi, Debbie," greeting, which tickled my mother pink since she looked nothing like Debbie Reynolds.

Jerry had previously given me a copy of his new album *Hollywood Brass* for my brother, and signed it before I mailed the record to England. My mother told Jerry that my brother had been thrilled to receive it, had played it over and over again, and bragged about it to his friends. He'd especially liked the *Spanish Flea* recording. Jerry explained that a young musician named Jules Werner, who played drums and percussion, had done the arrangement. He'd also originally written the tune, which had been a hit for Herb Alpert, and Jerry often called him in when he was making a record.

Jerry had warmed up to my mother immediately, I could tell. He smiled a lot. Well, she'd also brought him a bottle of Johnnie Walker scotch from the duty-free shop as a thank-you. Since Jerry was only two years older than my mother they also had World War II in common. Although Jerry hadn't actually served in the armed forces because of his health, he'd done his part for the war effort by working shifts at McDonnell Douglas in Santa Monica building airplanes by day and conducting his band on the radio at night. As we sat around the big kitchen table, my mother told him about the American Air Force bands she'd danced to at the air bases in England: Glen Miller, Tommy Dorsey. Camille and Essie listened in with rapt attention, while I re-listened to some of the stories I'd heard all my life. As sad and awful as the war had been, it had also been the most exciting time of my mother's life—as she had been so constantly fond of telling the family while I was growing up.

After breakfast, she slathered herself in suntan oil and laid out on a beach towel by the pool. Camille and I fixed food and drinks, which we stowed in the little poolside refrigerator, and spent an hour making a "Happy Birthday Joyce" banner that we hung across the lanai. We inflated the plastic pool toys Camille had bought at wholesale prices from the pool company Myra worked for. By the time Joyce and Barbara arrived, the swimming pool was

full of floating brightly-colored pool toys, including a giant
blow-up swan a person could ride, a garish green dragon, a
red and yellow canoe sans paddle I could lie down in com-
fortably, and a floating baby chair we popped a delighted
Claudia into. She soon learned that by kicking her legs in
the water not only could she propel herself around the
pool, but by flailing her arms she could cause a big splash
when her tiny hands and fists hit the water. When Claudia
got tired, she'd simply take a nap and bob around the pool
with her eyes closed and her head resting on her chest.
Rather than be in the pool, Elizabeth preferred to play in
her boat-shaped paddling pool beside the lanai. We'd filled
it water from the garden hose, but she discovered that by
filling up her beach bucket from the wide steps at the shal-
low end of the pool she could add water to her boat, too.

Elizabeth's cousin, three-year-old Dana, liked this
game as well, because she didn't want to get in the pool,
either. Her mother, Donna, sat on the pool edge and tried
to interest Dana in the delights of learning to swim every
time they visited, but the little girl wasn't interested.
Camille's brother, Brad, and his wife, came by with Dana
on the Sunday to meet my mother. Then Camille's mother,
Honey, dropped in with her sister, Pat, and their mother
Mrs. Reed to say hello. The two sisters wore shorts, and
had very shapely legs for women in their sixties. Camille's
grandmother got a mental thumbs-up from me for wearing snazzy capris and wedge-heeled sandals—remarkably
fashionable for a woman who was almost ninety. Camille's
female family members might not be in show business, but
they were decidedly glamorous. My mother was impressed
with the sisters' busy social life, especially when she found

out that Honey was still getting two or three marriage proposals a month.

Apart from Brad, it was an afternoon of sun and fun for females, including Rita, who dropped by with Sharon and her sister, Jannie. Jerry was working in the Dungeon writing music sixteen hours a day for four television series: *Run, Buddy, Run, Tarzan, Shane* and *Hogan's Heroes,* which was due to start showing in England soon. He surfaced at one point to wave at everyone as he escorted a musician colleague up the side steps and out the front gate, but declined to join us and drink a margarita. Jerry wasn't a pool person. Neither was Joyce. She liked sitting on the patio and being in the garden by the pool, but I never saw her in a swimsuit. Although she always wore mini dresses now, I never saw her in shorts, either.

My mother was in her element chatting to everyone. She eyed the mini beer barrel Camille kept by the pool, but along with Jerry and Mrs. Reed she passed on a drink. After Camille's family left, she took a nap on one of the blow-up pool beds, blissfully snoozing off jet lag as she floated in the water. At cocktail hour, she surprised me. Rita and company had already left, along with Camille's family, and we were sitting in the kitchen while Camille cooked dinner. She explained to my mother that Dan Dailey had actually taught her how to cook. Camille was also fixing cocktails and she offered my mother one, which she accepted! Gone was the supposed teetotaler I'd known for twenty years. Every night from then on, my mother sampled margaritas, various Jamaican rum drinks, and even martinis, her favorite being vodka and grapefruit juice. No more sneaking brandy tots in the kitchen larder.

34

Sight-Seeing in Southern California; Debbie's New Beach House

My mother's visit became a mini-vacation for both Camille and myself. Camille swapped her car with Leonard's station wagon so we could take Elizabeth and Claudia with us on our sight-seeing day trips, and they could lie down in the back for their naps. (Camille also hoped it would boost her claim that she needed a new car. Leonard was a very good business manager but notoriously tight-fisted; a good thing really as he was keeping the ex-wife and her lawyer at bay.) We drove down to Marineland in Rancho Palos Verdes and watched Bubbles, the killer whale, do tricks, ate hot dogs and drank Cokes, then stopped at the Wayfarer's Chapel in nearby Portuguese Bend, a glass chapel set in a Redwood grove high on a bluff overlooking the Pacific Ocean with a view of Santa Catalina island, and a popular place for weddings.

"Jayne Mansfield married Mickey Hargitay here," Camille told my mother, which seemed to impress her as much as *The Lord's Prayer* carved into the altar steps.

Our days alternated between sight-seeing and sun-bathing by the pool. The women my mother worked with had demanded she come back with a tan. We drove down to San Juan Capistrano to see one of the California missions and threw bread crusts from our sandwiches at the doves and pigeons. At Disneyland, Camille, my mother and I were as enchanted with the latest exhibit, *It's a Small World,* as much as Elizabeth and Claudia. We were mesmerized watching the mechanized dolls dancing and twirling.

One morning we headed north towards Malibu and Paradise Cove intending to have lunch at the restaurant on the beach.

"Debbie's just built a new beach house," Camille said as we drove along Highway One through Malibu, "Just about here somewhere. Oh, yeah, right there," she said pointing through some open gates as she spied Debbie's car. "Oh, look, she's home. Let's stop and say hello," she continued, pulling a swift and abrupt left turn into the courtyard.

Debbie answered the door in her bikini and invited us in. She was busy sorting plants and doling out cookies to her children and their friends. Debbie passed the cookie jar over to us then took one for herself. Camille and I declined, but Elizabeth eyed the jar enthusiastically and she wanted one, as did my mother, in spite of always watching her weight. Just as Camille had shown off her new home after we moved in, Debbie gave us a tour of her new house downstairs. I could tell my mother was dying to tag along when Debbie started upstairs and Camille followed. What a tidbit to tell her office friends when she got home! But, my mother hesitated, not sure of the protocol here regarding gawking at a film star's bedroom until I gave her the nod. The children were eating all the cookies now that Debbie's back was turned, and running in and out to the small swimming pool and the beach beyond. I thought it best I stay downstairs. Besides, I'd rather be out on Malibu beach than looking at someone's bedroom, even if they were famous.

We sat by the heated pool afterwards as Debbie held Claudia, dangled her feet in the water and chatted about her charitable work for The Thalians, and her latest film, *The Singing Nun*. She brought out a movie poster showing herself wearing a nun's outfit riding one-handed on a Lambretta, a guitar strapped to her back, while the other hand waved gaily at an imaginary audience.

I could tell my mother was in her element, observing all this. Debbie was very gracious to her and shook my mother's hand when we left, wishing her an enjoyable trip. In the car, my mother commented that Debbie had a lovely smile and "very penetrating green eyes" that "looked much prettier in person than on film." She also made mention that "Debbie hadn't made her bed," which made Camille laugh.

We saw Rita twice more during my mother's visit. The first time, my mother and I picked her up for a visit to *Knott's Berry Farm*, where we panned for gold and ate marionberry pie. The second time occurred when we took Rita and her three charges to the beach one afternoon at Playa Del Rey, where we swam in the Pacific Ocean and ate giant hamburgers from the greasy spoon take-out in the nearby parking lot. My mother struck up a conversation on the beach with an air force pilot home on six weeks leave from Vietnam. He'd been in London during World War II so they had plenty to talk about while Rita and I were watching the kids running in and out of the water. He had a half-blind Downs Syndrome daughter who was playing at the edge of the waves and asked us if we would kindly keep an eye on her, which of course we did, holding her hand and jumping small waves as they rolled onto the shore.

And then one evening when the children were in bed and Camille, my mother and I were sitting in Camille's bedroom watching television, something Camille and I often did, especially while we were sewing, Rita phoned me.

"Guess who I met today?" she said.

I said I didn't know.

"Elvis," she gloated, a smirk in her voice. I could hear Sharon and her sister giggling in the background as Rita rushed on filling in details. A friend of a friend's teenage daughter had been spotted by Hal Wallis while working at her mother's antique stall in London. Hal Wallis, Elvis's manager, had invited the young woman to Hollywood for a screen test, which the studio had apparently liked. She was given the part opposite Elvis in his new film. I'd met Annette a couple of times and she'd seemed a nice English girl who didn't care much for the California life, but appearing in an Elvis film was an exciting opportunity and a chance to earn enough money to pay for the wedding to her boyfriend back home, as well as buy a house. She'd invited Rita and any of her friends to MGM on her day off to watch the filming and meet Elvis. Rita had invited Sharon and her sister along.

"How nice for you all," I responded, puzzled, wondering what was really going on. This phone call sounded like a set-up that Rita had deliberately planned, and I didn't know why.

"She's jealous of you," Camille said after I put the phone down. We were sitting on her bed while my mother sat in a French provincial-style armchair, part of Camille's bedroom set.

"Why?" I wondered out loud. "I drive over to her place, we go out, she comes over here, you always invite her to stay anytime, and you've invited Sharon and her sister over to swim more than once," I said to Camille. "And you invited Rita's mother to dinner."

"She's jealous because you have a more glamorous life than she does," Camille replied. "You live in a bigger house with people who like and appreciate you. Your days are less run-of-the-mill and not so boring and conventional as hers. You get to mingle with show business people every day, enjoy cocktail hour and parties. Your life is consistently more interesting," Camille emphasized. "Rita's a more ordinary person living an ordinary life, and you're not. She's been jealous ever since you got here."

Camille was right. I had been deliberately left out of the invitation so Rita could one-up me in her mind.

"I didn't realize it was a competition," I said. I hadn't understood Rita was fuming behind our friendship. How sad. I recalled snide comments she and Sharon had made calling the Fieldings' house "the castle in the hills." She was probably jealous of Camille, too, and our friendship.

My mother had been busy admiring the framed 8" x 10" photograph of Debbie and her children on Camille's dressing table while I was on the phone. "I've heard that Rita often upsets people," she said. "I once saw your friend

Jackie crying on the bus home from work over a nasty comment Rita had made to her. This was before you both went to the States. I wouldn't bother with her. You've got much nicer friends."

My mother couldn't have cared less about Elvis. She'd already had a tour of CBS studios sound stages that afternoon, courtesy of Camille's father, Dick, who was working on a new TV show *The Wild, Wild West*. It wasn't filming this particular day, but people were still working. Robert Conrad, the star, who had the bluest eyes I'd ever seen, was looking at various guns with the prop master in one corner, and actors with scripts were sitting around having a read-through in another. This visit was just so my mother could have a look-see, not watch the filming or have a stop-chat experience, but she was thrilled enough. Tonight she was more focused on our sight-seeing drive around Hollywood the following day.

35

Hollywood Forever, Then On To San Francisco

$\mathcal{W}$e drove down the hill and stopped to look at the hand and footprints at Grauman's Chinese theater, then drove the short way along Hollywood Boulevard to the Musso & Frank Grill, where my mother ordered homemade chicken pot pie and I had their famous flannel cakes.

"Pancakes for lunch?" My mother associated pancakes with lemon juice and powdered sugar with Shrove Tuesday. She had fixed ideas about food, even though she'd liked hearing about it in my letters, and was aghast at the portion sizes when we ate out. "Much too large," she'd mutter. She hated sauces or "dressing" on anything. "I like my food plain so I can taste it. I don't like the taste covered up. Too much like the French."

"These are more like crepes," I said, liberally applying maple syrup. We'd slept in late and hadn't stopped for breakfast since the kitchen table was already crowded with Jerry's business manager, Leonard, and a couple of Jerry's musician friends. Camille was already brewing a third pot of coffee in the Corningware, Essie was making scrambled eggs at the stove, and the kids were chewing on toasted bagels and drinking their sippy cups of milk, with one dog sitting under each high chair alert for any falling crumbs.

After Musso's, my mother and I looked at a few star's names on the Hollywood Walk of Fame, then drove east along Hollywood Boulevard and up through Griffith Park, past the Greek Theater to Griffith Park Observatory, where my mother looked out at the panoramic view of Los Angeles and declared it was "similar to that from Camille's living room." She'd already kept commenting that California "looks like Spain" wherever we went. When I'd pointed out that Northern California didn't look like Spain, and that she actually was not in Spain, she'd replied that, no, it was different there. "The poor people live in the hills in Spain."

From Griffith Park we headed west along Sunset Boulevard and the Sunset Strip, where I pointed out a building one of Jerry's friends owned. The opening shots of a television show we'd enjoyed watching in the late 1950s and early 1960s, *77 Sunset Strip,* had been filmed there. I'd had an early teenage crush on the hair-combing hipster valet parking attendant, actor Ed "Kookie" Byrnes, who'd become so popular with the television audience that he'd graduated to being a private investigator on the show before the series was over. We drove into Beverly Hills and I pointed out where another star of that show, Efrem Zimbalist, Jr., lived "round the corner from Debbie," I told mum.

I turned Camille's Ford Fairlane onto Wilshire Boulevard, then swung into an alleyway shortcut through the swanky *Robinson's Department Store* and the *Beverly Hills Hilton Hotel's* shared driveway and parking lot onto

Santa Monica Boulevard, cutting out the long lines of vehicles waiting at the equally long traffic lights, before zipping
back onto Wilshire where it angled into the Beverly Hills
main shopping area. My mother had declined to stop and
shop at the department store because (a) she'd never heard
of *Robinson's*, it was not internationally famous; (b) it didn't
have a tearoom like *Harrod's* in London, my mother's favorite place for a mid-shopping snack; and (c) she couldn't
afford to buy anything there. I drove east through Beverly
Hills and the Miracle Mile district to the new Los Angeles
County Art Museum. We sat on the fountain rim in the
courtyard and watched people entering by the reflecting
pools that surrounded the complex.

It was very hot, one of what I called Los Angeles'
'white days' when the sun shone so vividly on the pale
stone buildings that the whole city seemed to shimmer
white in the view from the Fieldings' living room windows.
(Conversely, when it rained, the city took on a blue sheen
I'd noticed the previous winter.)

I'd parked on a side street next to the museum. My
mother wasn't interested in actually going in and looking
at any art. We stopped to look at the Pleistocene mammoth display in the park area surrounding the museum,
commonly known as the La Brea Tar Pits, on our way back
to the car.

"It always makes me feel sad," I remarked. "The large
mammoth and the baby mammoth are calling from the
edge of the black oily pond to the mommy-sized mammoth who's trapped in the tar and can't get out. You know
she's doomed. She'll sink down into the sticky goo where
her bones will lie for thousands of years until modern-day

paleontologists decide to excavate, which the City's planning to do," I told mum. "They figure there's tons of prehistoric bones down there." I looked out over the park, where children were running and playing. One accidental slip and fall too near the edge of the exhibit and down into the goo they'd go. "This whole area's one big giant tar pit underneath the surface. They even have tastefully camouflaged oil derricks in Beverly Hills, some at the back of Beverly Hill High School."

Large methane gas bubbles arose from the deep viscous pond, bursting just a few feet away. My mother's nostrils twitched. "It stinks of rotten eggs," she replied.

"Watch your step," I warned as we continued walking over to the car. "There's tar bubbling up in the cracks on the sidewalk, too."

My mother wasn't interested in archeology, and although she wasn't that interested in history unless it had to do with World War II when she was young, I'd chosen our next stop so she could take a little trip down memory lane.

"A graveyard!" My mother looked at me in amazement as we swung into the Hollywood Cemetery as it was known then before it became Hollywood Forever Memorial Park.

"Not just any graveyard," I pointed out as we parked. "It's right next door to Paramount Pictures. See their water tower beyond that boundary wall?"

Starting as a very young child, my mother's parents had taken her to the Duke of York cinema in Brighton every Saturday afternoon. She even remembered seeing silent films. My grandmother had initiated me to afternoons at the cinema starting when I was six years old. Ostensibly, my first movie, Danny Kaye and Farley Granger in *Hans Christian Anderson,* was a Christmas present. In reality it was a try-out to see if I could keep quiet and sit still for a couple of hours in a darkened theater while watching the screen tell a story. My grandmother needn't have worried. I was entranced by the singing and dancing as much as the vivid color, and didn't have any problem following the storyline. After that, I'd often accompany my mother and grandmother to the cinema on Friday evenings. I harbored fond memories of strolling along the promenade strung with little white lights on balmy summer nights in Brighton, listening to them discuss the most recent Doris Day musical while ocean waves gently rolled onto the shore.

Like its inhabitants, the cemetery was slowly crumbling to dust. But, the lawns were mowed and the flower beds were neat and tidy. As we wandered among the last resting places of the once rich and famous like Rudolf Valentino, Cecil B. DeMille and the Douglas Fairbanks mausoleum with its columns and laurel wreath in front of a reflecting pool, I thought about so many who had journeyed so far to fulfill their dreams, about all the striving and energy it had taken; the squabbles, the fights, the backstabbing. The tyranny producers and bosses tried to maintain over the creative forces of directors, actors and writers now mute and futile since they'd all been silenced and equalized, laying right here next to each other. But the arguments and creative wrangling still continued on through successive generations in and around studio offices all over town today. *Plus ça change, plus c'est la meme chose.* The more things change, the more things stay the same. Even the infamous had to have a resting place; mobster Bugsy Siegel now lay quiet and still in the Jewish section. My personal favorite was the grave of a prominent scientist I'd never heard of, which had a five-foot tall cement rocket for a headstone.

"Oh, look, Tyrone Power's here." We walked over to a grave covered in red, white and blue striped bows, obviously decorations leftover from July the Fourth. I took a picture of mum standing beside the stone sarcophagus of the heart-throb from her bygone youth. "Why don't you sit down on it, and I'll take another photo?"

My mother was grossly offended. "Oh, no! I couldn't do that," she said, shocked that I'd even suggest such a thing as sit down on a grave. "It would be sacrilegious."

Not in my books, but then I was such a cheeky heathen in *her* books no matter how many church services she'd dragged me to. My mother might wear a bikini to sunbathe in, but she was an Edwardian in high-necked dresses and long sleeves deep down inside.

"Let's go." She'd had enough. I'd invaded the tucked-away and fond narration of her youth by bringing her to the cemetery. It was too much. She'd mentioned she'd liked to see the Last Supper mural at Forest Lawn where a host of other famous celebrities were buried, but on the afternoon we'd driven there, she'd become insulted by the saccharin tackiness of it all, and had been horrified when I'd pointed gleefully to the ashtrays in the little gift area near the crematorium. She didn't care where anyone was buried or interned any more. She was only interested in live celebrities and the places they frequented.

We drove to the Brown Derby on Vine Street for dinner and ate Cobb salads while ogling the celebrity caricatures framed on the walls as we sat in mahogany booths under the chandeliers. Mum opted not to sample the famous grapefruit cake that I adored, but preferred to stop for dessert at C. C. Brown's ice cream parlor on Hollywood Boulevard. It sat just along from Grauman's, and was famous since 1906 for their hot fudge sundaes. It had been in this location since 1929. Alas, dessert was a great disappointment.

"It's just chocolate syrup on vanilla ice cream," she complained.

I couldn't imagine how she'd pictured actual fudge under the sliced almond topping. However, her mood picked up when I pointed out actor Richard Chamberlain from the television series *Dr. Kildare* chatting to some friends at a booth across room.

"I always watch that show," she said, filing the sighting away in her memory for hen she got back to England. I knew she'd now keep her friends at the office entertained all winter long. A live celebrity sighting! I'd redeemed the day and myself.

We took the train up to San Francisco for a long weekend and stayed at the Regent Hotel before visiting Mr. and Mrs. Anderson. As Mark Twain once remarked: "The coldest winter I ever spent was a summer in San Francisco." I had no idea it would be so cold there in July, and we hadn't brought coats. I almost froze in my cardigan on the boat ride over to Alcatraz, but my mother found it "bracing." She'd turned down my suggestion of a visit to Las Vegas in the desert, and also an invite from Joyce's brother, Gary, to visit Palm Springs, where he was a science teacher and football coach at the High School, and where it was currently 115 degrees.

"Too hot."

Frieda and Phil took us on a picnic to Jack London's Valley of the Moon property in Sonoma where you could wander freely without seeing anyone else, before it became a fee- paying and organized Historic State Park. Much of California was free like that before it became so densely populated by another avalanche of real estate investment property opportunists.

We visited Chinatown and rode the cable cars before the Andersons drove us to Oakland Airport. It was cheaper to fly back to Los Angeles than to take the train.

Florrie and Mick had called while we'd been gone. They'd left Phil Spector's and gone to work for a million-aire in Brentwood who'd given them a better salary and a much better car. I also suspected that the secret films Mick said Spector made of his sexual exploits, inviting Mick to "come and see what we did last night" when Florrie was busy elsewhere, had something to do with it.

They wanted to meet my mother and came to pick us up the day after we got back to Los Angeles. We then drove Downtown to collect their twenty-year-old nephew, Greg, who lived in an old clapboard Victorian that had been divided into apartments and rooms for rent. He'd lived in Los Angeles for six months and loved it, but was about to return to England before he got drafted into the Army and sent to Vietnam. A lot of young men went into the armed forces for a couple of years as a way of being on the path towards obtaining citizenship. Greg was upset about it. He didn't object to the Army, he just didn't want to be sent to southeast Asia. After watching the television news hour every night, I could sympathize with that. He'd probably be shipped back home in a body bag.

We drove to Santa Monica and walked along the promenade at the top of the cliffs above the beach.

"A lot of people retire in Santa Monica." Florrie told my mother as we watched some seniors on the shuffle board courts. There was a relatively new Senior Center to accommodate the retirees. A lot of them sat on benches, chatting, or at picnic tables playing cards. The demographics of Santa Monica have changed dramatically in the last fifty years. There aren't many seniors there now, although last time I looked there was still a Senior Center by the *Camara Obscura*. The City of Santa Monica has been an overpriced hipster community ever since people working in the film industry decided they wanted fresher air and moved closer to the beach starting in the 1980's.

My mother had been complaining to Mick and Florrie about the American food we'd eaten. "They ruin it with dressing," she said. We went to *The Mucky Duck* for a lunch of fish and chips. Florrie, my mother and I sat and drank Schweppes Bitter Lemon while Mick and Greg drank beer and played darts. My mother asked Florrie if she and Mick would stay in California.

"Our son and his wife are here, but we're saving to buy a house back in England," Florrie told her. She couldn't see living in California during her old age; it would be too expensive. "Medical bills in your senior years can wipe out everything you've worked for."

My mother nodded sympathetically. It hadn't cost her a penny for her back operation under the National Health, the rehabilitation therapy afterwards, the rest home for three weeks then another six weeks off work during which she'd collected her regular salary.

"Mind you, I'd slipped that disc moving a typewriter at work," she told Florrie. "Some of my friends said I could have got compensation, but I got paid for three months, all told. Even the Chairman of the company wrote and wished me a speedy recovery. They all encouraged me to take this vacation, too. I didn't want to bother with making a bigger fuss because I like my job."

Mick drove us home all the way down Sunset Boulevard. When we reached The Strip. Greg started reminiscing about the Friday and Saturday nights he'd miss, where he and his friends would drive up and down in their cars, along with hundreds of other young people, causing a traffic jam. The driving was slow enough for a guy to pass a note to a girl in a car that he liked the look of. If she agreed, she'd pass a note back and they'd make a plan to meet up at a coffee shop or one of the clubs.

He's going to really miss America, I thought to myself, as my mother looked pointedly at me, and I shook my head, *No, don't worry, I don't do that,* back at her. When I'd gone out with Karin and her friends, we'd never found it necessary to drive around. We'd found plenty of young men to talk to wherever we went. They always picked up on our European accents.

36

The Beatles Come To Town

The day after my mother flew back to England, Jerry's cousin Cynthia moved in. Again. After the brief time that she stayed when Claudia was born, and after Honey left, it seemed she'd never left. Cynthia often didn't call first; she'd just turn up whenever she felt like it. Camille and I would be in the middle of something, look up, and find Cynthia standing there without even having rung the doorbell. Camille thought she did it on purpose, although what Cynthia thought she might catch us doing we had no idea.

Cynthia said she was between apartments. She'd given notice and moved out of the old one, but the new one wasn't ready yet, she explained to Jerry and Camille. At least that was her excuse. Jerry thought she wanted to save some money. Camille thought she just wanted to hang out with us all at Maravilla Drive so she could gossip about her showbiz cousin and his friends at the nurse's station the following day; *not unlike my mother now she was back at the office*, I thought. Unlike Cynthia, people had liked my mother and were always asking after her, including Jerry's business manager, Leonard, who hardly liked anybody.

"Better not stand too close to her," he'd warned Jerry, making a crude joke the first time he'd met Cynthia. "You might get a little hot fat on your toes."

"You're disgusting, Leonard," Camille had snickered.

Even Jerry had cracked a smile. He wasn't a fan of this particular cousin, but, she *was* family and he loved her parents, his Uncle Jack and Aunt Ann back in Pittsburgh, so we all put up with the honking laugh, the silent sneaking up on conversations in her nurse's shoes, and the trail of cookie crumbs she left wherever she went.

Jerry's eldest daughters were wary of Cynthia. When the Beatles came to town, Jerry phoned someone he knew for tickets and asked me if *I* wouldn't mind taking the girls to the concert. I nodded my head: Sure, I could do that. My household duties had never turned out exactly to be like the ones described in the job description letter that Jackie at Continental Domestics Agency had initially sent me: "Laundry in the machine (I threw a load of baby clothes in once a week, plus my own stuff, bathing suits didn't require washing), "ironing" (thank God for drip dry clothing), "light housework" (I made my bed and vacuumed my room, Elizabeth's room, and Claudia's cubby hole, plus I cleaned our bathroom once a week), "light cooking" (Camille and I took turns trying out recipes from women's magazines and recipes printed in the *Los Angeles Times* and fixing cocktails), and "light childcare" (Elizabeth and Claudia played with their toys while Camille and I did our crafts, discussed politics, watched television and typed our letters and Debbie's fan mail, although Claudia's seizures did require constant vigilance). Taking Jerry's eldest daughters to see the Beatles would qualify as "childcare" in my mind. Everyone was happy.

The girls were happy they got to see a Beatles concert. Jerry was happy he didn't have to sit through the yelling and screaming of thousands of teenage girls listening to music he hated. Camille was happy she didn't have to deal with any of it, and I was happy to oblige as part of my job and get to see Dodger stadium. After that, I was the eldest daughter's friend for life as far as she was concerned. The younger one was a little more reserved about things but she did flash me one of her rare smiles.

I remembered when I'd first met them shortly after I'd arrived in Los Angeles, Georgia, the eldest had immediately asked me if I knew The Beatles, and never quite believed me when I said I didn't.

"But, I've danced to them," I told the girls. "And seen them in concert. Roy Orbison opened for them when they played Brighton." I'd also danced to the Rolling Stones when they'd played at the Railway Hotel in Horsham, although the place was so jam-packed that my friends and I could hardly move and it was more like jiggling and shaking in place to the music.

Jerry was so grateful that he drove us to Dodger Stadium, where we sat behind Edmund G. Robinson and his grandchildren, and had a very good view of the stage and all the antics around us from our seats. The only people who were well-behaved were the disc jockeys and members of pop groups who sat in our section. Everyone else went wild. I'd brought a pair of my mother's ear plugs she'd left behind as I knew American audiences were worse than the Brits, although didn't feel the need to use them in spite of the noise. Kids were jumping up and down, throwing things, hanging off the balconies, and three young people broke their legs during the concert. When they weren't screaming, people were singing; you could hardly hear the music, but that wasn't the point. The crowd didn't care if the young Englishmen played on key or not, or if they could even sing at all. They were *here* in the flesh, playing guitars with Ringo on the drums, and they looked just like they did on television, exactly like their photographs come to life. Young people weren't at Dodger Stadium just to listen to the music; they were there for the experience of it all. Jerry's girls were thrilled to bits with the whole scene. When they weren't screaming, they jumped up and down with excitement, and sang along with the rest of the audience. We love you. Oh, yeah. We absolutely do. When his eyes weren't on the stage, Edward G. Robinson, who sat in front of us with his grandchildren, was looking around as if he couldn't quite believe what he'd got himself into.

I'd never seen so many security guards and police. It was impossible to get onto the field and near the stage, but the first time two boys managed it and were dragged off, bent over double, the crowd cheered because someone had managed to get over the fence. The cops were kept very busy. When they ran over to take care of one trouble spot, some young people jumped into one of the grandstands that weren't in use behind the stage, then stood in a row and danced to the music. The Fab Four kept on playing and watching the action in front of them with the two boys being dragged off, their eyes darting only to the side of the stage in case they were being rushed from there. They didn't realize what was going on behind them as everyone started laughing and cheering. The laughing increased when one cop strutting around full of self-importance got something soft thrown at him that landed in the middle of his face.

"It was fun," I wrote to my mother. I didn't know it then, but the next night at Candlestick Park in San Francisco would be the last concert of their last tour, and we'd never see them perform live commercially in concert again.

★★★

After mum left, I felt homesick again. It started as I waved goodbye and watched her plane take off at LAX. Part of me felt empty inside. Before my mother had arrived, I'd taped her photo to the back of my bedroom closet door, along with other photographs of friends and postcards they'd sent me from Europe (the dressing table mirror had long ago run out of space). A week before she'd arrived, I'd pointed to mum's photo and told Elizabeth, "Betty" was coming to visit. Since she was talking coherently more every day now, when the closet door was open Elizabeth had pointed to mum's picture and pronounced, "Debbie." After the visit, and hearing my mother's name mentioned numerous times, Elizabeth had corrected herself. Now, she pointed to the photo and said "Betty." She remembered so much: the doll my mother had brought her (now called Betty), the book mum gave her, and that my mother had come and gone on an airplane. Elizabeth had been at the airport enough times in her short life to understand something about that. Betty was now at home in her house in a far-away place called England I told her. We also showed her all the photographs we'd taken during my mother's visit, many of which included her and Claudia.

"She may not understand all the details, but she never forgets and pieces it all together," I wrote my mother, not mentioning that Elizabeth had also pointed to a photo of entertainer Shari Lewis in a showbusiness magazine after she'd come to see Jerry, and called her "Betty," too. Everyone was Betty instead of Debbie now.

The Beatles concert didn't help that homesick feeling. It reminded me of what I missed about England. When you go to live in a new country it's very hard to ditch the old part of yourself entirely. You remain "half and half." Half of you here and half of you back there with what you grew up with. Rather like those two, three and four thousand year-old Bristlecone pine trees high up in California's White Mountains where new growth rubs up against the old growth as they reach for the sky.

My ex-office friend in New York wrote and said she missed her holidays in Europe; her interest in her au pair job was now "just about nil. After all, one can have enough of doing someone else's housework and taking care of someone else's kids. It's certainly an eye-opener for marriage, though," she surmised.

I missed Europe, too. Karin was now at home in Hamburg, working as a secretary, reminiscing about all the fun times we had spent together, and asking when I was coming to visit. She sent her regards to Jerry and Camille, and asked if I'd seen her prior employers, the Skaffs, to which I replied that Mrs. Skaff had moved to Palm Springs with the two little girls, and their house on Maravilla Drive was up for sale.

I loved the Fielding kids, and certainly liked Jerry and Camille and everyone else (Cynthia was tolerable), but the problems kept intensifying. The Fieldings now had four lawsuits going, including *Fielding v. Tarzan*. Just about everyone on that show was suing the producers, including the guy originally hired to play the lead. Jerry had written the music, but they refused to pay him. and maintained they didn't ask him to do anything in their Reply to the filed Complaint. Jerry's ex-wife was still suing the Fieldings, and had started up again with daily abusive phone calls, not only to Jerry, but to Camille, who was threatening to have her arrested.

Leonard was all for having everyone arrested. He came by so often, and sat in the kitchen drinking coffee while he complained about everything under the sun, I suggested Camille get him a coffee mug for Christmas with his name on it. Jerry should have a mug, too, with Bah! Humbug! written on it.

I don't know how Jerry managed to be creative and write music amongst all the problems. But the creative mind and spirit is a tenacious one and will not be denied. Especially when there are bills to pay. Writing the music for Peckinpah's project threatened actual fisticuffs between the two men at some point, but that was the way Sam liked it. Jerry never backed down from anything.

One Friday afternoon, a courier from the studios delivered an urgent manilla envelope for Jerry, and I took it down to his studio office. He was going over some music arrangements with Betty Hutton. One of the films I'd seen with my mother and grandmother when I was young had been *Annie Get Your Gun*. When Jerry introduced us, Betty was polite enough, but I noticed she had a hard, abrasive and unsmiling side to her, not unlike how she'd played her character Annie at the beginning of the film.

Later, as we sat down to dinner, Jerry said to Camille, "I think you should tell her."

"Really?" Camille replied. "D'you really want to pass those alcoholic rantings on?"

Camille turned to me. Apparently, Betty had seen sparks fly between our fingers as I'd handed him the courier envelope.

"They're having an affair," she'd informed Camille, who'd struggled not to laugh at the time, as she did now.

"What!" I was shocked that one of my childhood's film heroines had such a nasty mind and dabbled in unfounded accusations during our casual meeting of less than two minutes.

"She's crazy," Camille assured me, laughing it off.

"And how." Jerry assailed us with lurid tales of Betty and producers over the years all during dinner. "I remember when studio bosses used to stand round in a circle and piss on her."

This wasn't the first time I'd heard less than savory tales about people in show business. It was unnerving. There was a lot of predatory and lewd behavior from people in powerful positions, always men. Women were not treated very well in the Hollywood system, especially if they wanted to be an actress. A person had to be tough as granite, yet still remain vulnerable to be creative. As I listened to Jerry, I thought to myself *and they say women gossip!* He told stories about people just as much as Camille did, maybe more, and the juicier, the better. But then everyone in Hollywood gossiped about everyone else. And really, wasn't that just like life in a lot of places?

It was all getting too crazy for me. Little Doggie, too. He went missing after trotting off for a solitary walkies early one evening. By dinnertime, Camille was worried; he hadn't come back. We all went out and looked for him, but he was nowhere in sight, and none of the neighbors remembered seeing him. He didn't come back by the next morning. We combed the neighborhood for a week. Camille cried for days, and we all felt sad, even Essie, who was used to heartbreak. I felt guilty for every less than loving thought I'd had about that gray poodle. The only person who didn't show any visible sign of grief was Leonard. Even Solomon didn't seem to notice his little furry friend wasn't around. Theories about Little Doggie having been stolen morphed into the realization that he'd probably run afoul of coyotes wandering the hills and looking for dinner. But life moves on. Eventually we stopped searching and ended the inquiries.

★★★

My mother had had a wonderful time in California, had written and thanked Camille for her hospitality, but told me in another letter that she was glad to be back in England where she thought "people were more level headed and sensible, and if you had a bit of cash you could go anywhere for holidays." Her wealthy brother had told her, "he could live anywhere in the world as far as his capital went, but he would plump for England every time," she wrote. I was reminded that Uncle Dennis had toured America a few years before, and stayed at the Beverly Hills Hotel when he was in Southern California. My mother suggested I come home for a rest, that I could go to Paris with Avril, who was apparently showing sign of restlessness again, "do Europe," then go back to the States as a secretary when I was twenty-one if I wanted to and many of the obstacles about being underage had become moot. She also mentioned that the personnel manager at the firm I'd worked for (where she now worked) had told her I "had such a good name, 'they would take me back at a minute's notice,' which made *me* feel good!" she added. I felt that this was a bit of a stretch since I didn't remember any praise when I'd actually worked there, but it was nice to know I'd left behind some positive memories.

My mother had been surprised to find me in such high regard when she'd gone to work at the firm after I'd left for America. It had enhanced her image, especially when she read my letters to people. From the tone of her letters to me, it was as if I'd never left the place; she'd simply stepped into my shoes. It was the same with Camille. My mother was now writing her postcards, sending views of England she thought Camille would like, as well as letters enclosing photos she'd taken of us all. Essie asked me to be sure and thank my mother for photos she'd taken of her in my next letter home. Joyce got a separate letter with photos. My mother reported to me that Joyce wrote a nice note back saying Betty was missed at cocktail hour. Before mum had left, even Cynthia, who never spent a half-cent on anything if she could avoid it, had gifted my mother with some pink beads to go with a dress I'd bought for her and the pink Mexican bangles she'd bought in Olvera Street.

Everyone had liked my mother, who'd shown a social side of herself in Los Angeles that I'd never seen before, even at parties in England. My mother asked me to remember her to everybody and thank them for their kindnesses, that she had enjoyed meeting them all so much. In turn, they all kept asking after her, at the same time saying to me, "I expect you miss your mother." In a way I did. She was a woman typical of her generation in that she wouldn't have anything said against the church or the Royal family, but if we limited talk about those topics and kept it light, focusing more on things we had in common, like fashion, celebrities and losing weight, we got along fine.

My mother also wrote that she missed "those kids at times, especially holding that baby." She meant Claudia, although she thought Elizabeth was "a darling." Another surprise. My mother was notorious in the family for never having been keen on children or babies. In fact, she'd always maintained she should never have had children, which was not exactly comforting to me growing up. When we'd visited my aunt and her newborn, and the female relatives were sitting on chairs in a circle in the living room, the men having decamped to the pub, the new baby had been passed around the for a close-up look and cuddle while we gossiped. When the baby had been given to my mother she hadn't missed a beat, just kept talking to an aunt without looking down at the child and passed it on to another aunt sitting on the other side of her, as if the child was "it" in the English party game of Pass the Parcel.

Mum was now busy typing up an account of her Hollywood adventures for a talk at her local church group, the Mother's Union, that she referred to as "M.U." It became so lengthy she was only able to get through reading Part 1 at the first Friday night meeting, she reported;

the women had voted to wait until the following Friday for Part 2. She was still visiting my friends in the evenings, calling on them at home to show them photographs from her trip. My old school chum Marion, who'd asked me to find her a job similar to mine, and who had already turned down two as not satisfactory enough, had been accosted on the bus by my mother who then regaled her with stories of her adventures in Los Angeles. Marion wrote and said she thought my mother had seemed a bit muddled regarding some details, but the people on the bus sitting near them seemed to be listening in with rapt attention. Oh, and by the way, could I call Jackie at the agency and see if they had another job for Marion.

I missed Karin. I'd go and sit in the neighbor's garden to listen to the Hollywood Bowl concerts by myself and think about when we used to pal around together.

"I thought of you the other evening when I was watching Duke Ellington and his band from the neighbor's yard," I wrote to her. "It was crowded with portable lawn chairs and people drinking gin and tonics from coffee flasks. I sat next to a filmmaker Jerry knew, Haskell Wexler, who offered me a martini from his flask."

Karin sent back a postcard from Spain, where she was vacationing.

I'd only heard from Rita once. She'd left Myra and Harold's; they were now getting a divorce. Rita had moved into an apartment in West Los Angeles with two other women she'd met at the *Mucky Duck*, that bastion of Commonwealth ex-pats, which made me long for a real English pub where I could meet my friends and spend hours chatting and drinking before going dancing. Rita's parents regularly sent money to her, even though they complained to my mother about not having heard from her in two months. I was feeling a particular loneliness. I had people all around me, but it felt like I was on my own. I couldn't rely on Rita for anything anymore.

Before we'd left England for our au pair jobs just over a year ago, Rita and I had envisioned going down to Mexico after our year was up, lying on the beach and writing poetry. This dream had quickly morphed into another one—getting a second-hand car and driving across the USA before sailing home. Camille had put her two cents in on that, saying it wouldn't be safe for two girls to drive on their own through the south as "they had funny ideas down there." After the Watts riots and watching television's nightly news for several months, we'd come round to her point of view. That left another dream of going to Hawaii for a while, but the visits by our mothers had short-sheeted that idea, and left us both without much cash.

But now I needed to go home, touch base. It wasn't only to see family and friends. I missed the countryside at the edge of town where my parents lived: our lane with its avenue of trees, which I had walked along every day to catch the bus, the hedges and ditches running alongside filled with a trickle of water from snow in winter, bullrushes in spring, wildflowers in summer. I needed to ride my old bike into the countryside, feel the wind in my hair as I had done earlier in my life. I longed for the gritty smell of the hustle and bustle of London's crowded streets, a ride on a double-decker bus, the energy of journeying on a train rattling along the rails, swaying from side to side. A love of country is not the same as a love of government, or politics, or personalities. We are made from the soil we come from—the rivers, streams, the very air from the first breaths we took deep inside us, the stardust sprinkled invisibly over everything. It's hard to deny that, no matter where we're from.

It wasn't that I didn't love being in Los Angeles, in California, in America. I absolutely did. Most of the time I'd almost felt like I was on a long vacation. But one can get tired of being on vacation and long for home. Besides, living in Southern California, I missed the change of seasons. As I'd written to my family back in April: "The only way you know it's spring is because the temperature goes up slightly and instead of buying a new hat for Easter, everyone buys a new bathing suit."

And I loved the Fieldings, Camille's family, their friends. I loved the open-ness. In spite of all the many things I couldn't do because I was underage, I felt free. People had been kind and gracious, not to mention interesting. I loved the story of America with all its trials and tribulations, its struggles, its beauty, its vast landscape, imperfections and uncertainties, the possibility of something new just around the corner. It was a young and dynamic country, throbbing with limitless possibilities of the human imagination. I'd witnessed glamour and glitz as well as scuzziness and tackiness in Hollywood.

The truth was that after a year, when I'd left my teens behind and entered my twenties, I was a bit confused as to my next step. I needed to regroup, needed to sit down with Avril and other friends and catch up in person, talk over old times and adventures and think about new ones for the future. I felt I was now in two parts, the old and the new, and they were rubbing up against each other causing sparks to fly. A rollercoaster of emotions that I could not quieten down. I needed to go home. I needed to touch base.

37

Life Is Messy Everywhere

$\mathcal{I}$ flew back to England the week after Elizabeth and Claudia's birthdays. Since they were only a year and a day apart, Camille decided on a family party in the front yard with a few invited friends. Between them the kids had a pile of presents that I swear was larger than that at Christmas. Camille also provided a present for three-year-old Dana, so she wouldn't feel bad about witnessing her cousins' largesse, and so did I since I'd only given her a small gift for her birthday. All three kids got enormous dolls. Elizabeth and Claudia got a toy car, a rocking horse (the merry-go-round had been torn down because it was discovered to be rotting in a few places, plus Camille had now decided it was unsightly and not she image she wanted in the front yard), a little red wagon both of them could fit in, various stuffed animals, smaller dolls, games and toys to keep them entertained until their next birthdays, plus enough outfits and clothes for every occasion from now until next year. They each got their own birthday cake and separate tubs of ice cream.

Debbie Reynolds had come by the day before to drop off the girls' presents, along with Agnes Moorehead, an older actress currently playing a witch in the *Bewitched* TV series. To me she looked like a witch too, in her purple suit with her orange hair and unsmiling, stern face, although she and Debbie were impeccably dressed with hats that matched their suits and looked as if they were both on their way to a prayer meeting; which they probably were, both being very Christian.

Now that Claudia had turned a year old she was pulling herself up on everything, climbing on everything and practicing her walking as well as clearly enunciating many words, especially saying "no" and being disobedient on purpose. She loved twiddling the knobs on the television in my room, watching me out of the corner of her eye as she did it until I told her, "No." She ignored me. When I'd remove her from the set, she'd scream loudly with rage and throw a tantrum, but not shed any tears. Claudia had also discovered a love of dirt. I was now giving her two baths and shampooing her hair every day, and changing her clothes several times to keep her looking presentable. She behaved worse every day. When she found out she couldn't crawl out of the room under the baby gate, she started leaning against it and banging on it until it collapsed and she fell on the floor laughing.

"That's one strong kid," Camille remarked. Strong physically, and strong in temperament. We figured she'd have to be to survive that first uncertain year when her life hung in the balance so often with the convulsions. Along with everything else, it had taken an emotional toll on Camille every time her daughter stopped breathing and started shaking while her eyes rolled back in her head. Camille had felt powerless, and would burst into tears. Because Claudia wasn't my child (and maybe because of my

English upbringing), I didn't get caught up in my emotions as deeply and had no qualms about thumping Claudia on the back to get her breathing again, even though I privately hated doing it. We'd come to jokingly refer to it as the *Oliver Twist* method of child-raising and said that was why Claudia had survived and thrived; if she'd had a proper nurse right from the beginning and been treated with kid gloves she would have died.

Meanwhile, two-year-old Elizabeth was being better behaved every day, talking a lot more in complete sentences instead of babbling, and had learned to flirt, which she practiced on everyone. She was also potty-trained.

Sitting on the patio watching Camille's family interacting with each other—Maggie with her cigarette holder watching Honey through slits in her eyes that the cigarette smoke didn't quite conceal; Camille's father, Dick, not saying too much at all except to pinch my upper arm and say I was getting too thin; Donna smiling good-naturedly at everyone and talking away in her mid-Western twang that made sure no one felt left out of the conversation—I realized that becoming American just didn't happen overnight. As much as I liked them all, and no matter how kind and welcoming they had been to me, I didn't think I'd ever feel like one of them, not really. I was still just too English in my ways and in my thinking. Although I hated to leave, I had to go.

★★★

My mother threw a party the weekend I returned. Only she forgot to invite my friends. To be fair, they would have had trouble fitting into the living room. It was full of my father's family. Since his youngest brother had five children, the house was full of kids, along with his other four brothers and their kids, his sister's family, more kids, his parents and an elderly aunt. Mum did not invite her family, but they wouldn't have come, anyway. Her brothers had married one class up on the English class system scale, and she had married one class down. Not only did the two sides not mix, they didn't not even acknowledge the other's existence. Besides, my mother's brothers did not like the man my mother had married.

I was explaining this to Avril when we met up at a dimly-lit restaurant near her current London address. She apologized for not inviting me to the damp basement flat where she lived with John and six other people in what seemed to be a revolving door arrangement since Avril couldn't recall all their names. Not so different from the Fielding household, I thought, and almost said so, but remembered that a Hollywood mansion was on a totally different scale from a one-bedroom basement flat off the Fulham Road.

"Your mother seems to have enjoyed her trip to Los Angeles, although she told me she was terrified during the Watts riots," Avril confided, lighting a cigarette after flipping her latest Vidal Sassoon haircut out of her eyes. She looked much the same as she had done the last time I saw her although she swore she'd changed a lot.

"The Watts riots were last year, just after I got to L.A." I'd noticed my mother telling one of my aunts at the party about meeting Farley Grainger and a couple of other actors that I had written about in a letter home several months before her visit. She had never met him, but made it sound as if that were her experience, not mine.

Avril giggled. "She's getting your letters and her vacation mixed up. Maybe she's living subliminally through you. *Maybe* she's stealing your life!" Avril stubbed out her cigarette in the ashtray as our scampi and chips arrived.

"One thing I've noticed about my mother, both in L.A. and since I got back to England, is that she smiles a lot, but she rarely laughs," I mused.

I recalled something my mother had confided to me when she was in Los Angeles. On her previous job she'd only worked four days a week when everyone thought she worked five. On Friday, the fifth day, she'd dress for work and leave at the usual time to catch her regular train. At the station, she'd get a ticket to another town and spend the day exploring, having lunch, window shopping, seeing a movie, whatever she felt like. Then she'd come home at the regular time with no one the wiser. It was her secret delight. She had a parallel life, I realized.

"She can't help it if she's bored out of her mind married to my father," I told Avril as we ate. "She fantasizes. Everyone does it to some extent. I bet a lot of married women do, especially if they've been married a long time."

"So reading your letters to others is a way of getting attention for herself, giving herself a starring role, only it's your story, not hers?"

"Why is it easier to look at other peoples' lives, rather than examine our own," I mused.

Avril looked thoughtful for a minute. "Your father's a nice-looking man," she said. "All that black, wavy hair and blue eyes. He's got a million jokes and always makes people laugh. I can see why your mother was attracted to him. He must have been very handsome when he was younger."

"He was, according to my mother," I replied. "She says there was a shortage of men around after the war, and since he was so good-looking and seemed affable, that was enough for her."

How's he taking it, you're being back?"

"He told me I have to start paying rent. The water bill's gone up which he blames me for, plus I'm using *his* electricity."

Avril laughed. "What is it with our parents' generation and water? I swear my mother only uses three inches of water in her bath. I overheard my aunt complaining that when her grandchildren visit they take a shower *every day*! From her tone, you'd think it was sacrilegious to be clean."

"It's The War," I said. "It's still with us. My mother's the same. That generation were told to use as little hot water as possible to conserve energy because it was needed elsewhere for the duration. It wasn't only food that was rationed."

Indeed, since I'd returned to England, I'd noticed a whiff of World War II still lurking in the shadows everywhere I went. Except for most young people, who brightened up the atmosphere considerably in short skirts and colorful clothes, let alone a plethora of young music flooding the airwaves, I'd noticed a lingering air of stodginess lurking around the edges of most older people. Anyone older than about twenty-eight. There seemed to be a difference between those born before the war, and those born after, a different sensibility. I hoped they just needed a longer time to relax and catch up, but I wasn't going to hold my breath.

"I've been thinking a lot about marriage lately," Avril confided. Then she told me about her abortion.

I listened, stunned and horrified. The first doctor had told her it was a false alarm; she wasn't pregnant after all. It was all in her mind, after she'd told him her symptoms and he'd examined her. This in spite of morning sickness and a sudden fondness for tinned rhubarb. Avril called other doctors for a second opinion, all of them private, none of them on the National Health system, but most of them seemed to be abroad on holiday; she was three-and-a-half months pregnant by the time she had a test to confirm what she already knew. Then she found out it would cost £150.00 to get rid of "it." Boyfriend John had been made redundant by his firm, and Avril had just left her job in anticipation of them both going to Tangiers.

"In the end, I had to go to a back-street butcher, who actually turned out to be quite sweet," Avril said. "She gave me a soap and water douche, which turned out to be pain-less at the time, and charged me £30.00."

"At her house?"

"Yeah, on the bathroom floor. Quite sordid really."

I pushed my plate aside. Suddenly, I'd lost my appetite.

"Then about five the next morning I started to get violent cramping pains, utterly, utterly exhausting labor pains and I started bleeding. I can't really describe the feel-ing. This went on for about three hours, and because I was in such pain and screaming, one of my flat mates got me to the doctor, who gave me a shot of morphine and rushed me off to the hospital in an ambulance, sirens on and everything."

"Where was John?"

"He'd gone to visit his parents for the weekend."

I wasn't that surprised to learn this about her boyfriend. Absent when needed.

"At the hospital they gave me a blood transfusion. I was in labor until the next evening and guess what?"

"What?"

"I had twins. One on Monday, one on Tuesday."

Dear God.

"After I left the hospital, I got a temporary job for about a week, and then I collapsed with more violent pains." She nodded affirmatively. "Septic fallopian tubes and abscesses in my womb from the unhygienic abortion. Another two weeks in hospital."

I didn't know what to say. Avril had a knack for dramatic scenes and getting into trouble, but this took the cake.

"I now know everyone in the ob/gyn ward," she concluded. "And it's probably all for the best. John doesn't want children."

If you could even have them now, I thought to myself, but Avril abruptly changed the subject

"What about your love life?"

I told her about a grad student from UCLA I'd just broken up with who did a lot of drugs. He'd called one afternoon when I was out and ended up talking to Camille. I relayed part of their conversation to Avril.

"God, your boyfriend called and talked my ear off for an hour." Camille had told me. "What's he on?"

Benzedrine," I'd replied.

"And that's why I went off him in the end," I said to Avril. "He loved his Bennies more than he would ever love me."

"John and I are going to Tangiers next week now," Avril offered in response, going on to say she couldn't help it, but she couldn't let go of him even though she knew it was hopeless. He didn't want to marry her. He didn't want children. He looked at other women, but got annoyed if another man looked at her. I had no opinion to offer, since I didn't think much of him from what she'd told me. Avril was addicted to him for some reason that was beyond me. It was obvious we were not going to tootle around Europe together in the near future. Maybe I'd take Karin up on her offer from months back, and go visit her in Hamburg. She was always up for an adventure, and had also mentioned about going back to the States the following year.

We chatted about other people we knew. Tosia had come out of rehab and was living with her druggie boyfriend in Shepherd's Bush. Avril got phone calls from time to time.

"It's hard to understand what's she's saying. I think she's gone mad. Her mother's fed up with her and her sister. She's divorcing their alcoholic father and emigrating to Australia. By herself."

I left the restaurant feeling that a chapter in my life was over, and felt very sad. Avril was twenty; Tosia was nineteen. Her mother was forty-seven. Life was messy no matter who you were. Suddenly, the Fieldings' mess didn't seem *that* bad.

38

My Great Escape. Again.

A couple of days later I was riding on top of a red double-decker bus after buying a gift to send to Camille and Jerry and thinking about the experience I'd just had in the store.

"Are you American?" the shop girl had asked in an accusatory voice as she placed my purchase in a paper bag.

"No," I'd replied.

"Oh," she countered. "I thought I detected a slight accent."

"Well, I've just got back," I'd said.

"Hmmn," she'd sniffed as she rung up my purchase, mollified. I was not. Really, what was wrong with these people? They were downright rude, not to mention prejudiced. Whoever said the English were always polite? I'd gone on a temporary job interview the day before and the man had let forth a barrage of hostility against Americans when he'd found out I'd been in America, telling me about the time he'd been in New York on business for a week, how he'd been disgusted at his fellow office workers' behavior when they'd gone out to a nightclub.

"No morals," he grumbled. "Just like when they were over here in the war."

Oh, that again. The War. He looked to be about my parents' age. I'd heard the British men's mantra about the G.I.'s: "Overpaid, over sexed and over here." British women had not agreed with them, of course. Twenty years is a long time to hold a grudge, I thought, but realized it took a long time to recover when your world had been turned upside down, or from other violent episodes, and, perhaps a part of you never did recover. Working for this current miserable man, even for a few days would be a real pill, but, fortunately for me, he decided he didn't want anyone who'd been to America.

As the bus trundled along, I heard a political argument erupt between two men in the seats behind me, their voices rising. One of them had just dismissed the current prime minister as an idiot who would bankrupt the country.

"Rubbish, just 'cause he's for the Labor party. Won by a landslide! Clever of him to dissolve parliament and call a snap election so he could up his majority. Out-maneuvered the Opposition even though Ted Heath did go to Oxford."

"They both did!" the Conservative party supporter retorted.

"But Wilson's not an upper-class twit who wants us to join the European community like your boy Heath. Don't fancy that. We just beat the Germans."

There it was again, twenty years on, but just as if it was yesterday: The War. From thereon, the argument died down, both men agreeing they didn't want to join up with "the Frogs," either. I just hoped there weren't any Frenchmen on the bus. Was there anybody in the world

who hadn't had a derogatory thought against some-
body else who was from a different country, a different
culture, a different tribe, had a different color skin, a different thought or was of a different sex or different social
manners?

I smiled to myself. Really, this wasn't so different from
political conversation during cocktail hour or at the dinner
table in the Fielding household. British politics were as
foreign to me as American politics. You had to be twenty-one to vote in Britain, too, although there was talk of
changing the voting age to eighteen for the next election
in four years.

I glanced out of the bus window. The scenery looked
faintly familiar. I realized we were traveling through the
neighborhood where I'd lived as a young child, but it
looked totally different. In my mind's eye I remember pavements of gray concrete, the buildings as dull gray stone
row houses with slate gray roofs and sooty chimneys. In
my memory, the sky was usually gray, too, because it was
always raining, or was about to. Today the sun was shining, but I was still astonished at what I was looking at.
The houses weren't built of gray stone at all; they were
bright red Edwardian brick with cream-colored sconces
and curlicues surrounding front porches. The pavements
had a pinkish tone that sparkled in the sunlight; trees
were still in full green leaf lining the boulevard. I didn't
remember there being any trees at all when I was young.
As the bus trundled along, I noticed small front gardens
full of flowers in early autumn colors of dark reds, yellow,
rusts and gold: velvety snapdragons, mums, dahlias and
late-blooming summer roses growing profusely behind

green hedgerows. It was a beautiful, genteel area of town built in the early 1900's. Why had I remembered all this in shades of gray? What did that really say about my childhood? I thought of my six-year-old self, walking to school along these streets, and couldn't fathom it.

Sometimes we have to let go of that which no longer serves us. We like to think of home as a safe place. For many of us it is, but for far too many of us it is not. My home *looked* safe, as many homes do from the outside. Nice, normal, middle-class, churchgoing. But the man my mother married when I was four years old secretly hated women. He was an abuser.

I woke up thirsty just before dawn one morning and without turning any lights on, padded downstairs in my bare feet across the fitted carpet to get a drink of water. The house was in gray shadows.

I stood by the dining room window sipping my glass of water, looking out at the garden as night turned to day. The lawn was wet with dew, the trees and bushes shrouded in a dawn mist that hovered in gauzy white swaths around the trees like floating veils.

Suddenly arms came around from behind me, and hands covered my breasts. "Dreaming of your American boyfriend?" my father breathed into my ear.

Automatically, I dug my elbows back and quickly turned. Water from my glass sloshed against the front of his pajama jacket and trickled down his open pajama bottoms where his erect penis was exposed. He stepped back quickly. "Now look what you've done."

The accusatory mantra of my childhood. I could hardly breathe. My head felt like it was split in two. I felt like Alice falling down the rabbit hole. All was panic and confusion. Suddenly, I didn't quite know who I was as I found myself wandering through the charnel grounds of my unconscious. A scene from another time flashed across my inner vision. I saw myself at eleven or twelve years old, dressed in my school uniform, walking through the dining room on my way to the back door and out into the garden to collect my bike and ride to school. But first, I had to run the gauntlet. My mother had already gone to work. My father had not yet left. He turned as I came in. He was in his underpants, his penis in hand. As I ran past to get to the back door, a thick, sticky liquid spurted and hit me. Outside, I wiped the lapel of my school blazer dry with my handkerchief, then got on my bike and rode to school. This was my shame, not to be discussed with anybody because it wasn't done in those days, even if a child could find the words. It was always the female's fault and some form of sexual abuse was often to be expected at some point in a female's life, a normal occurrence. But it wasn't normal, it was just common. And nobody spoke about it. It wasn't done. But just because it's common that does not make it acceptable.

"I could never break you." His voice interrupted other scenes, other abusive visions from long ago bubbling up from deep down inside me like those malodorous gases rising from the La Brea Tar Pits, the place where all the bones were buried. I moved away from the window, feeling nauseous, yet strangely closed off.

"Why would you want to break me," I whispered, as the stinging sound of slaps and punches, malevolent threats and intimidating bullying throughout childhood when no-one else was around reverberated through my head.

He had no answer. He went into the kitchen and started making the morning cup of tea for my mother, who was still asleep. She wouldn't get out of bed until he'd brought it to her, and she'd drunk it.

Home is not always a safe harbor. Home for some is a dangerous place. People who are meant to love and protect you can be the biggest liars. Kind strangers can be loving friends. Sometimes reality is a nightmare, and a dream can be the best reality there is. When you leave the country of your birth it is not always clear why you are leaving, or what you are leaving behind. It becomes a leap into the great unknown, a gesture of faith in the universe, a supreme acceptance of fate and destiny, a vote of confidence in humanity as a whole, not a fractured part.

Somewhere, bells were ringing. But it wasn't bells; it was the telephone. I had automatically backed out of the dining-room, through the living-room and into the hall as other unpleasant scenes were trying to rise from childhood shadows. They would have to wait. It was too much to handle all at once. An old, and unconsciously practiced survival method, I shut them down and picked up the phone without thinking.

"Hello."

"Oh, goody. I've got you."

I heard a voice, an American voice. Camille.

The whooshing in my ears and the mist in my head subsided.

"Listen, I have to make it quick," she continued. "We're going to Mitzi's for dinner. You left your t-shirt dress in the dryer and a book down by the pool. Do you want me to send them to you...or are you coming back anytime soon? I know you said your green card allowed you to leave the country for six months and there'd be no problem getting back in as long as you didn't stay away longer."

"Er, Er." I was having a hard time thinking. I felt so far away from everything, including myself.

"I know you're probably having a good time, but I've got other news, so I'll cut to the chase since transatlantic calls cost a fortune."

"Um." Words escaped me. Then, "What?"

Camille ploughed on. "D'you remember meeting a composer by the name of Ernest Gold? He wrote the music for *Exodus, It's a Mad, Mad World,*" and a whole bunch of other films. His wife, Marni Nixon, is known as the "Voice of Hollywood" because she dubs many stars' singing in their films: Deborah Kerr in *The King and I*, Audrey Hepburn in *My Fair Lady*. Even Marilyn Monroe's high notes in *Diamonds Are A Girl's Best Friend* from *Gentlemen Prefer Blondes.* She's got a fantastic voice, and she's a nice person. You really liked her when you met her."

I was drawing a blank. I'd met so many industry people at Jerry and Camille's.

"Well, they remember you," Camille rattled on. "Jerry bumped into Ernest yesterday, and he asked after you. They need a part-time secretary, a personal assistant, someone who can type letters, do the banking and pick the four-year-old up from nursery school. They have an office in their home up above Laurel Canyon, not far from here. Jerry told Ernest you were on vacation, but he didn't know exactly when you were coming back. You *are* coming back, aren't you? We all miss you. Elizabeth and Claudia talk about you every day. My family always ask after you; so does Joyce, especially at cocktail hour."

"I miss you all, too." Silent tears slid from my eyes.

Camille lowered her voice: "It's been an eventful week around here. Joyce got arrested for shoplifting, and I had to bail her out. She tried to walk out of Magnins with two new skirts under the one she already had on."

I almost smiled to myself, but then Camille added in a solemn voice: "And Essie had a heart attack."

"Oh, my God!" Not dear, goodhearted Essie. Life was definitely not fair.

"She's all right," Camille assured me. "It was a small one, as those things go. She's taking it easy, and the doctor says she'll be able to go come back to work in a couple of weeks."

"Thank goodness. Give her my love." I was starting to space out again, but I had to stay grounded.

Camille rattled on. "Both Jerry and I would love to have you back. We talked it over. Forget about an apartment and the over twenty-one age problem. If you're coming back soon, you could live with us and do some babysitting for your room and board, and work for Ernest and Marni part-time. They only need someone for afternoons during the week. No weekends. And if that job doesn't work out, there's others. Jerry will give you a glowing recommendation. I know because I'll type it up and have him sign it."

Here it was again. An invitation to go walking in the world. And learning to rely on the kindness of strangers.

Early lessons linger and can rob us of our feelings of belonging and security. Pain from the earliest wounds go deep. I needed time to work things out emotionally, lots of time. Old scores would have to wait to be settled. But first, I knew I had to leave. I had to survive.

You don't always get to plan your journeys in life, there are always surprises. Entering my twenties did not automatically equal happiness. Being an adult did not equal happiness as I had naively thought it would as a young teenager. It brought up responsibilities I could never have guessed at. The journey to becoming an adult wasn't as instantly liberating as I'd once imagined it would be. It was hard work in all sorts of ways I couldn't have foreseen.

But I was getting clearer. I wiped my face dry with the palm of my hand.

"You're thinking, I can hear it," Camille said.

I came back to myself, or at least the everyday one I was familiar with. "I'll need a car," I replied.

"No problem. Leonard has a friend who owns a rental car company and they sell them off cheap after a year. And Jerry will co-sign for a loan at the bank. A couple of things have cleared up here and the Reklaw Drive house has sold, so we're not in the hole any more. Well, not as deep, anyway," she added."

They were so kind. Sometimes you get a second chance in life. And nothing's over until it's over.

"There's something else."

"Yeah, me, too," Camille replied.

"What?"

"If you make it sooner rather than later, Sam Peckinpah's having a barbecue at his house in Malibu in a couple of weeks. We're all invited. He's digging a pit and roasting a pig in the sand dunes. What's your something else?"

A beach party. In sunny Malibu. In November. It sounded like a wonderful dream.

"Uh, Camille, can you lend me the plane fare? I'll start paying you back out of my paycheck when I get one. Promise."

FINIS

Notes about the typefaces:

Annabelle, used for the headlines here, is a beautiful original script font from the type foundry Jukebox. Jason Walcott, the type designer, named the typeface after his mother.

Calluna, a serif face used for the copy, is a modern alternative to other old-style types. It combines the charm of classic design with the appeal of modernism. The type designer is Jos Buivenga, who spent 1-1/2 years designing Calluna.

Made in the USA
Las Vegas, NV
21 December 2022

63742659R10207